CHEMICAL WARFARE DURING THE VIETNAM WAR

Riot Control Agents in Combat

D. Hank Ellison

Routledge
Taylor & Francis Group

NEW YORK AND LONDON

First published 2011
by Routledge
270 Madison Avenue, New York, NY 10016

Simultaneously published in the UK
by Routledge
2 Park Square, Milton Park, Abingdon, Oxon OX14 4RN

Routledge is an imprint of the Taylor & Francis Group, an informa business

Typeset in Bembo by Wearset Ltd, Boldon, Tyne and Wear
Printed and bound in the United States of America on acid-free paper by
Walsworth Publishing Company, Marceline, MO

Library of Congress Cataloging in Publication Data
A catalog record has been requested for this book

ISBN13: 978-0-415-87644-5 (hbk)
ISBN13: 978-0-415-87645-2 (pbk)
ISBN13: 978-0-203-83113-7 (ebk)

NSF-SFI-COC-C0004285
The SFI label applies to the text stock.

I would like to dedicate this book to my father, MGySgt Vernon Lee Ellison, who retired from the Marine Corps after serving his country faithfully through both the Korean and Vietnam Wars. He is gone but not forgotten. Semper Fi Dad!

CONTENTS

ACKNOWLEDGMENTS

I would like to thank Arnie Bernstein and Brendan Boyle for their encouragement and insightful comments on the manuscript.

I would also like to thank my family, Rose, Sean and Sarah, for their patience, understanding and encouragement as I worked on this.

1

INTRODUCTION

Since the end of the war, the Vietnam-era chemical warfare program has been in and out of the news. Initially, concern focused on the potential long-term environmental damage from spraying herbicides on large sections of virgin jungle. It soon shifted to the toxic legacy left behind by dioxin, a minor but potent impurity in one of the herbicides. Because the principal ingredients in Agent Orange – a mixture of the butyl esters of 2,4-D and 2,4,5-T – were commercially available and considered non-toxic, there was little effort to prevent or even limit exposure during the war. As the world began to comprehend the extent of the damage, the impact to soldiers, civilians and now the next generation of Vietnamese children has been the topic of numerous medical studies, litigations and books. Dioxin's notoriety has in turn raised public awareness of military defoliant operations during the war.

There was another facet of the chemical program that remains unconnected to any toxic legacy and has largely been overlooked by the general public. Riot-control agents were used routinely during combat operations for a variety of tactical reasons and the lessons learned from these operations are still having an impact on US Military planning and policy today. An examination of this aspect of the program can provide insight into the development of current US military doctrine and the drive to make these weapons available to soldiers. As recently as the invasions of Afghanistan and Iraq, the Pentagon pushed for authorization to use non-lethal chemicals. Secretary of Defense Donald Rumsfeld told Congress on February 5, 2003 that, in his opinion, it would be "perfectly appropriate" to use riot-control agents in some situations that soldiers would likely face. He used examples of enemy forces hiding in caves, barricaded in buildings, or intermixed with non-combatants. "You would prefer to get at [the soldiers] without also getting at women and children, or non-combatants," he explained.

These were all situations that American soldiers faced during the Vietnam War and were often able to resolve with tear gas. The need for these weapons became even more acute when US forces prepared to enter Baghdad in the final days of the war. As one reporter put it:

> the potential use of tear gas in the war's pending assault into the urban jungle [of Baghdad's streets] has become a salient issue for Coalition commanders. US forces learned in the bloody Vietnam battle of Hue City that the judicious use of tear gas is a lifesaver when clearing close quarters of the enemy.[1]

Riot-control agents are chemical compounds that cause intense irritation and produce transient incapacitation. There are two general categories within this class of agents. The principle effects from exposure to the first class are uncontrollable lacrimation along with some difficulty drawing a deep breath. These materials are often simply referred to as tear gases. Effects from exposure occur almost immediately, and end within minutes of escaping from the agent cloud. The two tear agents used during the Vietnam War were CN and CS.

In addition to tearing, the second class also causes sneezing, extreme headache, chills, nausea and sometimes even regurgitation. This group is usually referred to as vomiting agents. Unlike tear agents, the effects from these agents do not show up until several minutes after the initial exposure and can also persist for several hours. Individuals often report that they also experience severe depression during this extended recovery period. The only vomiting agent employed during the war was DM.

Although they produce transient incapacitation, these compounds should not be confused with the class of chemical weapons known as incapacitating agents. An agent from this latter group was used by Russian Special Forces during the 2002 hostage situation when Chechen guerrillas took over a Moscow theater. Incapacitating agents mainly produce their effects by altering or disrupting the higher regulatory activity of the central nervous system. They may induce delirium (producing confusion, hallucinations and disorganized behavior), stimulation (essentially flooding the brain with too much information), sedation (depressants that induce passivity or even sleep) or even psychosis (producing abnormal psychological effects resembling mental illness). Symptoms from exposure to these agents, as well as the onset and duration of the effects, vary greatly with dosage and are difficult to predict on a battlefield. The only incapacitating agent in the US arsenal during the war was BZ, a powdered material that caused delirium lasting from two to five days.[2]

The agents and munitions used in Vietnam had their roots in World War I. The very first attempt to use tear gas on a modern battlefield occurred in August 1914 when several Parisian police officers serving in the French Army fired 0.26-caliber bullets filled with ethyl bromoacetate into the German positions.

For a number of years prior to the war, the Paris police department had been using these weapons against barricaded criminals who refused to surrender. Although these *cartouches suffocantes* produced good results inside a building, they were too small to be effective outdoors. Still the idea caught on and soon both sides were using tear gases to harass and wear down opposing soldiers.

To counter the effects of these and other chemical agents, the belligerents began wearing gas masks. Throughout the war there was a continual race between developing new agents and developing new masks and filters to counter their effects. Toward the end of the war, German researchers once again discovered a new class of agents, one they hoped would defeat the Allied masks. These "mask breakers" were actually non-volatile solids that had to be delivered as aerosols of micro-fine particles. Such particles were not absorbed by the charcoal in the filter elements used at that time and soldiers inhaled them with every breath. These agents caused violent sneezing and uncontrollable vomiting, thus forcing the affected soldier to remove his mask. When he did, he was exposed to other lethal agents that were fired on the target at the same time. Although the Germans used them extensively during the last year of the war, the design of their artillery shells was not effective at aerosolizing the powdered material. But even if they had solved the delivery issues, the results would have been a disappointment because the Allies had added a particulate filter to their masks.

Recognizing the potential of these vomiting agents, the Allies tried to synthesize their own. Unable to replicate the complex manufacturing process needed to produce the German agents, American researchers discovered a compound that was simpler to make and even more effective. Initially named for the American chemist who first synthesized it, adamsite eventually became known by the military code DM.

Concurrent with this discovery was the development of a new British munition that effectively generated a highly concentrated aerosol of properly sized particles. Known as the M device, it used a pyrotechnic mixture to generate hot gases that passed through the agent and distilled it into the atmosphere. As they left the canister, the vapors cooled and rapidly condensed into microscopic particles that remained suspended in the exhaust cloud. Filled with adamsite, the M device was a very potent weapon. However, the war ended before the Allies could get them into the field.

After the war, the fledgling security industry in the United States began offering police departments an assortment of weapons containing a variety of agent combinations. Unable to survive on the police market alone, these companies expanded their services and developed a host of novel products that they marketed directly to banks, armored car services and even individual citizens. The spectrum ranged from large systems that instantaneously flooded an entire room with gas to dual-purpose pens and mechanical pencils for personal protection.

Militaries around the world continued to pursue chemical programs and there were several conflicts before World War II, such as the Italian war with Ethiopia and Spanish colonization efforts in Morocco, when chemical agents and tear gases were used. Although the European powers did not use chemical weapons during World War II, the Japanese began using them against the Chinese as early as 1937. Along with lethal chemicals, they frequently used irritants to suppress enemy machine gun and artillery fire, as well as to disorganize enemy defenses prior to an attack. Unable to protect themselves or respond in kind, the Chinese could only plead with the rest of the world for support. In 1943, President Roosevelt issued a statement condemning the Japanese and threatening US retaliation in kind if they continued to use chemical weapons. Fearful of precipitating a full-scale chemical war that they did not think they could win, the Japanese acquiesced.

When the Korean War started, there were advocates on both sides of the chemical warfare issue. Many frontline commanders thought gas would be very beneficial against human wave attacks and for dealing with enemy soldiers hiding in the rough, mountainous terrain. Ultimately, no chemical weapons were used during the war except for limited application of tear gas as a means of subduing rioting prisoners of war.[3]

Over the years, various bodies and international conventions have tried to restrict the use of chemical weapons. At the time of the Vietnam War, the most successful was the 1925 Geneva Protocol. This document codified a common repugnance for these types of weapons and banned "the use in war of asphyxiating, poisonous or other gases, and of all analogous liquids, materials or devices." Despite this lofty proclamation, most signatories filed reservations when they deposited their ratifications stipulating that they could retaliate in kind if chemical weapons were used against them. A number also held that the restraints against chemical warfare were only valid between the actual signatories to the treaty. Mussolini, for example, used variants of both of these arguments to justify using chemical weapons in Ethiopia. In a practical sense, the Geneva Protocol was only a no-first-use agreement between the signatories that did not limit the development or stockpiling of chemical weapons.

When it had the chance to ratify the Protocol in 1926, the United States Senate refused because they were convinced other countries would continue to clandestinely stockpile chemical weapons and these weapons would undoubtedly be used in the next war regardless of the treaty. Forty years later, the United States was still not a signatory. Based on this failure, Washington was able to maintain throughout the Vietnam War that the US was not a signatory to any treaty or agreement that limited its use of riot-control agents in combat.

The present work chronicles the events surrounding the use of these agents in combat and evaluates the evolution of the weapons and tactics used to deliver them. This study provides an opportunity to determine if riot-control agents actually offer any real advantages on the battlefield and if there were any situations for which they were uniquely suited. It also provides some insight into the attitudes of soldiers, civilians, the press and politicians concerning their use, and the changes in each over the course of the war. Further, it offers an excellent case study to examine one of the key questions that is often debated when chemical warfare is discussed. Does the availability and widespread use of tear gas necessarily weaken the constraints on escalation to unrestricted chemical warfare? Since there have been allegations that the US did use other classes of chemical weapons, including nerve agents, did the US in fact slide down that slippery slope? If not, what were the influences that prevented the escalation? The answers to these questions bear relevance for future conflicts as the nature of wars continue to change and the need for less than lethal options becomes even more critical.

2
PRELUDE

The first chemical weapons used by Americans during the Vietnam War were herbicides. Although not directly connected to the eventual combat use of riot-control agents, it is critical to understand the decision-making process; the concern over public perception; and the response to the Communist propaganda campaign in order to put the events surrounding the initial use of riot-control agents in perspective.

The program began when President John Kennedy authorized the military to begin testing aerial application of herbicides as a means of increasing visibility in the dense jungle vegetation to reduce the potential of enemy ambushes. On August 10, 1961, the Combat Development and Test Center in Vietnam ran the first defoliation test by applying herbicides to a small patch of jungle using specially outfitted helicopters. Two weeks later, they conducted a second test on a larger section of jungle, but this time they used airplanes so they could increase the rate of application. In both cases, the targets were personally selected by South Vietnamese President Ngo Dinh Diem. Although the American evaluation team was not overly impressed with the results, they made a big impact on Diem and he became an enthusiastic supporter of the program.[1]

On September 29, shortly after the initial defoliation test, President Diem asked US representatives about using chemicals to destroy enemy food crops that being grown in remote, hard to reach regions of the country. The South Vietnamese Air Force had been trying unsuccessfully to use antipersonnel bombs and rockets to either destroy the crops or to drive off the Viet Cong tending the fields. President Diem told the envoys that he had heard the US had a "special powder" that would destroy the rice, but that President Kennedy had to personally authorize its use.[2] When he was informed that such materials were highly controlled and would not be approved for use in Vietnam, he became animated and declared that he did not care what was used as long as he could destroy the enemy's crops.[3]

The proposal to employ defoliants on a widespread basis, especially to destroy enemy food crops, caused a serious controversy in Washington. Although members of the Administration generally agreed that using herbicides did not violate any rule of international law, and even destruction of enemy food stores was an accepted tactic of war, many did not believe that it was worth the potential negative press and public outcry.[4] Ultimately, the question came down to whether the potential military tactical and strategic gains were worth the possible adverse propaganda and the subsequent damage to US long-term goals in the region. The destruction of food in a country that was suffering from a food shortage was seen as a particularly sensitive issue. Everyone involved recognized that the negative propaganda associated with crop destruction would be greater and harder to handle than any outcry associated with defoliation operations undertaken to reduce the capability of the enemy to ambush American soldiers.[5]

The Administration wanted to avoid anything that gave the impression that the US was resorting to biological or chemical warfare. Robert Johnson of the National Security Council Staff suggested to Deputy Special Assistant Walt Rostow that, "we must make the general character of the operations as open and above board as possible. Publicity ought to emphasize ... that the chemical agents involved are the same kind that are used by farmers against weeds." As the discussions continued, Under Secretary of State for Political Affairs Alexis Johnson advised Secretary of State Dean Rusk that "[w]e must also stay away from the term 'chemical warfare' and any connection with the Chemical Corps, and rather talk about 'weed killers'. Defense and the Chemical Corps entirely agree on this." They were afraid of a repeat of what Paul Neilson of the US Information Agency described as "the propaganda circus created by the communists on alleged US use of 'germ warfare' [during the Korean War]." He, along with many others in the Administration, was haunted by "the specter of charges that 'US imperialists are waging germ warfare on Asians'."[6]

During the Korean War, the Communists had charged the United States with using biological weapons, including agents that caused plague, anthrax, typhus and cholera.[7] The diseases were allegedly spread by dropping leaflet bombs filled with contaminated feathers and balls of cotton, or insect vectors such as flies, fleas and ticks instead of the usual propaganda flyers. The allegations began in 1952 after several outbreaks of cholera and plague occurred inside North Korea. The Communists immediately launched a vehement propaganda campaign, railing against the US in the press and even elevating the issue to the United Nations. Despite an equally passionate refutation, the United States was never able to unequivocally clear itself of the cloud caused by the charges, which lingered on into the Vietnam War.[8]

The controversy over crop destruction peaked in the summer of 1962. On July 28, the Joint Chiefs of Staff sent a memorandum to Secretary of Defense

McNamara stating that crop destruction would give the South Vietnamese Army a substantial military advantage over the guerrillas. After careful review, McNamara concurred with their conclusion and sent a recommendation to the President that the United States initiate a pilot program to see if it was plausible to destroy enemy crops with herbicides sprayed from aircraft. Since he was still worried about the potential damage that a Communist propaganda campaign might have on the international image of the United States, McNamara nuanced his recommendation with the caveat that American participation should remain as unobtrusive as possible and be limited to technical advice and assistance. He emphasized that all of the operational aspects, especially piloting the delivery aircraft, had to be handled by the South Vietnamese.[9]

As the military was preparing to move forward with both facets of the herbicide program, Rachel Carson published her seminal series of articles on the environment in the *New Yorker*. Although she never intended for them to be a commentary on the war, the Administration took note of their potential to start a grassroots outcry against the possible environmental and social impacts of deforestation and anti-crop operations. On August 16, Edward Murrow, Director of the US Information Agency, sent a memorandum to McGeorge Bundy, the Special Assistant to the President for National Security Affairs, noting:

> [a] series by Rachel Carson currently running in *The New Yorker* and soon to be published in book form sets forth with devastating impact the consequences of insecticides on insect–plant life balance and human health.... [I]f we launch a defoliation program in Vietnam our enemies and many of our friends will use this book against us. No matter how reasonable our case may be. I am convinced that we cannot persuade the world – particularly that large part of it which does not get enough to eat – that defoliation "is good for you."[10]

However, the feared public outcry never materialized. By the end of August, the Administration concluded that the public did not connect the events on the other side of the world with their concern over the damage to their own backyard. In November, the Administration relinquished direct control over jungle defoliation operations and delegated authority to authorize such missions down to Frederick Nolting, the US Ambassador in South Vietnam, and General Paul Harkins, Commander of the Military Advisory Command in Vietnam. Anti-crop operations, on the other hand, still required direct approval from Washington. The Administration continued to carefully monitor the Communist propaganda campaign for the rest of 1962 and throughout 1963 before deciding that it was ineffective and would have little impact on public opinion. Further, they reasoned it might actually be counterproductive to stop spraying since that could be interpreted as actually validating the propaganda claims made by Hanoi. In short, there was nothing to be gained by terminating the program.[11]

Emboldened by the rudimentary and uncoordinated Communist propaganda program, as well as the apparent apathy of the American public, the military began supplying South Vietnam with riot-control agents in 1962. Most of these munitions were in the form of pyrotechnic grenades containing CN, DM or a combination of these two agents. CN was the compound that actually inspired the term "tear gas" and was the standard US military tear agent until 1959, when it was replaced by the more potent CS. CN was also the key ingredient in the commercial formulation known as mace, the standard agent used by police forces worldwide and the protection industry in general. DM, on the other hand, was the standard vomiting agent stockpiled in the US arsenal at that time and also a component in several commercially available formulations. In addition to nausea and vomiting, effects from exposure also included severe headache and acute pain behind the eyes. The US military only used this agent when these more intense and longer-lasting effects were needed. Since both of these agents were commercially available and considered non-lethal, Washington did not require South Vietnam to consult with them prior to using them, nor did they place any restrictions on the way they could be used.[12]

Initially, the South Vietnamese government used these munitions to help break up the many domestic disturbances springing up in the newly formed country. President Diem, a devout Catholic, was facing major unrest from the Buddhist population in his country. Although on the surface it appeared to be solely a matter of religious intolerance, it was actually as much an internal political struggle as it was about freedom of religion. President Diem continued to give his fellow Catholics the same preferential treatment that they had received under French colonial rule. Under his administration, Catholics fared better economically and priests also had special political influence. Buddhists began protesting this situation on both religious and political grounds.[13]

On May 8, 1963, events began to deteriorate when government troops used tear gas and fired on protesters marching in the city of Hue. Nine people were killed when a civilian guard of the Deputy Province Chief threw a concussion grenade into the crowd. Although the government initially adopted a compromising tone and granted a number of concessions to the Buddhists, they refused to take responsibility for these deaths. Instead, they maintained Communist agent provocateurs within the Buddhist organizations had somehow orchestrated the incident. This led to hunger strikes and additional protests across the country.[14]

On June 3, about 12,000 high school and college age students staged another anti-government demonstration in Hue. When the demonstrators refused to disperse, troops leveled bayoneted weapons and moved forward as tear gas was fired into the crowd. While some of the protesters threw stones at the soldiers, many of them simply sat down on the street and prayed. The situation continued to degenerate as the troops tried to drag the protesters off the street. Frustrated, some of the soldiers poured an unidentified liquid from colored glass bottles onto praying demonstrators who were blocking the streets. Within seconds, the doused individuals were unable to see and could barely breath. Nearly seventy individuals were hospitalized; several eventually died of complications resulting from exposure to the liquid agent. Over fifty others suffered severe burns and blistering wherever the liquid had landed on their skin, leading to accusations that the government had splashed the protesters with a military blister agent. John Helble, the US Consul in Hue, visited the hospital and observed first-hand the skin injuries and respiratory distress of the victims.[15]

At that time, the only blister agents in military stockpiles around the world were mustard gas and lewisite. Both were legacy agents from World War I, although lewisite never made it onto the battlefield. Of the two, mustard gas produced signs and symptoms similar to those of the victims: eye and respiratory irritation followed a short time later by blistering of exposed skin. If victims inhaled a sufficient amount of agent vapor, their lungs would swell and then fill with fluid. Without timely treatment, these individuals would eventually asphyxiate.[16]

When he learned about the incident and the symptoms of the victims, Secretary of State Dean Rusk sent a telegram to the Embassy in Vietnam seeking additional information. In a typically truncated telegraph he informed them:

> We very concerned by report blister gas may have been used. As you of course aware adverse effects such action could hardly be exaggerated. Request you ascertain whether poison gas in fact employed and if so, under what circumstances. If blister gas used, would appear imperative for [Diem's Administration] to promptly disassociate itself from such action and announce intention investigate and punish those responsible. If report true, believe we must also consider best means indicating our thorough disapproval while at same time not appearing to withdraw general support from [South Vietnam].[17]

The possibility that the United States could be associated with an incident involving toxic chemical warfare agents was catastrophic and made concerns over the potential fallout from destroying enemy crops with herbicides seem truly insignificant.

On June 4, William Trueheart, the Minister-Counselor and Deputy Chief of Mission in Vietnam met with Nguyen Dinh Thuan, the Vietnamese Secretary of State at the Presidency and Assistant Secretary of State for National Defense, to sort out the details of the event and determine what types of agents had been used. Thuan was not aware of the allegations concerning a blister agent but promised to relay the information to President Diem immediately. Within hours, Thuan notified Trueheart that an investigative commission had been appointed and was already en route to Hue. He also stated that he had been in touch with authorities in Hue and they assured him tear gas was the only chemical agent used during the riots. They also suggested the "chemical burns" were misdiagnosed thermal injuries caused by the burning pyrotechnic fuel in the tear-gas grenades.[18]

As the US mission in Vietnam delved into the incident, they asked reporters to delay sending out the story until the investigation was completed and the full facts were known. Despite the request, both the Associated Press and United Press International released stories alleging that the South Vietnamese military had used a toxic blister agent on the protesters. To the relief of American diplomats in Saigon, the articles did not specifically try to implicate the United States as either having a direct hand in the incident or in potentially supplying the blister agent to the South Vietnamese. When these stories appeared in newspapers back in the United States, the general public took little notice.[19]

On June 6, the commission completed its investigation and determined that the agent poured on the protestors was a tear gas taken from old stocks left behind by the French.[20] In order to be absolutely certain, the Embassy had samples of the material sent back to Edgewood Arsenal for analysis, where army chemists confirmed that it was indeed a type of tear gas used during World War I.[21] Although not specifically identified, the material was likely bromobenzyl cyanide, also known by the military designation CA, which became the standard French lacrimatory agent in July 1918. Because it had a tendency to corrode many common metals, it was often stored in glass containers. Direct exposure to the agent liquid, or even prolonged exposure to very high vapor concentrations, could produce blisters on exposed skin similar to those caused by mustard gas. This effect would have been exacerbated by the hot and humid summer conditions.[22]

The Kennedy Administration breathed a huge sigh of relief. However, despite the palpable drain of tension among US diplomats in Vietnam, the political situation there was still exceptionally tense and needed to be resolved rapidly. The continued draconian actions by Diem's regime led to an escalating cycle of public protests and police crackdowns. Ultimately, the Buddhist crisis marked the beginning of the end for President Diem and became one of the key factors leading to a coup that eventually claimed his life and that of his younger brother Nhu.

Since the American military had not placed any stipulations on how the riot-control agents they were supplying could be used, the South Vietnamese Army began issuing them to combat units. Although the South Vietnamese Army had used riot-control agents many times against protesters, they did not have any tactical experience with them and only a rudimentary understanding of how they could be used effectively in combat. Further, many of the individual soldiers were not only nervous about using the agents, they were anxious about having to wear the claustrophobic protective masks in battle. Unfortunately, their American advisors had little practical advice to offer since the US itself did not have a comprehensive chemical doctrine with a well-defined role for non-lethal agents, and the advisors had only received familiarization training with chemical agents, typically limited to confidence-building measures involving exposure to tear gas in a training chamber.

Initially, the agents were only used haphazardly by individual units, frequently depending on the whim of the local commander. In these situations, the results were often marginal or even counter-productive. As an example, it was not uncommon for Viet Cong guerrillas facing a larger or better-armed government force to intermix with non-combatant villagers, forcing the soldiers to either allow the Communists to escape or engage them and risk killing the civilians. Often the commander chose to engage the enemy regardless of the risk to the lives of the village women and children. On one occasion, however, a commander decided to use tear gas to blind the guerrillas so that they could move in and capture them without endangering the civilians. However, the unit only had a few gas grenades and the soldiers did not understand how to deploy them properly to maximize their effect on the target. The wind blew the agent cloud away before it had any noteworthy effect and they had to resort to the standard higher-casualty method of trying to shoot around the non-combatants.[23]

In another common situation, guerrillas took refuge in tunnels as the South Vietnamese soldiers approached. Because of the booby traps and high risk of ambush, the soldiers did not like to enter these confined spaces and preferred to wait for the enemy to emerge on their own. However, since these shafts usually had more than one exit, the Viet Cong often got away. In a foreshadowing of things to come, some units tried to force the guerrillas to evacuate the tunnels by tossing a tear-gas grenade as far as possible down the entrance shaft. Even though the cloud filled the tunnel near the entrance and billowed back out at the soldiers, it did not penetrate much deeper into the passageway and had little effect on the enemy concealed underground.[24]

Sometimes the government even used riot-control agents to deliberately target civilians that were interfering with their operations. In one such instance, the South Vietnamese Air Force wanted to clear approximately 6,000 non-combatants out of an area that was going to become a free-fire zone. Although the province chiefs were warned about the impending reclassification and the risk that it posed to their communities, only two of the three leaders moved their constituencies out of the area. In order to force the remaining occupants to evacuate, the Vietnamese Air Force repeatedly dropped tear gas onto their villages. To make matters worse, the residents were not warned they would be gassed because the air force feared it would give the Viet Cong time to move anti-aircraft weapons into the area. Ultimately, the combination of riot-control agents, psychological harassment and the fear of the "poisonous" defoliants that would soon be used on the surrounding jungle convinced most of the holdouts to move to strategic hamlets located in territory controlled by the government.[25]

The next significant combat use of riot-control agents occurred at the end of 1964 when the South Vietnamese Army began conducting rescue operations to recover American advisors that were being held at Viet Cong prison compounds. The first attempted rescue occurred on December 23 in the An Xuyen Province. Prior to ground forces entering the compound, helicopters used the troop landing smoke screen system (TLSS) to drop nearly 200 tear-gas and smoke grenades to incapacitate and confuse everyone in the area.[26] However, the camp was unoccupied and no contact was made with the enemy.[27]

The second rescue attempt occurred two days later in the Tay Ninh Province. On this occasion helicopters used the TLSS to drop 550 CN-DM grenades and 100 CS grenades onto the camp, and also used aerial dispersers to spray it with an additional 300 pounds of bulk CS powder. The rescuers hoped that this massive dose of agent would instantly incapacitate everyone, prisoners and captors alike. As the cloud swirled around the compound, a South Vietnamese rescue force, equipped with protective masks and led by Special Forces advisors, assaulted the camp. Once again, however, the camp was empty.[28]

While the overall operation was a failure, one aspect turned out to be very enlightening. The agent sprayed above the jungle canopy with the dispersers took an excessive amount of time to migrate down through the dense foliage and reach the ground. After further experimentation the military found that it took an unacceptable amount of time for either liquid or finely powdered agents sprayed above the canopy to penetrate the foliage in sufficient quantities to achieve an incapacitating concentration. For example, they determined that in twenty minutes, less than 60 percent of a micropulverized powder released above the tree-tops would reach the jungle floor, certainly not the proper delivery parameters to achieve incapacitation during a surprise attack.[29]

To the advisors and others associated with the rescue attempts, it seemed obvious from these failed attempts that either the intelligence data in both instances was excessively flawed or, more likely, the Viet Cong were being alerted to the rescues attempts. On January 29, 1965, the US secretly attempted its own aerial rescue of an American POW. This time they were specifically looking for Captain Nick Rowe, a Special Forces advisor to a South Vietnamese unit operating near the U Minh Forest at the time he was captured.[30] He had been taken prisoner along with two other Americans on October 29, 1963 after a heated battle with a large guerrilla force. Over the following year, the prisoners were moved frequently from camp to camp to prevent them from being located and rescued. However, early in 1965, Captain Rowe was seen by a credible source and a rescue mission was quickly organized. This time, even the pilots were not briefed on the precise location until the helicopters were in the air. Once again the plan called for a swarm of helicopters to descend on the camp and flood it with tear gas. Then, when everyone in the camp was incapacitated, a single air ambulance helicopter would land and the flight crew would quickly search the compound for Captain Rowe and any other

American prisoners. Unfortunately, the crew of the air ambulance had very little experience flying while wearing protective masks. To make matters worse, proper aviation protective masks that would have allowed them to use their on-board communications system were not available and they had less than an hour to practice with a set of standard infantry masks prior to the rescue. The pilot found it particularly difficult to communicate with his crew and the other helicopters, and the distortion caused by the lenses tended to give him vertigo when he was flying.

The first helicopters arriving at the camp began spraying the area with tear gas. The jungle cover was relatively thin and the compound was quickly saturated. Protected by numerous gunships, the air ambulance landed and the crew immediately jumped off to search the area. Although they found evidence that Captain Rowe had recently been at the camp, it was deserted at the time of the rescue and the mission was a failure. Unfortunately, back on December 23, the camp where Captain Rowe was imprisoned was mistaken for a Viet Cong training facility and attacked by helicopters and AD-6 Skyraiders. Afraid that the Americans would come back, the Viet Cong continually kept him on the move over the next month, rapidly transferring him between a series of camps throughout the region. The source that tipped the Americans to his location had seen him at an interim stop and not realized that he had been moved again. Ultimately, it would not be until December 31, 1968 that the now Major Rowe would escape from his captors and make it back into friendly hands.[31]

By April 1965, Operation Ban Thai I, which occurred on January 28, 1965 in the Phuyen Province, was the only significant combat mission where riot-control agents were an integrated part of an operational plan. The mission objective was to drive Viet Cong out of heavily fortified positions along the Phu Lac Peninsula. These fighting positions had been constructed near a village and, because of their proximity, there was concern that there might be non-combatants intermixed with the guerrillas. The South Vietnamese commander planned to initiate his ground assault with a heavy dose of tear gas and vomiting agents to suppress the enemy fire and allow his forces to quickly close with the enemy. He hoped that this would minimize the risk to any villagers who might be nearby. Soldiers were also issued tear-gas grenades to help neutralize any small pockets of enemy resistance they encountered, especially if villagers were present.

The initial phase of the operation took place as planned and, at 8.00 a.m. the helicopters were ready to deliver the riot-control agents. The weather conditions were almost perfect for a chemical attack – the sky was overcast, the winds were slight and there was an atmospheric inversion layer that would hold the agent cloud down on the ground. Unfortunately, the assault was delayed for over three hours, and during that time the conditions changed. The wind picked up and the heat from the sun created convection currents that would rapidly carry the cloud up and away from the target.

When the infantry was finally ready, the helicopters descended on the enemy positions and dropped a total of 900 CS and CN-DM riot-control grenades. A second series of helicopters flew over and sprayed the enemy with an additional 300 pounds of CS powder. The cloud of agent generated by the combination of grenades and bulk agent covered the enemy fortifications and rapidly incapacitated them. However, the South Vietnamese commander was inexperienced with gas operations and ordered his soldiers to wait a full ten minutes after the tear-gas attack in the mistaken belief that the delay would ensure the enemy suffered the full effects of their exposure. During the delay the unfavorable weather conditions dissipated the cloud and allowed the defenders to recover. The assaulting soldiers, still wearing their masks to protect them from the non-existent gas cloud, were at a disadvantage because their masks made it difficult to breathe, affected their vision, and prevented effective communications between officers and men. Although the assault was eventually successful, in this case gas was more hindrance than help and probably made the operation more costly than it should have been.[32]

All of these operations were undertaken at the discretion of local Vietnamese Army commanders. Even if they had been consulted, the US military would not have considered the use of riot-control agents an issue since they did not believe the non-lethal agents were covered by the 1925 Geneva Protocol. Further, neither the United States nor the Republic of Vietnam were signatories to the Protocol, and in their opinions that meant that they were not legally bound by any prohibitions contained in the treaty. This attitude, coupled with the lingering desire to keep any reference to chemical warfare out of the public eye, unwittingly set the stage for the greatest controversy on the subject the United States would face during the war. By the time it was over, Secretary of Defense McNamara, articulating the feelings of the entire Johnson Administration, declared that he would rather "lose the war" than authorize the use of any more tear gas. "If by itself it would save the situation, I wouldn't [use it].... My God, I don't want to go through that again."[33]

During the summer of 1964, public concern mounted about the potential for chemical and biological warfare to erupt in Vietnam. Discussions appeared in professional and scholarly journals, and scientific literature. Various factions weighed in offering opinions about the potential viability of using such weapons. On one side, experts cited the potential usefulness of the agents:

> [T]he time has come to distinguish between nonlethal chemical agents and the lethal chemical agents that recreate the old picture of WWI gas warfare.... Chemical agents provide a discriminating weapon for use in areas in which friendly or semi-friendly natives are located. The proper agent may help separate guerrilla forces from the support of the local population, avoiding bloodshed and property damage.... Tear gas ... could be used to flush the guerrillas from suspected areas or to break up

> guerrilla action taking place among the local population.... It could be used to break up ambush attacks along the trail, to turn back surprise attacks against a village, strong point, or observation post.... Tear gas could be used as a lesser measure of force.

Others were not persuaded. To some it was not so much the specific use of non-lethal agents as it was the appearance that the United States was secretly testing new weapons and tactics. The Federation of American Scientists, an organization founded in 1945 by scientists who had worked on the Manhattan Project to advise both the public and policy leaders of potential dangers from scientific and technical advances, were previously primarily concerned about controlling the development, testing and use of nuclear weapons. However, in the June issue of their newsletter, they published a statement opposing chemical and biological warfare in Vietnam:

> [W]e are concerned with reports of the field use of chemical weapons in Vietnam.... [R]eports that defoliating agents have been used ... have been confirmed by ... the Department of Defense. These charges give rise to the broader implication that the US is using the Vietnamese battle-field as a proving ground for chemical and biological warfare.... We are further opposed to experimentation on foreign soil and also feel that such experimentation involving citizens of other countries compounds the moral liability of such actions.

Further, claims that mustard gas had actually been used on the Buddhists in Hue still occasionally surfaced and invoked concerns that even the use of non-lethal agents might escalate into full-blown chemical warfare.[34]

In February 1965, General William Westmoreland, the Commander of the Military Assistance Command in Vietnam (MACV), came down on the pro-side of the argument. He believed that in a number of instances using riot-control agents would have prevented guerrillas from overrunning South Vietnamese units and killing or capturing their US advisors. Without fanfare, he notified the senior military advisors in Vietnam that US soldiers could use riot-control agents for self-defense and ordered them to issue protective masks and CS grenades to all their subordinates.[35]

As the South Vietnamese Army continued using riot-control agents and began to incorporate them into more of their operations, many in Saigon became concerned that the news would eventually break and could spark a fresh round of Communist propaganda even stronger than the one seen when herbicides were introduced. In December 1964, information officers began suggesting that the MACV Office of Information preemptively marginalize any future propaganda program by briefing newspaper correspondents about the growing use of these weapons. They felt an official statement on the properties of the agents and the reasons they were being used would avoid the impression the story was being suppressed and help dissipate any negative perception that might be generated if the press uncovered the information on their own. The Departments of State and Defense, however, disagreed. They thought it might unwittingly precipitate the propaganda campaign that they were hoping to avoid. Also, since many of the operations had involved efforts to rescue American prisoners of war, they were sensitive to potentially embarrassing questions and the impact such a story might have on the public back in the States.

Inevitably, newsmen did hear rumors that South Vietnamese troops were using unspecified chemical weapons against Viet Cong guerrillas in remote jungle areas. Early in 1965, Associated Press Reporter Peter Arnett contacted MACV about the rumors but they refused to acknowledge the incidents or provide any information on the nature of the chemical agents available to the South Vietnamese Army. Even though he could not get any official information, he continued to track reports and follow up on leads. On March 20, one of his colleagues, Associated Press Photographer Horst Faas, heard that a South Vietnamese unit was about to attack a Viet Cong stronghold in Binh Duong Province and were supported by helicopters equipped with sprayers filled with a nausea-producing gas. According to his source, the helicopters would fly over the enemy and spray them with the gas just prior to the infantry assault. Faas joined the unit to check out the story and possibly get some pictures of the helicopters spraying the enemy positions.[36] As he traveled with the soldiers, he saw that they were indeed armed with gas grenades and carrying protective masks. He also thought that they seemed unusually nervous about the operation and surmised that they were uncomfortable about attacking the enemy through a cloud of gas. Although the attack was called off and the chemicals never used, he told Arnett about the incident when he returned to Saigon. Arnett used the information to write a story about US and Vietnamese military forces experimenting with non-lethal chemical agents in South Vietnam. The Associated Press dispatch was sent out on March 22, 1965.[37]

The story was carried in papers throughout the United States and the rest of the world, and in many cases appeared on the front page. Although each paper truncated the story in different ways, they all included Arnett's major assertions. First, that the US and South Vietnam were conducting experiments with secret chemical warfare agents.

> The nature of the gases is classified information.... US and Vietnamese military forces are experimenting with non-lethal gas warfare.... Some of these experiments have succeeded, it was reported, but others have failed.... US helicopters have been used in some experiments, spraying gas in powdered form or laying down a barrage of gas grenades.... In one experiment held in 2nd Corps regions [troops fled in disorder when they

received fire from an area they believed was neutralized by the gas].... Informed sources pointed out that the use of gas is still in the experimental stage.... The experiments are expected to continue.

Second, that there was a lack of proper training and equipment for the South Vietnamese troops:

[During the mission observed by Faas] there proved to be a major shortage of gas masks. One tank unit had fifty-one masks [for] one hundred sixteen men. Those without gas masks were given pieces of lemon and handkerchiefs. An infantry battalion ... had one hundred seventy mask for its four hundred men. The Vietnamese troopers obviously were unfamiliar with the gas masks.... [Vietnamese officers said] gas was not used [during the operation] because their men were not familiar with it.

And, third, that the United States knew that it would be difficult for the world to accept the use of chemical weapons: "[One military source said that] [e]ven if [gas] does work over here, there are real problems of getting it accepted. The difficulty is in getting the American public used to the idea."

Despite the increase in public awareness and discussion on chemical warfare the previous summer, Washington was caught completely off-guard when Arnett's article appeared in papers throughout the country. The Administration had been lulled into complacency by the apparent lack of public interest in the defoliation program and even in the reports of the alleged use of mustard gas on protesters during the summer of 1963. Further, they did not consider the use of riot-control agents to be particularly newsworthy since they were used by police departments around the world. If anything, they felt the story should have been about soldiers using non-lethal weapons to help reduce the risk to noncombatants in the area.

When he heard about the story, Secretary of State Dean Rusk hurriedly called William Bundy, Assistant Secretary of State for Far Eastern Affairs, and then McGeorge Bundy to discuss the factual basis of the article, the current situation and the potential crisis. Concluding that an immediate coordinated response was essential, they decided to address journalists in both Washington and Saigon. While the State Department prepared a statement addressing the broader international implications and stressing that the use of such agents was "not contrary to international law and practice," the Pentagon directed Admiral Ulysses Sharp Jr., Commander in Chief of the United States Pacific Command, to provide the press with information on the types of agents and the reasons they were used. His press spokesman called the MACV Office of Information and told them that the Secretary of Defense wanted a press release issued to reporters in Saigon within the hour.[38]

Pressured by the deadline, the statement was vague and jargonistic:

In tactical situations in which Viet Cong intermingle with or take refuge among non-combatants, rather than use artillery or aerial bombardment, Vietnamese troops have and use a type of tear gas in the area. It is a non-lethal type of gas which disables temporarily, making the enemy incapable of fighting. Its use in such situations is no different than the use of disabling gases in riot control.

In an attempt to further distance the United States from the events in the article, the spokesman also told the reporters that "Americans have not used it, [only] the Vietnamese employ it."

Instead of dissipating the controversy, the statements were seen more as a confirmation of Arnett's version of the story than as a rebuttal. In many of the follow-up articles appearing on the front pages of papers the next day, reporters often blended the claims from the Associate Press dispatch with the text of the military press release, making it appear that the military was admitting that it was indeed experimenting with new chemical weapons. Some journalists continued trying to connect the events in Vietnam with the horrors of World War I with statements like: "Washington and Saigon confirmed the experiments, launched half a century after the Germans introduced poison gas to modern warfare at Ypres in World War I."[39]

One critical piece of information that was not released at the briefing was the identity of the specific agents used. The rhetoric about experiments coupled with this lack of specificity led some journalists to speculate the military was also using other classes of chemicals, such as the highly lethal nerve agents. When this question was put directly to the military spokesman in Saigon, he did not deny the claim but merely cast doubt on reports they were used. Since he claimed the identity of the agents was classified and refused further comment, even reporters accepting his statement that the chemicals were only riot-control agents assumed they were something exotic and did not believe they were available to civilian police departments. Although the Pentagon rectified the situation the next day by providing complete details on the agents, the perception of experimentation and cover-up persisted. This perception was amplified when military press officers, acting on orders from the Pentagon, refused to answer further questions about chemical agents or their potential use in Vietnam.[40]

The North Vietnamese took advantage of the uproar and launched a propaganda campaign decrying the use of chemical weapons. At a press conference in Hanoi, they appealed to "all progressive people of the world to rouse public opinion everywhere to stay the bloody hands of United States imperialism." Even though riot-control agents were used in a number of earlier operations, this was the first time that either the North Vietnamese or the Viet Cong expressed any indignation. They were apparently as surprised as the Johnson Administration over the vehement outcry in the press. The day after the press conference, Communist newspapers in China and the Soviet Union took up the campaign, running stories about the "new crime of American imperialism" declaring Americans had an "utter disregard for international law and the most elementary principles of humanitarianism, and show them up as fascist criminals," comments that were soon echoed in left-wing newspapers throughout the world. Reacting to allegations that there was a Caucasian versus Asian element to the incidents, the propaganda had a significant impact in Southeast Asian countries as well as other nations that had suffered under European colonialism. On April 5, North Vietnam attempted to stoke the fire by claiming the US had actually used "lethal asphyxiating gases," dropping "adamsite, alpha-chlora-ocetophone [sic] and thiophosgene" earlier in the year during Operation Ban Thai I. Although the new charges were carried by pro-Communist newspapers around the world, it added little to the ongoing controversy.[41]

Stunned by the growing storm both at home and abroad, the Administration hastily arranged a series of press conferences to try to control the situation. At each briefing, the speaker stressed the key points that the Administration thought would dissipate the crisis: that the South Vietnamese had only used the agents as a means of limiting casualties in situations where guerrillas were intermixed with non-combatants; that the agents were the same as those used by police agencies throughout the world; and even that there was no Federal law prohibiting US citizens from purchasing tear-gas dispensers for personal protection. They gave numerous examples where the agents were safely used and even pointed out that, eighteen months earlier, Secretary McNamara deliberately walked into a cloud of CS so that he could experience the effects first-hand. Officials were careful to avoid using the word "gas," strictly referring to the compounds as riot-control agents. They also tried to deflect the focus of the controversy back onto Arnett's choice of wording in his article, saying that his emphasis on experimenting gave the impression that "something new and esoteric and weird" was going on, and he was therefore responsible for arousing unwarranted fears about the start of a chemical war.[42]

As the controversy grew, George Reedy, the President's press secretary, tried to distance the White House from the events by telling reporters the President was not consulted before the agents were used. "That's not the sort of thing that comes up for [his] approval. For many years, this kind of authority has been delegated to area commanders." However, this plea of ignorance sparked a controversy of its own. As Former Vice President Richard Nixon pointed out, it merely gave the impression that the military was out of control and making policy decisions on its own. Senator Mike Mansfield wrote the President to express his disbelief in such an assertion, stating it was "beyond [his] comprehension how any American in an office of responsibility would not realize the vast significance, beyond immediate military considerations, of this act and, therefore, seek the highest political authority before taking such a step."[43] The President, however, did not waiver in his response to these criticisms, stating flatly that he did not agree with the suggestion that the military authorities in Vietnam should have sought [his] personal approval before making the limited, specific use of riot-control gases which they authorized in an effort to save lives. These episodes have been blown up out of all proportion by critics who do not seem to be troubled by the killing of civilians in city streets by terrorist bombs.[44]

Newspaper editorials around the country continued to be negative, questioning the political, moral and ethical judgment of the Administration. The *New York Times* summed up the typical US sentiment very well, stating that, while it was possible to argue that using non-lethal weapons could save lives,

> ordinary people everywhere have a strong psychological revulsion, if not horror, at the idea of any kind of poisonous gas, even a temporarily disabling type that only causes extreme discomfort.... In Vietnam, gas was supplied and sanctioned by white men against Asians.... No other country has employed such a weapon in recent warfare. If the United States believed that people everywhere would be logical and "sensible" and would understand that nonlethal gas constitutes really only another form of warfare and even a relatively humane one, someone has blundered grievously.... The United States claims to be fighting in Vietnam for freedom, right, justice and other moral principles, as well as against Communism and for the security of the United States and the free world. By using a noxious gas – even of a nonlethal type – the Johnson Administration is falling back toward the old axiom that all's fair in war. But this happens to be a war in which the moral stature of the United States is at least as vital as bullets, shells and bombs. Gas is a wretched means to achieve even the most valid ends.[45]

Other editorials from around the country raised similar concerns:

> The general feeling in this country is almost certain to be that whatever temporary advantage may have been gained by the use of the gas is microscopic in comparison to the damage that has been done to the image of America.
>
> *Scranton Times* (Pennsylvania)

> The danger in using gas, even in this limited way, is that it breaks down the restraints that warring nations have put upon the use of gas since the First World War. If nonlethal gas is used by the South Vietnamese, the Communists may look upon this as an excuse to use poison gas.
>
> *Nashville Tennessean*

The obvious peril is where to draw the line when once this form of warfare is adopted. It is not too far from tear gas to a toxic gas, and if the enemy responds to a nonlethal gas with a more virulent type, escalation in terror is under way.

Detroit News

Compared to bombs, napalm, antipersonnel mines or plain bullets, it is merciful indeed; a war fought with such weapons could result in fewer casualties than a normal football season. Unfortunately, there is no guarantee that a billion Asians – not to mention Africans, Europeans and Latin Americans – will reach that conclusion, obvious as it is.

Chicago's American

Internationally, editorial comments mirrored these concerns and focused on the same visceral issues – secret gasses, experiments and Caucasians verses Asians. Some left-wing papers even raised comparisons to infamous historic figures such as Hitler and Mussolini.[46]

In the midst of the uproar, a few reporters decided to follow Secretary McNamara's example and experience the effects of CS for themselves so they could accurately describe the effects for their readers. While no one enjoyed the experience, some were more surprised than others, and described the effects of exposure as making

the subject feel like he has been unexpectedly hit by a flying tackle [in a football game] … he cannot breathe, though he has an overpowering desire to get air into his lungs … in a few seconds, he is helpless, truly incapacitated, because his one thought is to be relieved of this surprisingly terrible feeling which may be similar to the way a man feels when he is drowning.

Others were less colorful but more realistic, pointing out that although the gas made them sick, it was "not so bad," and they "prefer[red] it to being shot or shelled."[47]

Many in the scientific community also raised protests over the cavalier use of any chemical weapons, regardless of their effects or the circumstances surrounding their use. For example, in their March newsletter, the Federation of American Scientists weighed in on the issue, condemning

in the strongest possible terms the use of chemical and biological [*sic*] warfare agents in the Southeast Asia area.… We find it morally repugnant that the United States should find itself the party to the use of weapons of indiscriminae [*sic*] effects, with principal effectiveness against civilian populations. The justifications of such weapons in warfare as "humane" will, in the long run, hurt the security of the United States, even if military effectiveness in a specific situation can be demonstrated.... [T]he use of United States produced chemical and biological [*sic*] weapons in Asia will be interpreted widely as "field-testing" of these weapons among foreign people and will hurt our efforts immeasurably in good will and moral respect all over the world.

They even turned what the Administration saw as a key benefit of using the agents, the ability to limit casualties in situations where guerrillas were inter-mixed with non-combatants, into a vilification by stating that "news stories coming out of Saigon confirm, in fact, that gas attacks have been mounted against civilian populations suspected of harboring Viet Cong elements. The characterization of such applications as 'humane' is incomprehensible, to say the least."[48]

Congressmen also received a marked increase in the number of letters harshly critical of the Johnson Administration's Vietnam policy, particularly with regards to employing chemical agents. For example, a businessman in Media, Pennsylvania, wrote:

[w]hen the United States makes war on people who use poison arrows as part of their weaponry, something is wrong. When, in addition, the United States employs poison gas upon these same people, everything is wrong. Bad means cannot accomplish a good end.

A physician in Bay Shore, Louisiana, wrote: "[t]he incredible announcement that we have ordered gassing of innocent men, women and children, and then defend it as humane, can only invoke the memory of Hitler."[49] Responding to this uproar, six Republican members of the House of Representatives wrote to the President deploring the use of chemical weapons in Vietnam and requesting the military immediately cease using them. They charged using chemical agents, even non-lethal ones, was turning world public opinion against the country and inviting Communist reprisals with lethal chemicals.[50]

As the White House maneuvered to stabilize and defuse the situation within the United States, the international political outcry mounted and forced the Administration to expend even more time and energy defending itself. On March 26, the Central Intelligence Agency sent out an Intelligence Information Cable concerning the attitude of the Permanent United Nations Representatives on the Vietnam Crisis:

The introduction of gas into the Vietnam conflict has, allegedly, aroused the Soviet Union's interest in possibly introducing not the whole Vietnam question but the issue of the use of gas in the Vietnam conflict. Apparently the issue of gas warfare is so emotionally charged that it is generally felt by the United Nations Permanent Representatives that if the USSR were to introduce the issue to the Security Council, the USSR would be able to get a strong and widely supported condemnation of the United States for allowing the use of gas in Vietnam.... A condemnation of the United States, whether passed as a resolution or not, would be an achievement in solidifying the growing criticism of the United States for escalating the conflict in Vietnam.... [T]he image of the United States, according to the opinion of United Nations Representatives, is at its lowest ebb today.[51]

Nikolai Fedorenko, the Soviet representative, eventually brought up the issue during a meeting of the Committee to Define Aggression, charging the United States with a "gross violation" of the universally recognized rules of international law and the "elementary principles of morality and humanity" for using "poisonous gas" in Vietnam. US representative Francis Plimpton vehemently denied the charge, stating the United States had never used poisonous gases in Vietnam and had no intention of ever using them. He emphasized the non-lethal characteristics of the agents and stressed that they were often used by police around the world. He accused Fedorenko of laying down a "familiar smokescreen of propaganda" to cover the campaign of terror, murder and kidnapping the North Vietnamese were waging in South Vietnam. Ultimately the verbal battle degenerated into more generalized accusations of the efforts of both countries to dominate the world. Since the Soviet Union never attempted to bring up the issue before the Security Council, the United States avoided an official condemnation and further damage to its international image.[52]

While it was obvious the Soviets would try to do as much damage to the image of the United States as possible, a much more grievous denouncement came from an unexpected quarter. While Great Britain was usually one of Washington's staunchest allies, this tumult had the Members of Parliament in an uproar. They were inundating Washington with protests "denounc[ing Americans] for resorting to barbarous and horrible weapons." The volume and vehemence of the British response surprised the Administration and created a substantial strain on relations between the two countries.

On the day after Arnett's article hit the news stand, British Foreign Secretary Michael Stewart was in Washington and gave a presentation at the National Press Club. During his comments, he related how he had just come from a meeting with the Secretary of State where he expressed to Mr. Rusk the "very grave concern" felt in Britain and other countries about the use of gas in Vietnam. Stewart continued his remarks noting that the choice of weapons employed by the US should be based not only on their military characteristics but also on world opinion. "I am, in fact, asking your Government – to quote your own Declaration of Independence – to display a decent respect for the opinions of mankind."[53]

The comment, particularly the choice of wording, stunned President Johnson personally. The next morning, McGeorge Bundy telephoned David Bruce, the US Ambassador to the United Kingdom, and told him to draft a letter to Prime Minister Harold Wilson expressing the President's indignation over Stewart's comments, especially his quotation of the Declaration of Independence in conjunction with British objections to the use of riot-control agents. Bruce protested, pointing out the Prime Minister was always a strong supporter of the Administration. However, at this time Wilson was receiving pressure from both the left and center elements of Parliament to take a harder and more critical stand against American activities in Vietnam, and a disparaging letter about a ranking member of the British Government would provide him with an excuse to pull his support from the US. Fortunately for the Administration, Johnson's advisors convinced him to reconsider before the letter was sent and Bruce was spared the "undignified and unnecessary" task of delivering it.[54]

On March 24, members of the British House of Commons packed the chamber to debate the issue. During the debate, the Labour Party called for Prime Minister Wilson to condemn the US for using gas and, further, to dissociate Britain from American policy in Vietnam. Sir Alec Douglas-Home, leader of the Conservative Opposition, asked Wilson for his assurance that tear gas was the only chemical agent used and not something more lethal. After reassuring the House that the United States had not violated any international conventions by using riot-control agents, the Prime Minister deflected calls for immediate action by reminding House members that Foreign Secretary Stewart was at that time in Washington meeting with Secretary of State Rusk to discuss the situation in Vietnam, and that the Foreign Secretary was the best conduit to convey the sentiments of the British Government to the Johnson Administration. Immediately after the session, a contingent of the Labour Party called the Foreign Secretary in Washington and urged him to express their "horror and indignation" to the Americans. Another group went to the American Embassy in London and met with US representatives to press for negotiating a peaceful settlement in Vietnam.

Later in the day, the tenor changed as reports circulated that the British themselves used tear gas in several dependant territories, including Cyprus, British Guiana and Singapore. Several days later, in response to a question from the House floor, Anthony Greenwood, the Colonial Secretary, confirmed that Great Britain had used the same agents employed in Vietnam in over 120 incidents in English territories over the previous five years to "disarm persons who ran amok, to quell prison disturbances, to apprehend armed criminals and to disperse rioters." Faced with their apparent hypocrisy, one member of the House quipped that perhaps it really was "better to cry than die." As Sir Douglas-Home noted, it was not really the application of riot-control agents per se that caused the fervor but their description as "gas," which aroused intense emotions because of experiences in World War I.[55]

The Wilson Government continued working to abate the controversy and move away from a confrontation with the United States. Despite their progress, President Johnson continued to fume about the initial British response, especially some of their comments that appeared in the press. When his preoccupation began to become counterproductive, McGeorge Bundy admonished Johnson to keep things in perspective and stop being bitter:

> On a number of occasions you have showed your skepticism when one or another of us has remarked that the British have been very solid and helpful on Vietnam.... Moreover, you feel the wounds of ... what Michael Stewart said about gas, although everyone else has long since forgotten.... It remains a fact that every experienced observer from David Bruce on down has been astonished by the overall strength and skill of Wilson's defense of our policy in Vietnam and his mastery of his own left wing in the process.... The only price we have paid for this support is ... keeping them reasonably well informed... This is not a very great cost.[56]

During an April news conference where the President outlined his Administration's efforts on education and the economy, he was still being asked to "set the record straight."

> Well, I think the record's pretty straight on it already. They filed a story out there that indicated – the first story filed – that America was engaged in gas warfare. The implications of that story were that we were using poisonous gas to ... kill people. And it took the Government about two weeks to catch up with that story.... The type of gas that is a standard item in the South Vietnamese military forces ... can be purchased by any individual from open stocks in this country just like you order something out of a Sears and Roebuck catalogue.... The Chief of Police in Washington has it now and in the interest of saving lives and protecting people it could be used.... But if you wrote a big story and made a big broadcast, and said the Chief of Police is using gas warfare ... it would excite people; because the word "gas" is like the word "dope" – it is an ugly word. And until you get all the truth, the whole truth, and nothing but the truth, you have a lot of people making misjudgments. Now, I knew nothing about the gas. No one told me that the South Vietnamese were going to use a tear gas ... but there's no reason why they should. If the United States military forces were going to use poisonous gas, of course the Commander in Chief would know about it... I think that Senator Fulbright ... after a full hearing on it, pretty well summed it up when he said that somebody made a mountain out of a molehill. And I just wish [people were as concerned about] our soldiers who are dying as they are with somebody's eyes who watered a little bit, particularly in an effort

that ... the South Vietnamese were making, to save some of their people and some of our people.[57]

The maelstrom eventually subsided, but the Administration was truly shaken. Public and political response to the article had caught them like an old-fashioned naval broadside, and they were unprepared for the magnitude of the conflagration. At one point, it became so frustrating for President Johnson that he asked the National Security Council if the whole incident could have actually been a "Communist plot," prompting Carl Rowan, Director of the United States Information Agency, to point out that "Peter Arnett of the Associated Press didn't write his story out of the blue. We should find out about his background."[58]

Part of the problem was the wording of both Arnett's article and the press releases issued in response, and part was the way the Administration attempted to deflect the blame. As *Time* magazine summed up the events:

> [w]ithin hours, Arnett sent clattering out over AP's wires a dispatch that began: "US and Vietnamese military forces are experimenting with non-lethal gas warfare in South Vietnam." ... Hardly anybody noticed the word "nonlethal." ... But the words "gas warfare" and "experimenting" stirred macabre memories.... When the story first broke, the US was inept in its efforts to soften criticism.... Press Secretary George Reedy took great pains to let it be known that the gas was first sent to South Vietnam before Johnson became President, which is irrelevant, and that it was used without his knowledge, which is inexcusable.[59]

Even though the story won Arnett and his co-writers, Horst Faas and Malcolm Browne, a Pulitzer Prize, the poor quality of the writing was recognized by their peers. For example Jack Raymond, a contemporary journalist in Vietnam, wrote an article the following year discussing the inherent conflicts that arise between the press and the military during a war. As one of his key points, he described how both the tone of an article and the manner that facts were presented could cause serious problems. He concluded his article using the Arnett story as an example, observing that

> the reporting last year of the use of nonlethal gases, similar to those used by police, was dramatized as though these were poison gases. The stories did not say they were poison, but the tone of the reporting implied that.

Arnett also repeatedly used key words that created negative images for his readers. For example, he made reference to "experimenting" six times in his relatively short article, and as General Earl Wheeler, Chairman of the Joint Chiefs of Staff, pointed out, "[t]o the uninformed, all gas is poisonous and an experiment is something conducted by a mad doctor in a secret laboratory." Barry Zorthian, the chief spokesman for the US mission in Vietnam, who later retired as Vice President of Time Inc., was more blunt. He described Arnett's story as deliberately negative and designed to create worldwide anti-American sentiment.[60]

Ultimately, Washington established new press guidelines to help Saigon deal more effectively with the rapidly proliferating number of journalists that were moving into the war zone. They also withdrew General Westmoreland's authority to use riot-control agents and instructed him to postpone any upcoming defoliation missions except ones that were deemed critical, and then only in remote areas that were unlikely to draw much attention. If such an operation was undertaken, then he was to use "maximum measures to reduce publicity" and to prepare "to meet any inquiries [from the press] with a full rationale."[61]

3

OPERATION STOMP

The first combat units arriving in Vietnam were largely unprepared for the type of war they were facing; not only for the tactics of their elusive enemy but also for many of the venues they would eventually fight in. This deficiency was often compounded by insufficient or inaccurate intelligence prior to their arrival, an extended chain of command that often intermixed the different service branches, physical isolation from other American units, and simple culture shock. In September 1965, these factors came together in a situation ultimately opening the door for widespread use of riot-control agents by the United States and its allies.

Along with other battalions of the 3rd Marine Division, the 3rd Battalion of the 9th Marine Regiment was stationed in Okinawa as a rapid response force to the Korean peninsula should the ceasefire end. When its rotation ended in the summer of 1964, the battalion was transferred en masse back to California where its designation was changed to 2nd Battalion of the 7th Marine Regiment (abbreviated 2/7). This "transplacement" process was designed to ensure deploying combat units maintained a stable cohort of officers and men. When they arrived at Camp Las Pulgas, however, most of the personnel – including all the battalion staff, all the company commanders and nearly half of the enlisted marines – were either transferred to other duty stations or discharged from the Corps. Many of the replacements with orders to fill the vacated positions were recruits fresh out of boot camp reporting to their first duty station. Essentially a new battalion, 2/7 became one of nine infantry battalions making up the 1st Marine Division.

After the Bay of Pigs and Cuban Missile Crisis, Washington was afraid Fidel Castro might order an attack on the naval base at Guantanamo Bay to drive the final vestiges of the United States out of his country, so one mission of the 1st

Division was to act as the reactionary force to any hostilities erupting in Cuba. On a rotational basis, one of the nine battalions was always on standby for immediate deployment to Cuba; they were prepared to be airborne within eight hours of an alert. A second battalion was on standby to follow the first no later than twenty-four hours later. If the situation warranted, four additional infantry battalions would board ships and sail to the island within seventy-two hours of the alert. While a battalion was in one of these three alert categories, all of its equipment was packed and ready for deployment; all assigned personnel were required to remain within a few miles of the base. Field training, or any other activity that might delay demarcation, was postponed until the battalion rotated out of alert status. Following its arrival at Camp Las Pulgas, 2/7 assumed its part in this rotational standby system.

In September, after only a few months in the United States, 2/7 began training for redeployment back to Okinawa the next summer. This training was specific, focusing on the conditions and situations the marines expected to encounter should the war in Korea resume. They spent a great deal of time on cold weather operations, mountain warfare and even amphibious assaults. Due to the limited training budget, many of the field exercises were abbreviated and there was significant simulation. The marines also attended several classes on counterinsurgency and guerrilla warfare, since 2/7 could deploy from Okinawa to South Vietnam during an emergency. The primary focus of their training, however, was fighting a classical confrontation against a massed enemy force.

By April, 2/7 completed its training cycle and the marines were waiting for orders to deploy back to Okinawa. However, on May 18, they received orders to deploy to Vietnam instead; departing San Diego Harbor for Vietnam a mere six days later. Concurrent with the change in mission orders was an unusual and unexpected change in command. Lieutenant Colonel J.K. McCreight, the officer who commanded the battalion through all the training at Camp Las Pulgas, was replaced by Lieutenant Colonel Leon Utter, who had been the operations officer of the 7th Marine Regiment. A veteran of both World War II and the Korean War, he was personally selected to lead 2/7 by the commanders of both the 1st Marine Division and the 7th Marine Regiment. He assumed command of the battalion as the ship left San Diego Harbor and put out to sea. Utter spent the next forty-five days at sea getting to know his officers, inspecting his men and their equipment, and preparing for the battalion's arrival in Vietnam.

Since their pre-deployment training focused almost exclusively on the conditions and enemy they expected to face in Korea, the marines scrambled to compile everything they could about guerrilla warfare and the Viet Cong while sailing to Vietnam. They pored over training manuals and reviewed tactics used fighting the Japanese during the island hopping campaigns of World War II. Unfortunately, much of the information they found on guerrilla warfare and counterinsurgency was outdated or did not apply to the conditions in Vietnam;

and most of what they knew about the Viet Cong was from watching TV back in the United States, reflecting both the cultural and martial bias against developing countries presented there.[1]

The 2/7 Marines landed at Qui Nhon, the capital of Binh Dinh Province, on July 7, and became part of Task Force Alpha, an assignment placing them under the operational control of Major General Stanley Larsen, United States Army. Qui Nhon was located on National Route 1, about 270 miles northeast of Saigon and sixty miles southeast of Da Nang, next to a key harbor MACV was going to develop as a deepwater port. After a Viet Cong sapper attack in Qui Nhon killed more than thirty Americans earlier in the year, one of the reasons General Larsen sent the marines to the city was to provide protection for the construction workers building the naval station.

When they sailed into the harbor, the marines were prepared to conduct an amphibious landing under hostile fire from an entrenched, well-armed enemy defending the beachhead. Instead, the Americans received an unexpected fanfare from the local villagers, including hundreds of laughing women and children, shouting to them from the beach. The marines were in shock, the first of many to come as they adapted to their new environment.

The marines immediately began building a battalion defensive compound a short distance inland and away from the civilian population. After three days, all the battalion's equipment was unloaded from the ship, moved off the beach and into the new compound. The marines also set up security checkpoints and road blocks along the section of National Route 1 running through their area of operation. The constant press of civilians moving through the area was a serious concern since the Americans worried Viet Cong spies were intermingling with the residents and mapping out the battalion's defenses. Once the marines felt their base of operations was secure, they began patrolling the nearby countryside.

Training the marines received prior to deployment was useless in their current situation and it took time for the Americans to adjust to life in Vietnam. Along with learning the customs and routines of their new neighbors, the marines also had to adapt to the animals inhabiting the wilderness around them. In addition to insects, unusual birds and poisonous snakes, there were apes that threw both rocks and excrement at them. There were also large lizards, some up to four-feet long, foraging at night for food among the sleeping soldiers. The inexperienced and jittery marines engaged in many "firefights" during early encounters with these intruders.[2]

Other than jungle, the terrain around Qui Nhon consisted of mud flats, rice paddies, manioc fields and hills. Scattered throughout the hills were a number of caves the locals used as hideaways to store crops and supplies. These caves also served as a refuge when their villages were threatened by the war; a practice common in many parts of Vietnam. Such caves were also ideal for Viet Cong operations. The entrances were usually well camouflaged and difficult to spot;

utterly invisible from the air. A convenient place to store food, weapons and medical supplies, caves provided a concealed assembly point, shelter from the weather and protection during a firefight.

Marines learned how to fight enemy soldiers barricaded in caves the hard way during the island-hopping phase of World War II. In 1945 on the island of Peleliu, the Japanese abandoned the conventional strategy of defending the beach against an amphibious assault; instead waiting for the marines in fortified caves and pillboxes across the interior of the island. This battle heralded a change in Japan's defensive strategy, foreshadowing operations on Iwo Jima, Okinawa and Luzon.

After suffering a staggering number of casualties, the marines eventually developed an effective technique to force the defenders out of these heavily fortified positions. The initial version of what became known as the blowtorch and corkscrew method involved pumping gasoline down a ventilation shaft into the main cave chamber and then igniting it with a phosphorus grenade. The waiting marines shot the defenders trying to escape the flames. Then the marines began using flame-throwers. A marine armed with one of these weapons would crawl as close as possible to the cave opening and shoot the flaming fuel into the cave. The thickened fuel was particularly effective because it would cling to every surface and even flow around corners. These features reduced the need for accuracy and made it easy to target the small openings the defenders fired through. The flaming mass not only burned the enemy soldiers, but also quickly used up the oxygen inside the cave and asphyxiated anyone who was not killed in the conflagration. To complete the blowtorch and corkscrew, when the flames died down the marines threw in a satchel charge, collapsing the cave and ensuring it could not be reoccupied. At the start of the Vietnam War, this technique was still the preferred method of dealing with caves and bunkers. Now referred to as the "3Bs," which stood for "blind 'em, burn 'em, and blast 'em," the only modification was using smoke grenades to cover the approach of the flame-thrower gunner.[3]

About two months after landing at Qui Nhon, Lieutenant Colonel Utter received approval from Task Force Alpha headquarters to conduct a minor search and clear mission along a ridgeline about ten miles north of Qui Nhon. He wanted to drive a local Viet Cong unit out of a series of caves they were using as a base of operations. His plan was relatively simple. First, two companies of marines would envelop the ridgeline, then move through the area, capturing or killing the guerrillas they found and destroying the enemy's equipment. Whenever possible, the marines would also destroy the cave systems to prevent other Viet Cong moving in after the operation was over. While the operation was straightforward, there were a couple of serious complications he worried about. First, since local villagers were also using caves in the area for storage, the marines needed to verify the status of any cave occupants before moving in to search the cave. He wanted to minimize the potential not only of civilian casualties, but also of his men being ambushed by guerrillas posing as non-combatants. Another concern was the Viet Cong seizing civilians and using them as hostages. All the tactics the marines used to neutralized fortified caves were based on the premise everyone inside was hostile and could be engaged without discrimination; thus the marines would likely kill most, if not all, of the hostages. If faced with this scenario, the only option available to the marines was convincing the guerrillas to surrender; a skill the marines were not training for.

As the operations section developed the plan and considered the alternatives, a battalion ammunition sergeant suggested using the tear-gas grenades the battalion carried as part of its standard equipment.[4] These gas grenades resembled a softball and looked like a cheap plastic toy. Unlike pyrotechnic tear-gas grenades, resembling a can of shaving cream and using an incendiary fuel to volatilize the agent, these grenades exploded and instantly dispersed a dense cloud of CS powder into the surrounding area. If the guerrillas refused to surrender, the sergeant reasoned, the intense irritation caused by exposure to the agent would drive them out of the cave and into the open. Even if the Viet Cong were not fully incapacitated, the marines waiting at the cave entrance would have no trouble capturing and disarming them. Using the grenades also reduced the risk of injuring any hostages that might be in the cave.[5]

Since landing in Vietnam, the commander and staff of 2/7 operated with minimal guidance from their army counterparts at Task Force headquarters. Unaware American forces in Vietnam were prohibited from using riot-control agents, and that only General Westmoreland had the authority to override this restriction, the operations section solicited comments from the battalion's officers and senior sergeants. Since every marine was exposed to tear gas as part of his basic training, none of them had any doubts about its effectiveness. Company commanders and platoon leaders endorsed anything driving the enemy out of a cave; eliminating the need for the marines to fight their way in. The chaplain added his blessing, noting tear gas would save lives on both sides. Based on these comments, Lieutenant Colonel Utter accepted the suggestion and approved the plan to use tear gas during the upcoming operation. The gas grenades were issued to the marines in addition to the smoke grenades, flamethrowers and explosives needed for the 3Bs.

The mission was designated Operation Stomp and began on September 5, 1965. Company H crossed the mud flats of Qui Nhon bay on tracked amphibious vehicles similar to those used to assault the beaches of Iwo Jima, while helicopters carried Company F into position on the back side of the ridge so they could prevent the Viet Cong from escaping. The operation proceeded just as planned, trapping the guerrillas between the two forces. During the initial phase of the operation, the marines killed twenty-six enemy soldiers and captured three others.

As they were searching the area, the marines found a huge cave and tunnel complex occupied by a large Viet Cong force. As they tried to convince the guerrillas to surrender, the marines realized there were also numerous hostages in the cave and the guerrillas were planning to use them as shields if the marines attacked. Aware that the intense effects of CS were only temporary and unlikely to cause serious injury to the women and children, Lieutenant Colonel Utter ordered the marines to use the CS grenades. When the grenades went off in the caves, the results were immediate and spectacular. As fast as possible, everyone exited the caves and stumbled into the open. The guerrillas were quickly disarmed and segregated from the civilians without any fighting. By employing tear gas instead of more traditional alternatives, seventeen guerrillas were captured and all of the hostages, approximately 300 women, children and old men, were rescued unharmed.

Using non-lethal grenades also helped introduce the relatively inexperienced marines to some of the unusual hazards associated with fighting in caves. For instance, in one incident a marine threw a gas grenade into a cave before he entered to search for Viet Cong. Unfortunately, there was a short connecting tunnel at the back of the cave leading to an adjacent part of the complex. The grenade bounced through the tunnel and went off among a group of marines clearing the adjoining area. Had he used the fragmentation grenade called for in the traditional protocol, all of those marines would have been killed. As it was, their injuries were limited to coughing, sneezing and crying.[6]

In a concurrent but contrasting example to Operation Stomp, highlighting the need for alternative methods of clearing caves, Company B of the 1st Battalion, 7th Marines was part of a search and destroy mission to clear the Batangan Peninsula. After capturing a Viet Cong field hospital hidden inside a large cave, the marines came under heavy fire from guerrillas barricaded deeper within the cavern. Unable to convince the barricaded guerrillas to surrender, the marines threw satchel charges into the cave; the explosions killed the sixty-six Viet Cong hiding there. While searching the cave for weapons and enemy intelligence, six marines passed out because the blasts had displaced the oxygen in the deeper recesses of the cave. One of them died as a result of asphyxiation.[7]

Aware that Secretary of Defense McNamara had sworn he would never again authorize American soldiers to use riot-control agents in Vietnam, an Associated Press correspondent covering the operation asked Lieutenant Colonel Utter if MACV gave him permission to use tear gas. The colonel replied he decided to use the weapons based on his own authority. MACV was caught by surprise when reporters asked about the mission; demanding to know who had authority to authorize using riot-control agents. The staff in Saigon immediately initiated an investigation to determine if Utter knowingly violated United States policy and ignored the ban on using such weapons. Information officers scrambling to avoid another press fiasco, attempted to put a positive spin on the incident by calling attention to the battalion commander's concern for the hostages intermixed with the Viet Cong guerrillas. They stressed the need for a humanitarian option, contrasting the lethality of traditional methods of clearing caves with flame-throwers and explosives to the uncomfortable but relatively harmless effects of exposure to tear gas. To buy time, military spokesmen asked reporters to hold the story until the investigation was complete so as not to preemptively convict Lieutenant Colonel Utter and ruin his career if it was unwarranted. However, after the magnitude of the controversy less than six months before, reporters disregarded the request and the story appeared in papers the next day.[8]

As anticipated, North Vietnam attempted to capitalize on the propaganda value of the incident and rekindle the fire that burned through the press during the previous March and April. On September 8, Radio Hanoi rewrote the events and charged the marines had "imprudently used toxic gas, killing or seriously affecting many civilians," a charge echoed by the Communist China News Agency and Soviet TASS. Hanoi also filed a complaint with the International Control Commission, the body formed to oversee the elections that would merge North and South Vietnam. As visions of another international outcry flashed before their eyes, officials in Washington braced for the fallout.[9]

A swarm of newsmen descended on Qui Nhon to cover the story. The marines were in shock over the level of media attention the battalion was receiving and the apparent worldwide interest in such a minor tactical operation. They were not around for the March controversy and did not grasp the sensitivity of the situation. In addition to the obvious issue involving the unauthorized use of tear gas, the incident gave the impression the military was out of control; combat officers could do as they pleased, ignoring the regulations and policies established by higher command.

Reactions among military officers to Lieutenant Colonel Utter's decision to use tear gas were mixed. Some believed he should be disciplined since he had used weapons specifically banned by the Secretary of Defense and his actions placed the United States in a potentially compromising position. These officers wanted him removed from command and possibly even court-marshaled. Although the investigation quickly established the marines never received the directive prohibiting the use of riot-control agents and Lieutenant Colonel Utter was indeed unaware of the ban, many in MACV still unsympathetically castigated him for failing to get clarification from his superiors. As a member of General Westmoreland's staff noted, "[e]veryone knew how [General Westmoreland] felt about it and had [they asked for permission, it] would have been denied."[10]

Other officers were more empathetic to the difficult decisions Utter had to make during the hostage situation. With only limited options, they supported his methods as the best way of minimizing the risks to both the civilians used to shield the guerillas and American soldiers. Well before the current controversy, soldiers were pointing out the unique advantages riot-control agents offered in these situations. As an article in *The Marine Corps Gazette* suggested:

> [c]hemical agents provide a discriminating weapon for use in areas in which friendly or semi-friendly natives are located.... [R]iot control chemical

agents might be considered to gain control without exposing the local population to undue hazard. Tear gas ... could be used to flush the guerrillas from suspected areas or to break up guerrilla action taking place among the local population. The effects of CS, though temporary, are immediate.

A number of American commanders in Vietnam also endorsed using these agents in their combat after action reports. One in particular noted:

[m]any of the casualties sustained by this Brigade in operations thus far and much risk to civilians in the area of operations, could have been avoided through the use of riot agents. The use of riot agents would serve to incapacitate the VC long enough for US troops to get to them; it would provide a good tool for flushing the numerous underground fortifications that this unit has encountered. It would increase the proportion of prisoners captured and it would prove invaluable for use when the VC use civilians as a shield. Finally, it would materially reduce the number of US casualties sustained on offensive operations.[11]

Unaware of the serious predicament his counterpart in 2/7 was in, but recognizing the need to develop additional tactics marines could use to force guerrillas out of caves and other enclosed areas, the battalion commander whose soldier died of asphyxiation in the cave on the Batangan Peninsula recommended to General Lewis Walt, commander of the 3rd Marine Division, marines be authorized to use riot-control agents to save both American and enemy lives. The suggestion was met with a cold silence.[12]

Attempting to put an end to the controversy, General Larsen sent a message to MACV backing Lieutenant Colonel Utter and the decision to use tear gas to protect the hostages. He noted even his office did not have any directives specifically banning the use of tear gas and it was therefore impossible to claim Utter was not following orders. He went even further, declaring although he had not been specifically briefed on the proposal to use gas grenades during the operation, he would have endorsed it as the most humane way of dealing with the tactical situation the battalion faced. MACV, however, proceeded with their investigation and the pressure continued to mount on Lieutenant Colonel Utter. Feeling a scapegoat would ultimately be required to end the controversy, he prepared the farewell remarks he wanted to deliver to his battalion.[13]

As the inquisition proceeded, the gaggle of journalists who had flocked to Qui Nhon began sending stories back to the United States. But this time, instead of insinuations of experimentation and secrecy, reporters tended to focus on the unique value of the agents to the operation:

The concussion from a demolition charge can cause bleeding from the mouth, nose, ears and anus, but a really professional and trained soldier can take that and keep on firing. He may be permanently deafened but a good soldier will continue to fight. But if you attack a man's eyes and his breathing he will come out of the hole.

They also keyed in on the humanitarian side of events and contrasted the brutality of the Viet Cong with the restraint shown by American soldiers. In some instances, articles even endorsed using tear gas; pointing out it could be considered inhumane not to use it. For instance, *Time* magazine reported:

> [a] tragic but inevitable feature of the ground war in Vietnam is that civilians are all too often caught up in the shooting. Time and again US troops are fired upon from the huts of peasant families, from villages that the Viet Cong have commandeered. Should the response be a blast from every deadly weapon available? Or should the troops hold their fire for fear of hitting innocent civilians, and risk letting the Viet Cong escape?... [A] reluctance to use tear gas is an unnecessary and even inhumane restriction in doing what is one of the most unpleasant and difficult jobs in the world.

When it came down to the issue of why tear gas was used in the first place, most reporters dismissed it as an unintentional error since Lieutenant Colonel Utter was unaware of the ban. The marines used tear gas because it was simply the best method available for dealing with an otherwise impossible situation.[14]

Ultimately, it was the undeniable success of the operation, especially the safe recovery of all the hostages and lack of American casualties, that produced a low-key and relatively favorable reaction in the media; a reaction echoed by the public. Encouraged by the positive response, MACV discreetly asked Washington to reconsider the ban on riot-control agents. When the media heard about the request, some journalists began to suggest the entire incident was actually a well-orchestrated plan to resurrect the chemical war that was condemned and shut down earlier in the year. Pentagon officials countered these allegations somewhat disingenuously by stating the United States had simply refrained from using the agents and never actually abandoned its right to utilize them in combat. Unable to substantiate their accusations, these reporters could only grumble about being duped into testing public opinion for the military and how MACV was preparing to use the agents on a regular basis without needing to hide their operations.[15]

On September 22, Secretary of Defense McNamara forwarded the request to the President's office.

> General Westmoreland has requested a reaffirmation of his authority to use standard riot control munitions in certain specified combat situations in South Vietnam and Ambassador Lodge has supported his request. This

authority would extend only to lacrimatory agents (tear gas) known as CS and CN. Use of nausea-producing agents DM and CN-DM would not be authorized. The agents would be used primarily to clear tunnels, caves, and underground shelters in cases where their use will lead to far fewer casualties and less loss of life than would the combat alternatives which involve high explosive or flame munitions. Of particular importance would be the reduction in casualties to civilians who are inevitably mingled with hostile military elements as the result of VC tactics.... Secretary Rusk concurs in this recommendation. If you approve, the Department of State will send a message to all posts informing them of the decision and providing public affairs guidance.

Taking special note of the change in attitude toward the humane aspects of employing the agents, he continued:

I agree with General Westmoreland that the use of these riot control agents far outweighs disadvantages that may accrue; in fact there is every indication that we may be in for censure if civilian casualties should accrue because we didn't use tear gas. The disadvantages to which I refer are the likelihood of some sharp international criticism, spurred by Communist propaganda, of the US Government authorizing the employment of what will inevitably be called "poison gas."[16]

General Wheeler sent a message to both Admiral Sharp and General Westmoreland notifying them that the request had been sent up to the President and expressing optimism it would be approved.

This has been a most difficult and complicated hassle. Nevertheless, ... I am satisfied that we are on the way to achieving a satisfactory policy which will untie [General Westmoreland's] hands and permit him to use riot control agents when he believes it necessary.[17]

After reviewing McNamara's memorandum, McGeorge Bundy sent it to President Johnson with his endorsement:

Secretaries Rusk and McNamara join in recommending that [General Westmoreland] be given clear authorization to use tear gas ... but not the more violent nausea-producing gases.... As you know, Ambassador Goldberg has had reservations about this recommendation, and in deference to his wishes, the recommendation has been held up until after his initial speech. But now ... we all think it is time to go ahead. If this recommendation is approved, our plan would be to have no announcement in Washington, but to have Westmoreland make it clear in due course ...

that tear gas (and tear gas only) is authorized in cases where it is more humane, and especially with respect to civilians. There will be some international criticism, but even the *New York Times* is resoundingly with us on this. I do not worry you with the pros and cons because it seems to me that the common sense of the matter is so clear.... Can we go ahead?

The President accepted their recommendations and approved reauthorizing the use of tear gas within the limits proposed by Secretary McNamara.[18]

Late in September, MACV told the press in Saigon that the Pentagon had reviewed the policy on using riot-control agents and it was now unambiguous; tear-gas munitions could be used in situations when they would be more humane than other available options. The military spokesman also told reporters there would not be an official announcement in Washington because this was not a new policy, it was only a clarification. General Westmoreland had always had the authority to use tear gas, he had only received informal instructions not to use them during combat operations.[19]

Despite their statements expressing a lack of concern over a potential international outcry, the Administration began to plan ways to avert any vociferation. During a luncheon meeting with the President on September 29, Press Secretary Bill Moyers told him he believed the Administration had been too defensive about using tear gas. He wanted a more aggressive public relations campaign focusing on the humanitarian aspects of the agents. "We should remind the world that the Viet Cong slit throats and bomb children and that any human being in one of the Vietnam caves would prefer to cry from tear gas rather than be killed by hand grenades." Undersecretary of State George Ball and William Raborn, Jr., the Director of Central Intelligence, agreed. McGeorge Bundy reminded the group how important it was to use the proper phrasing during public statements in order to prevent a repeat of the March catastrophe. It was imperative everyone – military spokesmen, press secretaries and even politicians – refrained from using terms like "non-lethal" or "riot-control agents." Everyone should refer to them by the less technical sounding and more benign term "tear gas"; stressing the agents were a humanitarian option for difficult circumstances.[20]

Back in Qui Nhon, the cloud over Lieutenant Colonel Utter dissipated. General Westmoreland issued a statement that "Lieutenant Colonel Leon Utter has been exonerated by me. No disciplinary action has been taken and none is contemplated." In October, while visiting Qui Nhon, Westmoreland told Utter it was the successful use of tear gas by his battalion that changed world opinion on using the agents in combat. General Westmoreland considered the results of this minor battalion-level action so significant for American operations in Vietnam he specifically mentioned it, and the successful employment of CS to limit civilian casualties, in his summation report of combat operations occurring between January 1964 and June 1968.[21]

Eventually, tear gas became a standard tool for clearing caves. In many instances, it proved to be highly effective and the results were everything soldiers expected. However, it was never a panacea and at times determined or extremely scared defenders would refuse to evacuate the cave despite the irritating effects of the agents. In these situations, soldiers were forced to revert to traditional lethal alternatives. Such a situation occurred on January 19, 1967 when soldiers of the 1st Battalion, 14th Infantry heard the voices of women and children coming from caves in the Suoi Ca Valley. These caves, later determined to be the Viet Cong political headquarters for the Binh Dinh Province, were under double and triple canopy jungle and escaped detection during aerial reconnaissance of the area. When a company commander was killed investigating the caves, the Americans surrounded the entrances and attempted to force the guerrillas out into the open with smoke and tear-gas grenades. The defenders refused to surrender, however, and even while coughing and choking in the irritating atmosphere, continued to fire blindly out through the openings. Unable to force the guerrillas out of the caves and unwilling to risk further casualties in an assault, the Americans used flame-throwers to deplete the oxygen in the caverns and suffocated everyone inside.[22]

There is no evidence to support the suspicion expressed by some journalists that Operation Stomp was a well-planned way to reintroduce riot-control agents into the Vietnam War. At that point in the war, tear gas was not seen as a sufficiently useful combat asset to make it worth the risk of another public outcry like the one that occurred only six months prior. It was simply a combination of disorganization and bad communication, the result of an inappropriately trained marine battalion attached to an army task force and working in geographic isolation. Without specific orders to the contrary, the marines simply used the weapons they had on hand to accomplish their mission in the most efficient way possible.

4

TUNNELS

In late September 1965, Secretary of Defense Robert McNamara gave General Westmoreland a one-time authorization to use tear gas during an unspecified future operation of his choice. Almost immediately, members of the Administration began urging McNamara to direct the General to use it quickly so Washington could capitalize on the encouraging press generated by Operation Stomp. At a September 29 luncheon meeting, Undersecretary of State George Ball brought up another reason to push the General to use the gas quickly when he pointed out the International Red Cross was holding a conference in Geneva in early October and would almost certainly issue a statement condemning tear gas as a chemical weapon. Since such a statement would add fuel to the Communist propaganda campaign and likely stimulate journalists to revisit the issue, he urged the President to have Westmoreland conduct the operation within the next few days. McNamara, however, insisted the specific operation had to be selected for purely tactical reasons despite the potential political implications. If Washington forced Westmoreland to use tear gas in a timely but inappropriate situation, it could backfire and once again open the Administration up to intense public and political criticism. After the events of the previous March, it was just not worth the risk. McNamara felt it was imperative the general have the freedom to select the appropriate mission to continue emphasizing the humanitarian properties of tear gas and making the agents a reasonable alternative to traditional weapons. In the end, McNamara was able to convince the President to wait and give the General time to select the proper mission. The mission General Westmoreland ultimately chose was an operation to clear the enemy out of tunnels and bunkers hidden deep in a key section of enemy controlled jungle.[1]

Even though tunnel warfare had been used for millennia, it was only during the American Civil War that the United States military actively used mine and countermine tactics in combat.[2] While tunnels were used by both sides during World War I, American soldiers did not participate significantly in such operations. During World War II and the Korean War, they only encountered short tunnel systems and essentially treated them as elongated caves. During these latter wars, they used artillery or aerial bombardment whenever possible to collapse tunnels and kill the occupants. If such assets were unavailable they relied on the 3Bs, the tactics developed by the marines while fighting the Japanese, to kill the enemy near the entrance and then collapse the opening. They left any enemy soldiers sealed in the tunnel to either suffocate or starve.[3]

This lack of experience was reflected in the early attitude of the American advisors toward Vietnamese tunnels. For example, during a meeting on September 7, 1962, South Vietnamese President Diem lamented to General Harkins, as long as the Viet Cong operating in the foothills of the Annamite mountain chain could retreat back into their caves and tunnels they felt safe from South Vietnamese helicopter patrols. The general simplistically told him the answer to the problem was to have his soldiers go into the tunnels after them. It would still be several years before the United States learned how extremely dangerous combat underground was, and about the unique mental and physical demands it placed on soldiers. In its defense, the primary concerns of the US military at that time were how to refight the classic battles of World War II if the Warsaw Pact decided to invade central Europe, and on ways to fend off more human wave attacks in the hills of Korea if the cease fire was broken. There was very little consideration on how to fight a guerilla war against small bands of insurgents who hid in a jungle, and there was certainly no thought given to fighting a burrowing enemy. The American military simply viewed tunnels as a tactical anachronism.[4]

The target area selected by General Westmoreland for the pivotal mission was located approximately twenty-five miles northwest of Saigon in the Binh Duong Province. Nicknamed the "Iron Triangle," it was a heavily fortified enemy stronghold allowing the Viet Cong to control all of the essential transportation routes passing through the surrounding area. The Saigon River formed the southwest side of the imaginary triangle, the Thi Tinh River formed the eastern side, and their confluence the southeast corner. The third side was a line drawn on a map from the village of Ben Suc, located on the Saigon River at the northwest corner, to the city of Ben Cat on the northeast corner. It was a roughly forty-square-mile tangle of jungle, briar and muddy marsh sandwiched between the Mekong River delta to the south and the foothills of the central highlands to the north. Unbeknownst to the Americans at that time, it contained one of the largest and most complex of the enemy's tunnel systems.

It was a historic stronghold for the insurgents. When the Viet Minh were fighting the French after World War II, the guerrillas made the area an unconquerable citadel by building a large interconnected network of tunnels, bunkers and trenches. Initially the tunnels were simple hiding places used by the guerrillas and their families to avoid French patrols. Over the years, the tunnels evolved and the complexity of the systems increased as the insurgents continued to dig. Soon the insurgents connected the short, simple family tunnels and the system expanded both horizontally and vertically. They also constructed bunkers and fighting positions on the surface; connecting them to the tunnels so the guerrillas could operate these defensive positions and fight intruders without first having to pour out of the ground like a disturbed anthill. These connections also allowed them to escape back into the tunnels when the fighting positions were no longer tenable. Together, the tunnel and bunker complexes were much more than a static bulwark. These systems allowed the guerrillas to move undetected around the battlefield, confusing their attackers and frustrating their enemy's efforts to force them to stand and fight. Tunnels allowed the guerrillas to "attack the enemy from the center of their formations or keep fighting from different locations." Guerrillas could pop out of a tunnel, fire intensely for a few minutes, then disappear before their enemies could find them and effectively return fire. After rushing along a tunnel for a short distance, the insurgents reemerged through a different trapdoor and continued firing from the new location. These tactics enabled just a few guerrillas to pin down, or at least stall, a much larger force and prevent the enemy from deducing the actual number of guerrillas they faced.[5]

When the French were finally driven out of Vietnam, the need for the underground fortresses faded and the tunnels were largely abandoned. However, when South Vietnam began to actively campaign against the Communists and started seeking out their operatives, a new faction of insurgents took up their shovels. In the early 1960s, the Viet Cong repaired and updated the old tunnels; they also started digging new ones. By 1965, they added over ninety miles of new tunnels in and around the Iron Triangle. Based on their twenty years of combat experience, the insurgents incorporated a number of unique, battle-tested features into the new systems; features designed to make the tunnels harder to detect, and to improve survivability of the occupants should the tunnels be discovered. Some of the larger systems covered nearly forty miles and contained training facilities, kitchens, hospitals, armories, manufacturing centers and large storage rooms.[6]

The conditions in the Iron Triangle and the surrounding area were perfect for digging these elaborate passageways. The water table in the area was typically sixty-five feet below the surface so the guerrillas could dig multilevel systems with little risk of groundwater flooding the lower levels. Most of the soil was laterite clay, which was relatively soft and easy to dig through when it was damp but became extremely hard after it dried out. Even the walls and floors of the deeper sections of tunnel were smooth and hard as rock. The shallower sections, which were the most prone to collapse, were further stabilized and reinforced by the thick mesh of intertwining roots from the jungle vegetation.

Sometimes the Viet Cong dug the tunnels themselves, but they often allowed local village "volunteers" to do the excavation for them. The miners worked in teams of three as they excavated a passageway. One individual dug the shaft, the second moved the pile of excavated dirt down the tunnel and back to the exit, and the third hoisted the dirt out of the tunnel and piled it beside the entrance. Other workers quickly hauled the freshly excavated dirt away – dumping it in bomb craters, freshly plowed fields or nearby streams – to prevent outsiders from seeing the pile of discolored earth and realizing it was from a tunnel. Normally, miners could only excavate less than three feet of tunnel in a day. If digging occurred near an opening so fresh air could come in from the surface, then they might dig a little farther.[7]

In order to appreciate the problem these tunnels ultimately posed for American soldiers in Vietnam, it is important to understand the complexity of some of the larger systems, and also to realize the wide variety of innovative techniques different units used in their efforts to destroy them. Camouflage was the primary first line of defense for a tunnel. To prevent discovery, the entrance was often covered by a superbly camouflaged, tight-fitting trapdoor. In the jungle or woodland, it was frequently hidden in the middle of a clump of bushes or beneath a pile of dead bamboo branches. In villages, entrances were commonly hidden under large storage jars, piles of firewood, in animal pens beneath manure and even in grave yards. They were also found part-way down the side of a water well or even underwater in the bank of a nearby river or stream. In the latter instance, the only way into the tunnel was to swim through the opening.

To circulate air in the tunnels, the Viet Cong dug ventilation shafts at regular intervals from the upper tunnels to the surface; fresher air reached the deeper levels via internal ventilation shafts dug down from the upper levels. Just like the entranceways, the surface openings of these ventilation shafts needed to be hidden or camouflaged so Allied soldiers could not trace the tunnel from above. One ingenuous method of digging such an air hole was to simply attach a topless cage containing a borrowing animal to the ceiling of a tunnel. To escape the cage, the animal dug its way up to the surface and in the process made an air shaft that was extremely difficult to identify from the surface.[8]

The tunnels themselves were typically very narrow, usually thirty to forty-eight inches in diameter, and were virtually impassable to many Americans. The floors were uneven and the walls were angled with numerous small alcoves allowing guerrillas to hide or take cover from anyone looking down a tunnel. These alcoves also offered some protection if there was a firefight. Tunnels had frequent sharp turns, typically at intervals of no more than sixty feet, to increase their strength and to prevent the enemy from firing down the length of the tunnel. These turns also helped to dissipate the shockwave of the explosives used to collapse a tunnel's entryway and limit the number of guerrillas killed further along the shaft.

The length and complexity of a tunnel depended on the size of the guerrilla unit using it as a base of operation. The simplest and most basic tunnels were dug by squads. These passageways were generally less than six feet below ground and usually no longer than 100 feet. For a company-sized element, the tunnel was considerably longer, but still had a relatively simple layout. It might contain a few rooms for sleeping and storage but was not extensively compartmentalized. The larger, more complex tunnels were typically built to house battalion or larger-sized units. These systems could extend more than fifty feet underground and contain six different levels. These complexes had living quarters, conference rooms, hospitals, cooking facilities and large storage areas. Some even contained rooms for manufacturing or repairing equipment and weapons. These larger systems were built in a compartmentalized or cellular fashion so discovery of one section of tunnel did not necessarily compromise the entire system. Sections were connected by secret passages accessed through camouflaged trapdoors or through an apparently dead-end passage where excavation of the last few inches of earth opened a way into another tunnel. These latter passageways were designed as emergency exits and used when enemy soldiers entered the tunnels. There were also numerous false side tunnels, many leading to booby traps, adding to the maze and increasing the confusion of anyone unfamiliar with the system. Larger systems were sometimes interconnected by long communication tunnels extending for up to forty miles.

South Vietnamese soldiers were familiar with Viet Cong tunnels and did almost anything to avoid confronting the enemy in their underground warrens. The South Vietnamese usually preferred to simply surround the entrance and wait for the guerrillas to come out. If the soldiers became impatient, they attempted to suffocate the inhabitants by collapsing the entryway. In these instances, one of the soldiers ventured into the passageway as far as the first side tunnel, typically eight to ten feet from the entrance, and placed explosives at the intersection. In addition to collapsing the entrance, placing the explosive charge at that location also ensured the lethal shockwave from the blast traveled the maximum distance down the rest of the tunnel. Once the South Vietnamese were confident all of the occupants were dead, the soldiers were willing to go into the tunnel to search for weapons and intelligence. Having collapsed the only way in, they had to dig a new shaft down to the still intact section of tunnel. Needless to say, the South Vietnamese method of dealing with a tunnel was a very time- and labor-intensive operation.[9]

Soon after the United States began supplying the South Vietnamese Army with riot-control grenades, a number of their patrols tried throwing grenades down the entry shaft of a tunnel in an attempt to force the occupants to come out and surrender. However, with little or no air circulating along the passageway, the cloud generated by this type of grenade did not penetrate very far into a tunnel and generally was not very effective.[10] These failures did not dissuade MACV, however, because American advisors concluded the poor performance of riot-control agent in virtually every operation thus far in the war was due to the inexperience of South Vietnamese soldiers and not the utility or effectiveness of the agents. This conclusion was only strengthened when the marines used tear gas successfully against the cave and tunnel complexes encountered during Operation Stomp. An operation against the tunnels in the Iron Triangle would provide an opportunity to test the American supposition while still highlighting the humanitarian aspects of using riot-control agents.[11]

The well-planned and executed operation was one of several closely coordinated actions in the Binh Duong Province designed to find and destroy heavily fortified enemy strongholds. Beginning on October 8, 1965, the 173rd Airborne Brigade, in a joint operation with the 1st Battalion of the Royal Australian Regiment, began scouring the Iron Triangle for enemy fortifications. Although they found an abundance of bunkers, trenches and tunnels, and seized large stores of rice, soybeans, peanuts, salt and a considerable number of enemy documents, there was surprisingly little contact with the enemy. By the end of the operation, only ninety-three Viet Cong were captured and seventy-eight others killed. The prisoners told their captors many of the guerrilla units normally in the area left when warned about the impending attack.

Due to the lack of contact, the Americans only used tear gas twice during the entire offensive. Soldiers dropped a single gas grenade in each of the first two tunnels they found but neither of the tunnels was occupied. Even though tear gas was not a major contributing factor in any tactical aspect of the operation, from the standpoint of promoting the image of it as a non-lethal weapon and removing the appearances of secrecy and experimentation, the operation was an overwhelming success. This was largely due to the extraordinary public relations effort put forth by MACV. As Ambassador David Bruce summarized the crisis the previous March:

> [t]he chief trouble [was] that no warning was given in advance from Saigon of its prospective utilization.... From a public relations viewpoint, the Saigon authorities ... behaved idiotically. "Gas" is widely regarded as a dirty word, and everywhere evokes images of World War I brutalities.[12]

This time, the military went to great efforts to avoid such mistakes. Spokesmen briefed the press on the upcoming mission and the intention to use tear gas a full twenty-four hours in advance. Information officers also avoided using words and phrases that might give a negative impression. As directed by Washington, everyone involved with the mission refrained from referring to the compounds as "riot-control agents" and even from using the word "gas" by itself. Instead they exclusively used the more innocuous expression "tear gas" whenever they were responding to questions from reporters. Whenever reporters asked if nausea-producing agents such as DM would be used, spokesmen told them emphatically that only CS and CN were authorized for the mission.

Emphasizing the humanitarian reasons for using tear gas, when Brigadier General Ellis Williamson, commander of the 173rd Brigade, addressed journalists during the pre-mission briefing he stressed:

> [t]ear gas may be used on this operation if the local unit commander feels that its employment will assist in accomplishing the operational requirement with fewer casualties to friend and foe. It is anticipated that the use of the tear gas will be restricted to small areas where the enemy is holed up in bunkers or trenches.

Noting these efforts, one journalist quipped this relatively minor operation "was mounted with as much detailed planning in public relations as normally goes into a major battle." When the operation was over, the limited usage and sheer lack of drama convinced journalists there was nothing spectacular or mysterious about combat operations with tear gas. They moved on to other aspects of the war.[13]

In January 1966, the United States began Operation Cedar Falls and reentered the Iron Triangle with the intention of eliminating the longstanding enemy stronghold. This operation ultimately turned into the single largest US ground offensive of the war, involving nearly 30,000 Allied soldiers. General Westmoreland wanted not only to drive the enemy out of the area but also to destroy all of their infrastructure and installations, making it difficult if not impossible for them to reestablish their control over the region. It was during this operation that Americans had their first encounter with truly complex tunnel systems and began to grasp the tactical problems these subsurface structures posed.

The first phase of Operation Cedar Falls began on January 8 and consisted of several different missions. One involved a raid on Ben Suc, a key Communist-controlled village forming the northwest corner of the Iron Triangle, whose residence had a long history of aiding the guerrillas. To prevent them from interfering with the rest of the operation, American and South Vietnamese forces captured the village and forced all of the residents to relocate to a refugee processing center at Trung Lap. Once the residents were gone, soldiers razed the village as part of the effort to eliminate the guerrillas' infrastructure, preventing the Viet Cong from using the village as a safe hiding place in the future.

Another component of the first phase was designated Operation Crimp, a joint operation involving a total of approximately 8,000 soldiers from the US 1st Infantry Division, the 173rd Airborne Brigade and from the Royal Australian Regiment. Their mission was to find and destroy the headquarters of Viet Cong Military Region IV, which was located in Ho Bo Woods, a rubber plantation across the Saigon River to the west of the Iron Triangle. The operation began with a preparatory aerial bombardment by B-52s from Guam followed closely by an intense artillery barrage and tactical air strikes. After the preparatory fires lifted, helicopters inserted the infantry soldiers into the target area.

As the helicopters settled down onto the landing zones, they were hit by small-arms fire from Viet Cong hiding at the edge of a nearby groves of trees. Strangely, when the soldiers moved forward to engage the guerrillas, the enemy seemed to melt away into the relatively open surroundings. Throughout the first day, snipers continually harassed the Allied soldiers advancing through the area; always disappearing before the soldiers could fix the enemy's position and close in on them. Although it was evident the soldiers were chasing a large enemy force, guerillas were only seen occasionally and then only at a distance. As the American units moved through their sectors, soldiers found an increasingly complex series of trenches, bunkers and fighting positions; all were unoccupied. The Australians made the only serious contact of the day, engaging a Viet Cong company fighting from a well-constructed bunker and trench system. The ensuing battle lasted from around noon until well after sundown. As night fell, enemy fire dissipated and then stopped as the insurgents melted into the darkness.

On the second day of the operation, the Australians solved the mystery of how the snipers were able to move around the battle field undetected, vanishing in the relatively open woodlands. They found a trapdoor leading down into a series of interconnecting underground passageways appearing to crisscross beneath the jungle. After alerting the Americans about their discovery, the Australians began a careful and systematic search of the elaborate tunnel system. The soldiers quickly uncovered huge stores of food, medical supplies, weapons and equipment. Even though the Australians knew tunnels were often several hundred feet long with false tunnels, hidden passages and even multiple levels, nothing they had seen before compared to the scope and complexity of what they began to uncover.

The soldiers moved cautiously through the myriad passageways, marveling at the expanse and sophistication of the system as they mapped it out. Despite crawling through what seemed like miles of tunnels, they never encountered anyone. They concluded the Viet Cong were fleeing; abandoning the tunnels as the Australians moved into them. Then, as the soldiers climbed down into a deeper section of tunnel and moved around a corner, they came face to face with several guerrillas hiding in the dark. Momentarily stunned, the soldiers hastily backed out of the tunnel and returned to the surface. After recovering from the shock, the Australians began shouting down into the shaft, calling for the Viet Cong to come to the surface and surrender. After a few minutes of silence, the Australians spread out and tried to trace the passageway from the surface, looking for another trapdoor that would let them into the system behind the guerrillas. Despite a careful search, the soldiers did not find anything on the surface they could use to trace the tunnel. They called back to their battalion for a Mity Mite.

The Mity Mite, also known as the M106 dispenser, was a commercially available agricultural backpack sprayer/duster first used during the previous mission into the Triangle. When used in combination with smoke grenades, the Mity Mite aided soldiers trying to trace tunnels from the surface. To follow a tunnel's path, soldiers placed grenades in the entrance and used the blower to force the smoke along the passageway. Following the path of least resistance, the blower pushed the smoke up through air holes and camouflaged entrances along the length of the tunnel. This time, within minutes of starting up the blower, smoke was rising out of numerous ventilation holes over a large area fanning out from the entrance they were guarding. The complex was obviously much larger than they anticipated. Unable to trace the tunnel even with the aid of the Mity Mite, they threw tear-gas grenades into the entrance and used the blower to force the agent cloud through the system, expecting anyone without a gas mask to quickly find the nearest exit to the surface. After several minutes the gas was boiling out of the ventilation holes with the smoke and beginning to taint the air above ground. Still there was no sign of the guerrillas. Unable to delay their mission any longer, the Australians placed explosives a short distance along the shaft and collapsed the tunnel leading away from the trapdoor. Although the Australians believed the overpressure from the blast killed the stubborn guerrillas, it is more likely the Viet Cong escaped through an adjacent passageway and regrouped with their comrades to continue fighting somewhere else on the battlefield.[14]

As more and more tunnels were identified and the danger posed by the extensive network became clear, the operational objectives were modified to incorporate clearing and destroying all of the tunnels the Allies found. At first, American troops simply did a perfunctory search of each tunnel before setting the charges and moving on to the next location. However, it rapidly became apparent the tunnels also contained a treasure trove of enemy intelligence and the searches became more thorough. In one tunnel alone they found four truck-loads of enemy maps, documents and training pamphlets.[15]

Initially, units relied on volunteers to search tunnels and anyone could step forward. Some were motivated to volunteer to prove their courage, while others felt a desire to get back at the enemy who had tormented them over the past few days. It was soon apparent not everyone was cut out for underground exploration. Some obvious limitations included things like size and claustro-phobia. Tunnels were not constructed to accommodate the build of most Westerners and only smaller individuals could pass through them. In these extremely constricted areas, even individuals who were not normally affected by enclosed spaces could become claustrophobic. Panic underground could quickly become fatal for the stricken individual and his teammates. Also, since the tunnels were cohabitated by numerous indigenous animals and insects, another less obvious limitation included fear of such things as spiders, centi-pedes, snakes, rats and bats. In the confines of a tunnel, even an apprehension of such creatures could become amplified into a phobia. As one soldier put it, "[i]t's as close as I want to get to hell."[16] Eventually, the unique complexities and dangers of underground warfare led to the establishment of formal training and earned the graduates the distinctive title of "Tunnel Rat" if you were American or "Tunnel Ferret" if you were Australian.

When they entered the tunnels, soldiers not only had to locate and deactivate all manner of booby traps, but also had to be prepared to respond instantly to an enemy attack. The Viet Cong had hiding places at key locations along the narrow passageways and would lie in wait to ambush passing soldiers. As soldiers crawled through the tunnel, guerrillas would materialize from behind a trapdoor and stab or shoot one of the searchers. At other times, they simply dropped a fragmentation grenade into the passageway. In the narrow tunnels, there were not many places offering cover from the blast.[17]

To avoid these confrontations, it soon became standard practice to throw tear-gas grenades into the entrance and use the Mity Mite to force the gas down into the recesses of the tunnel. Used singularly, the cloud generated by pyrotechnic grenades did not penetrate very far along the passageway and was relatively ineffective in all but the simplest tunnels. However, by blowing the tear gas into the tunnels, it became a big problem for the occupants. The Mity Mite drove the gas deeper into the system and also pushed it through the tunnels at a much greater rate. This made it harder for lurking guerrillas to avoid exposure and greatly reduced the threat of ambush.

Using the blower to clear a tunnel was relatively simple. If a horizontal entrance was found, then a poncho was used to cover the opening and dirt was shoveled around the edges of the poncho to hold it down. Then the nozzle of the blower was inserted through the hood of the poncho and tied into place. After the blower was started, an edge of the poncho was lifted and a tear-gas grenade was dropped into the tunnel entrance. Additional grenades were used as needed. If a vertical entrance was found, then a hole was cut into the bottom half of a five-gallon can and the nozzle of the Mity Mite was pushed through the hole. The blower was started and a tear-gas grenade was thrown into the entrance. The can, with the nozzle blowing through it, was wedged into the entrance. The can was removed momentarily whenever an additional grenade was added. If a five-gallon can was unavailable, then some other field expedient plug was fashioned.[18]

Unfortunately, using tear gas to clear tunnels could also make life more difficult for a Tunnel Rat. It forced him to wear his protective mask while making a search. The mask reduced his field of vision, made it difficult to communicate with the surface, made it more difficult for him to breathe in an already stifling environment, and increased his heat load, making him more susceptible to dehydration and heat injuries. It also added to his feeling of isolation and enhanced any latent claustrophobia.

Gas also caused problems when the Viet Cong used animals as part of their tunnel defenses. The agent irritated the animals just like it did people, and the creatures became even more aggressive than usual. For example, on one occasion a Tunnel Rat began his search just after tossing a tear-gas grenade into the tunnel entrance. As he moved past the first turn, he came face to face with a pit viper tethered to a stake. The snake was exceptionally agitated, writhing about and striking at anything nearby. The soldier returned to the surface, cut a long length of bamboo, and used it to dispatch the snake. Then he moved deeper into the tunnel and proceeded with his search.[19]

Another significant problem that rapidly became obvious to the Tunnel Rats was the lack of ventilation and fresh air in the tunnels. Although the Viet Cong dug ventilation holes, without equipment to force air through the system they had to rely on natural air currents to bring fresh air in from the surface and cycle it throughout the tunnel complex. To increase the volume of air moving down into the system, they dug some of the surface ventilation shafts at angles, hoping to take advantage of any breeze moving through the jungle. While this might have helped increase circulation in the upper tunnels, it did nothing to improve the air quality in the deeper levels. In order to draw air down the internal air shafts and into the lowest sections of the system, the guerrillas lit a candle at the bottom opening of one of the deeper ventilation shafts. The idea was the air heated by the flame would rise up the shaft, thereby drawing fresher air down through another nearby ventilation hole. Although this method of circulating air was used with great success during several historic mining operations, those miners used more elaborate ventilation systems with much larger fires. The convection current created by a candle flame would only draw down a very limited volume of air and the benefits would not be much greater than the oxygen consumed by the flame or the smoke created by the candle.[20]

The limited circulation also allowed the odors associated with human occupancy to accumulate; in fact, air in the tunnels could get quite foul. There were the odors from sweat and human waste, stagnant water in water traps and animal cohabitants. Food rapidly went bad in the damp environment and there was often the smell of rotten rice, fish or other staples. Food preparation was also a serious problem since the special chimneys intended to disperse the smoke from cooking fires above ground typically allowed the fumes to leak back into the tunnels. There were also sections of tunnel used as graveyards where fallen comrades were temporarily interned after a pitched battle on the surface. However, if the Allies continued operations in the area and prevented the Viet Cong from transferring the bodies to cemeteries above ground, then the remains rapidly decomposed in the damp heat and the sections of tunnel with the shallow graves became permanent crypts.

The dangers posed by the poor ventilation were driven home in the most tragic way on January 11. Shortly after using a Mity Mite to blow smoke and tear gas into a tunnel to look for hidden entrances and drive out any hiding guerrillas, Corporal Robert Bowtell of the 3rd Field Troop, Royal Australian Engineers, donned his protective mask and entered the passageway to search for enemy weapons and equipment. When he attempted to crawl through a particularly narrow trapdoor, he became stuck and was unable to free himself. Within minutes, he felt lightheaded and could not catch his breath. Although he was able to call to the surface for help, by the time his comrades arrived he was unconscious. Despite all efforts to save him, he suffocated before he could be freed from the confines of the trapdoor. Six of the would-be rescuers were also hospitalized as a result of their efforts in the hypoxic atmosphere.[21]

The depressed oxygen level was caused by a combination of the inherent poor ventilation in the system and the use of pyrotechnic munitions, which produced carbon monoxide and carbon dioxide as byproducts of combustion.[22] Driven by the Mity Mite, these hot gases replaced some of the ambient atmosphere in the tunnels. The standard military protective mask was not effective in these conditions. The masks did not supply oxygen to a user; the filter elements simply blocked or adsorbed chemical warfare agents before the materials could be inhaled. Unfortunately, the activated charcoal in the elements was not effective against all hazardous chemicals. The filters did not absorb carbon monoxide or carbon dioxide; like oxygen, these gases were inhaled by the wearer. To avoid these hazards, some teams tried using self-contained breathing apparatuses (SCBAs) during a search. However, the increased logistical burden associated with bringing compressed air cylinders into the jungle as well as the more serious problem of trying to wear them in the tiny tunnel passageways made SCBAs impractical for most operations. A more practical solution was to flush the system with fresh air before the Tunnel Rats crawled down into the tunnels. Soon after the Bowtell incident, it became a standard practice to use the Mity Mite to blow out all of the smoke, tear gas and combustion byproducts prior to the first entry.[23]

After a tunnel was emptied of all equipment, supplies and useful intelligence, it was destroyed or rendered unusable to the enemy. Initially, the Americans simply threw CS grenades into the entryway, used a Mity Mite to blow the agent cloud as far down the passageway as possible, and then collapsed the entrance with explosives. The soldiers thought the agent would remain active in the sealed tunnel and discourage anyone from reoccupying it. In reality, the small amount of CS in the grenades did not produce any significant residual contamination and what was left behind rapidly degraded in the damp environment. Shortly after the Americans left the area, the Viet Cong were back to dig down to the undamaged sections of tunnel and resume operations.[24]

The Americans soon learned the only way to permanently eliminate the threat from a tunnel was to collapse the entire length of the shaft. Soldiers tried to accomplish this with a number of innovative methods. They tried using tank dozers and the Rome plow to dig through the roof of a tunnel and induce a collapse. Such heavy equipment worked well on tunnels that were dug only a few feet below the surface, but was useless against the deeper passageways in more complex systems. They also tried flooding the tunnels with water. This technique was limited to complexes near a large river and was further thwarted by features engineered into the tunnel systems, such as the airlocks isolating individual sections of tunnel and internal drainage systems preventing flooding during the monsoon season. Without opening all of the trapdoors between the interconnecting passageways and sealing all of the drains, the volume of water needed became overwhelming. Both of these options also depended on access to heavy construction equipment, which was difficult to transport to remote locations in the dense jungle.[25]

The most efficient method of collapsing an underground tunnel was with explosives. One particularly effective method was to place dynamite or blocks of C4 at regular intervals throughout the tunnel passageways and tie them together with detonating cord. Depending on the complexity and depth of the system, explosives were also attached to any shoring and to the roof. The timing of the explosions was critical; the charges in deeper tunnels had to detonate first to ensure the entire complex collapsed. The amount of explosives needed for a single tunnels could reach several thousand pounds. During Operation Crimp, special demolition teams kept helicopters working overtime ferrying in explosives to meet the demand. As one of the engineers observed, "[t]here isn't enough dynamite in Vietnam to blow up all of them."[26]

The Americans tried to come up with alternatives to traditional military explosives, such as a fuel/air explosive gas mixture. It was fast, simple and minimized the amount of time the engineers spent in the tunnels. Engineers used a Mity Mite blower to force acetylene gas throughout the system and then set off a small explosive charge to detonate the gas.[27] Unfortunately, this method did not generate the same kind of destructive force as traditional military explosives and was limited to tunnels dug no more than ten feet below the surface. For deeper systems, it was back to variations of the contaminate-and-collapse technique.[28]

One of the key factors affecting the length of time contamination remained effective in the tunnel was the quantity of agent spread along the passageways. The amount of agent in a cloud generated by gas grenades was simply inadequate to create a persistent hazard. In January 1966, the US began using bulk CS powder to increase the level of contamination. One very effective method of dispersing the agent was to use the bags of CS straight out of the shipping drum in conjunction with detonating cord. Tunnel Rats laid the cord along the floor throughout the system and then placed the ten-pound bags on top of it at each sharp bend in the tunnel, every intersection with a side tunnel, and otherwise at intervals of about every 100 feet. This method ensured the system was filled with a massive amount of agent and was significantly faster than having engineers emplace all of the explosive charges necessary to completely collapse a system. As the Tunnel Rats backed out of the system, they trailed the detonation cord behind them, dropping bags of agent at key locations. Then they set forty-pound cratering charges inside every tunnel entrance. The explosions from the charges collapsed the entrances and the detonation cord ruptured the bags of agent, spreading it throughout the tunnel where it stuck to the walls and floor. When the Viet Cong dug down to an intact section of tunnel to rebuild the system, they aerosolized the thick layer of residual contamination, forcing them to abandon their efforts. The tunnel was unusable to unprotected personnel until the agent degraded.[29]

Even though this method was highly effective at preventing reoccupation of the tunnels, it still required a considerable amount of time and hard effort, especially dragging the eight-pound bags of agent through long stretches of tunnel. It was hazardous as well. If one of the bags tore open during the process, the Tunnel Rats would be covered with the bulk agent. In the hot, humid conditions the powdered agent rapidly caused serious chemical burns on exposed skin that were both painful and slow to heal. Soldiers in the 173rd Airborne Brigade quickly realized the operation would be safer and easier if they transferred the agent from the eight-pound shipping bags into a more manageable three-pound bag. They also pre-wrapped these smaller bags with short lengths of detonating cord and used an electric blasting cap to set off the detonating cord. The electrical wire was much easier, quicker and safer to string through a system than the bulkier detonating cord. The Australians adopted a similar system but preferred to use old ration cans filled with the loose powder and dispersed the agent with a quarter-pound stick of TNT. All of these configurations were very effective for contaminating a tunnel.[30]

The other key factor limiting the duration of effectiveness of subterranean contamination was the rate of hydrolysis of the agent in the high humidity found inside the tunnels. Both CS and CS1 were hydrolyzed relatively quickly; even with heavy residual coatings, the guerrillas could begin rebuilding a tunnel after as little as seven days. Once the Americans realized this, the military began searching for ways to extend the persistency of the contamination. The results of one line of research led to the development of a stabilized gelatin foam laced with CS. Within minutes of being sprayed into a tunnel, the foam expanded to fill the passageway and became rigid. Anyone attempting to dig through the foam released the entrained tear agent and suffered the usual effects of exposure. This foam was effective for at least thirty days after it was applied. Although the army went to the trouble of getting a patent on the foam, there is no record it was ever used in Vietnam.

A broader line of research focused on finding a way to increase the persistency of the powdered agent itself. When the military began coating the micropulverized powder with a special silicon additive during the manufacturing process, the material became extremely hydrophobic and resistant to hydrolysis. Designated CS2, it remained effective for five-to-six months in a tunnel once the entrances were sealed.[31]

Another drawback to these operations was soldiers had to make multiple entries into the system to emplace the charges and position the bags of agent. Each additional entry delayed the overall combat operation and increased the risks to both the entrants and to the soldiers on the surface guarding them. The solution was to pare down the number of entries to the minimum number necessary to search the system and remove all the usable intelligence; then to contaminate the system from the surface. Initially the Americans thought this could be accomplished with the Mity Mite blower, which was capable of dispersing ten pounds of CS powder in three-to-four minutes. However, the Mity Mite was a small unit and only effective in tunnels less than 500 feet long. It quickly became apparent the blower did not have the power to force the agent throughout the large complex systems soldiers were finding in the Iron Triangle.

The military began searching for another commercially available blower providing the necessary power to distribute the agent down through six levels of tunnel, but light enough to carry through the jungle. Suitable candidates also needed to be reasonably easy to operate and maintain, able to operate for extended periods, and capable of delivering fresh air uncontaminated by the exhaust from the motor. A number of blowers were field tested, including the Buffalo Turbine, the Perkins Generator, the Resojet blower and the Mars generator. Ultimately, the Mars generator was selected; the others were disqualified because of excess weight (the Buffalo Turbine weighed 800 pounds and the Perkins Generator weighed 350 pounds) or because of operational considerations (the Resojet only operated for fifteen minutes on a tank of fuel and could not be refueled while running). Unfortunately, the Mars generator did not meet the requirement for delivering fresh air and could not be used to ventilate a tunnel. The air blown into the tunnel was not only contaminated with the engine exhaust, but also heated to a temperature of nearly 1,000 degrees Fahrenheit. The evaluators matter-of-factly observed these conditions were "considered to be unsafe if friendly personnel [were] in the tunnel."[32] Eventually, however, ever-resourceful soldiers realized this drawback was actually a valuable bonus and began using the superheated air as a weapon to rapidly drive out or kill guerillas hiding in a tunnel.[33]

There were two particular engineering features of a tunnel that could prevent a blower from forcing smoke or tear gas throughout the system. The first of these was the trapdoors hiding the entrances to adjacent sections of the tunnel. The Viet Cong constructed these doors to fit into their frames without leaving any telltale gap around the edges. While this was primarily done to camouflage the passageways, the tight seal formed when the doors were in place effectively eliminated air movement between the sections and isolated the cloud of agent. As Tunnel Rats explored the system, they had to ensure all of the doors were removed so the cloud could flow freely down all of the passageways.

The other was the water traps. At regular intervals throughout many of the systems, guerrillas dug the tunnel so it took a deep, downward "U"-shaped bend and then completely filled these depressions with water. These U-bends forced anyone crawling through the tunnel to dive below the surface of the water, scramble underwater for the length of the bend, then come up on the other side. They also stopped agent blown in from the surface and prevented the contamination of the rest of the system. Some have suggested they were specifically built for this purpose, but tunnels containing these traps were dug long before Americans began using blowers for tunnel operations. A more likely explanation is these bends were initially dug to help minimize the effects of explosive charges used to collapse the tunnel entrance. When the explosives went off, the shockwave from the blast also traveled down the intact section of the tunnel like a bullet down a rifle barrel, killing anyone hiding deeper within the system. South Vietnamese soldiers were trained to place the explosives at the first side tunnel to maximize this effect. The water in the traps would absorb and dissipate much of the overpressure, limiting the danger to anyone on the other side.[34]

While the Mars generator was described as a portable unit, it still weighed nearly 200 pounds. Coupling limited availability of the units with the difficulty of moving them through the jungle, an inability to use them to ventilate the tunnels during the search phase of the operation and the existence of features engineered into the tunnels eliminating the universal applicability of all blowers, it was not long before most units opted to go back to contaminating tunnels using bags of agent in conjunction with explosive charges.

Although the Iron Triangle contained the largest concentration of tunnels, they were a problem throughout Vietnam. By the end of 1970, nearly 5,000 enemy tunnels had been discovered. There were even instances where the United States unknowingly built a firebase on top of a tunnel system, thus giving the enemy a way past the defensive perimeter and into the middle of an otherwise secure compound. At night, enemy soldiers seemed to materialize in the heart of the camp, attacking sleeping soldiers, destroying equipment and then disappearing into thin air. These incidences led the army to conclude "the presence of a tunnel complex within or near an area of operation poses a con-tinuing threat to *all* personnel in the area. No area containing tunnel complexes should *ever* be considered completely cleared" [original emphasis].[35]

On rare occasions, the insurgents also used tunnels offensively when they laid siege to a fortified position. This happened at the battle of Dien Bien Phu, the climactic battle ultimately leading to the end of French colonialism in Vietnam. In addition to hiding their artillery in tunnels to prevent the French Air Force from targeting the guns, the Viet Minh also tunneled under the French defenses and came up inside the base perimeter. Another example occurred in 1962 when the Viet Cong dug a tunnel almost two miles long in an effort to breach the perimeter defenses of a strategic hamlet in Dinh Tuong Province.[36]

As part of the 1968 Tet Offensive, the Communists laid siege to Khe Sanh. Just as they had done against the French at Dien Bien Phu, the Communists dug extensive bunkers, tunnels and trench works. As the siege progressed, enemy surface trenches extended to within fifty yards of the base perimeter. In late February, an enemy rocket landed in the perimeter wire and the explosion uncovered a freshly dug tunnel six feet below the surface. The tunnel was far too narrow for an American to crawl through to investigate so the marines threw a tear-gas grenade into the shaft and filled the opening with barbed wire. Afraid the enemy might be digging into the compound, soldiers devised ways to locate the tunnels. Some marines drove stakes into the ground around the perimeter and used a doctor's stethoscope to listen for sounds of digging. Others resorted to even more questionable means and attempted to use divining rods to dowse for the tunnels.[37] Although far-fetched, under the circumstances even individuals with a less rural upbringing bought into dowsing. "I thought it was a stupid idea at first, then I practiced over a culvert and found that it actually worked," said Lieutenant Marshall Wells. Colonel David Lownds, the base commander, added:

> No matter how stupid anything is, and I don't say the brass rods are stupid, we use it. If some country boy from the Kentucky hills says he has a gadget that he used to hunt foxes with and wants to try to find tunnels, I say go ahead. I try everything.

Finally, a team from the Recon Marines went to Khe Sanh with a geophone, a device the operator connected to microphones driven into the ground so he could listen for the tell-tale sounds of tunneling. The team was unable to detect any further efforts to tunnel under the wire.[38]

Throughout the Vietnam War, the American military struggled to established a realistic, workable doctrine to locate, trace and destroy tunnels. They tried to locate and trace them with specially trained dogs, electronic sensors and even dowsing rods. They tried to destroy them with bombs, artillery, explosives, excavation and flooding. They tried to render them uninhabitable by contaminating them with chemicals. There was no single answer. Ultimately, it was a combination of all of these on-the-ground efforts, along with Ranch Hand defoliation missions over high threat areas and concentrated bombing campaigns by B–52 squadrons, that eventually led to the attrition of insurgents hiding below ground and destruction of their morale. Many of the tunnel systems were never destroyed.

5

ESCALATION

Since there was no public outcry after the successful, but tactically insignificant, use of tear gas during the October 1965 operation in the Iron Triangle, the Pentagon notified General Westmoreland on November 3 that he could once again use riot-control agents to support general military operations in South Vietnam. They specifically limited the authorization to the tear agents CN and CS, continuing the ban on the more toxic vomiting agent DM. In January 1966, along with its continued use as a means of dealing with tunnels in the Iron Triangle, he authorized the 1st Cavalry Division (Airmobile) to use it during Operation Masher–White Wing.[1]

It was the first major US action incorporating tear gas as an integrated component of a battle plan. The operation began on January 25, 1966 and continued until March 6 of that year. It took place primarily in Binh Dinh, a coastal province at the northernmost edge of II Corps. The province was largely under the control of the Viet Cong and, in some sections, such as the An Lao Valley, there were no Allied patrols in the past year. The Communists took advantage of this neglect and built a number of well-fortified compounds protected by bunkers, deep trenches and tunnel systems. Operation Masher–White Wing was a search-and-destroy mission; the objective was to simply capture or kill all of the Communists the Americans could find and destroy all of their installations.

This was the first time the 1st Cavalry Division had conducted combat operations in an area where a large number of civilians might be present and potentially intermixed with the enemy. All of the unit's past experience was in uninhabited or very sparsely populated areas where it was safe to assume anyone the Americans encountered was a member of the Viet Cong. To overcome this lack of experience, the commanders set very strict rules of engagement. Within populated areas, the Americans had to clearly establish the status of each individual. In order to accomplish this without putting their own soldiers at undue risk, the commanders would rely heavily on tear gas. Throughout the operation, soldiers used CS grenades when searching houses and tunnels to drive out anyone who might be hiding inside, allowing the Americans to safely question the occupants and search the hiding space. As a result of these efforts, there were very few civilian casualties. As the commander concluded in his after action report, "[the use of tear gas as a] limited response technique undoubtedly resulted in reducing the number of noncombat[ant] deaths in this highly populated area. It also greatly shortened the time for clearance and probably reduced friendly casualties."

On occasion, soldiers also used the non-lethal gas as a means of warning civilians against interfering with the operation. For example, during the first few days of February, someone in one of the villages near the operations center sporadically fired a rifle at helicopters passing overhead. Tired of the harassment and afraid a lucky shot might cause some damage or even wound someone, one of the helicopters flew over the village and dropped enough CS grenades to envelop it in a cloud of gas. Then an interpreter called down with a loudspeaker and told the villagers not to shoot at helicopters any more. He left the threat of stronger retaliation open-ended. There was no further gunfire from that village for the rest of the operation.

As soldiers gained experience with CS, they began testing its effectiveness in more traditional combat situations. One such instance was when they used it as a form of reconnaissance by fire. Classically, a reconnaissance by fire was the tactic of firing artillery or even small arms on a suspected enemy position in the hope that hidden soldiers would give themselves away by either firing back or running for better cover. Tear gas offered a number of advantages over traditional munitions. The agent cloud quickly covered a large area, diffusing into the most hardened fighting positions. Even if the unprotected enemy did not break and run for fresh air, it was almost impossible for guerrillas not to sneeze or cough and reveal their location. The intense eye irritation also limited their ability to shoot accurately at the Americans searching for them in the jungle. The US soldiers, on the other hand, could don their protective masks and move through the cloud unaffected by the agent.

In one example occurring on February 4, the Americans used a helicopter equipped with a TLSS to drop 300 CS grenades on the suspected location of a Viet Cong field hospital. The intent was to drive combatants out into the open where the enemy soldiers could be engaged without posing any serious risk to the wounded being treated in the hospital. In this instance, intelligence about the location of the hospital was inaccurate and nothing happened when the Americans dropped the gas grenades.

Later on the same day, soldiers used the technique again to help find a hidden Viet Cong trench and bunker complex concealed somewhere in a square-mile section of jungle in the foothills north of the An Nao River. To reduce the risk of an enemy ambush as soldiers searched the thick vegetation, several helicopters saturated the area with a CS cloud generated by dropping over 600 grenades. Before the cloud could dissipate, other helicopters inserted soldiers at key points throughout the area. After a brief search, the Americans located the bunker complex. Suffering from the effects of the gas, the Viet Cong offered only limited resistance before abandoning their defenses and fleeing into the jungle. This was the first time helicopters were used to ferry soldiers into a cloud of agent during a combat mission and served as a model for many future operations, especially inserting patrols into landing zones where the enemy was likely to set up an ambush. Although highly effective at subduing enemy fire, one drawback was such an operation obviously required all personnel involved, including the helicopter pilots, to wear their masks during the attack. As would be echoed throughout the war, the pilots disliked wearing a protective mask while flying because the masks were uncomfortable, limited the pilot's vision and made communications nearly impossible.

During Operation Masher-White Wing, soldiers of the 1st Cavalry Division also faced the same two situations prompting the marines to use tear gas during Operation Stomp – civilians intermixed with combatants and guerrillas fighting from caves. In the first instance, Viet Cong hiding in a small village began firing at an approaching patrol. Unable to engage the guerrillas without risking the lives of the civilians, the Americans used a helicopter to drop CS grenades in and around the village. As the cloud enveloped the gunmen, soldiers wearing their protective masks charged into the village and overpowered the guerrillas. The Americans successfully captured all seventeen of the enemy soldiers, injuring only one of them during the brief confrontation. Other than discomfort from exposure to the gas, none of the villagers were injured during the attack.

In the second instance, forty-three Viet Cong barricaded themselves in a cave and refused to surrender. Unable to determine if there were also civilians hiding in the cave, the Americans surrounded the entrance and threw in several CS grenades. The gas quickly forced everyone out of the cavern. Only one of the insurgents was killed when he attempted to fight his way out of the cave, the rest of the badly disoriented guerrillas were quickly disarmed and subdued.

Perhaps the biggest tactical innovation developed during the operation was a technique that became known as "flushing." About twelve miles south of the city of Bong Son in the southeast corner of the Kim Song Valley, there was an enemy strongpoint soldiers of the 1st Cavalry began referring to as their own iron triangle because of its roughly triangular outline on a map and the strength of the enemy defenses. Inside the triangle was a system of well-built and heavily fortified tunnels and bunkers defended by a Viet Cong battalion reinforced with a heavy weapons company. Despite its relatively small size – the longest side of the triangle was less than 400 yards – after four days of intense fighting (including thirty-three ground attacks, hundreds of artillery barrages and thirty-nine tactical air sorties), the Americans had not breached the enemy perimeter. At this point in the fighting there were twenty-three dead Americans with another 106 wounded.

Unable to crack the enemy defenses with his own assets, the division commander arranged for a B-52 strike late in the afternoon on February 21. From past experience the Americans knew, even with the incredible destructive power of the 750-pound bombs the jets would drop, it would take a direct hit to destroy one of the tunnels or bunkers and many of the guerrillas hiding below ground would survive the intense bombardment. For the bombs to have the maximum effect, somehow the soldiers had to get the Viet Cong to come to the surface. The planners decided to try a tear-gas strike, hoping the agent would drive the guerrillas out into the open looking for fresh air. If everything went according to plan, when the helicopters flew over to deliver the gas, the enemy would go to their fighting positions in preparation for an attack. The Viet Cong would not realize it was a gas attack until it was too late. Once the gas began flowing over their positions, even if the guerillas did try to retreat back below ground, the cloud would follow them into their sanctuaries, blinding and irritating and forcing them back to the surface. Timing would be a critical factor. Not only would the helicopters have to drop enough grenades to quickly create a thick blanket of gas over the entire triangle, but the cloud would have to remain intact until the bombs began falling or the Viet Cong would recover and go back into their underground positions. Since a gas grenade typically burned for about thirty-five seconds and the cloud would begin to dissipate within minutes after it burned out, there would not be much time for the helicopters to complete the attack and then clear the target area before the bombs would begin falling.

The pilots executed the plan perfectly. Just before the B-52s arrived, the helicopters swarmed over the triangle, peppering it with grenades. Almost immediately Viet Cong began crawling to the surface trying to get away from the irritating gas filling their bunkers and tunnels. Then the ground began to erupt as the B-52s started their bombing runs. The next day, two battalions of soldiers cautiously moved through the area; they met only very light resistance. Scattered among the remains of the enemy fortifications were the bodies of over 300 soldiers. Based on the additional remnants strewn about the complex, the Americans estimated the total number of enemy killed was closer to 700.

Following their victory at the iron triangle, the 1st Cavalry used the flushing tactic several more times, but in combination with a barrage of artillery shells or aerial rockets. In each instance, the gas greatly increased the effectiveness of these traditional weapons. In his after action report, the division commander noted these successes and recommended the technique be considered by other units whenever they faced a fortified area where the enemy did not have access to gas masks or when the guerrillas would be caught by surprise.[2]

Despite the enthusiasm of MACV and the success of Operation Masher-White Wing, most commanders did not incorporate tear gas into their battle plans during 1966 and it was typically only used spontaneously at a critical moment in a battle. One such instance occurred on July 2, while two companies from the 2nd Battalion of the 18th Infantry Regiment were on a search-and-destroy mission near the Cambodian border about sixty-five miles northwest of Saigon. Just before dawn, the Viet Cong began pounding the American positions with heavy mortar and machine-gun fire. As the barrage lifted, the enemy attacked the camp from opposite sides, forcing the Americans to keep their heads down and limiting their ability to shift their forces inside their perimeter. As the battle progressed, the guerrillas focused their attack on a section of the perimeter near to where the battalion reconnaissance platoon happened to be fighting. Frequently on patrol well out in front of the battalion, members of the platoon carried CS grenades for breaking contact with a larger enemy force. As the situation became critical and it appeared the Viet Cong were about to break through the perimeter, the platoon leader ordered his men to don their protective masks and then threw six gas grenades into the section of jungle from where the heaviest concentration of enemy fire was coming. As the gas disoriented the Communists and their volume of fire dropped off, platoon members were able to crawl forward and stabilize the perimeter. In the words of a *New York Times* reporter covering the story, the gas "worked beautifully."[3]

There were two fundamental reasons why commanders failed to use tear gas more extensively during this period. The first was a lack of doctrine giving them guidance on how to effectively employ it in a guerrilla war. In July 1966 the army began correcting this deficiency by publishing training circular 3–16, *Employment of Riot Control Agents, Flame, Smoke and Herbicides in Counterguerrilla Operations*. The expressed intent of the manual was to give "commanders a consolidated source of information on the technical aspects and employment concepts for experimental and recently standardized items of equipment and munitions.... [This manual] consolidate[s] and supplements the limited amount of [available] information." At the time the training circular was published, the only standardized delivery systems available in Vietnam were grenades, three sizes of dispersers and the TLSS.[4] Experimental or newly developed equipment included the Mity Mite, a backpack-sized multiple rocket launcher called the E8 and the E158/159 canister clusters that were dropped from helicopters. The manual explained the operational features of each of these systems and briefly outlined tactical situations where each weapon might be useful.

The second, and perhaps more pragmatic, reason was, during this time, the only CS munitions available in Vietnam in sufficient quantities to have a tactical impact were the M7 and M25 hand grenades. This severely limited the size and type of targets that could be engaged. Without a helicopter equipped with a TLSS, grenades could only be used to engage local point targets.[5] Even with access to a TLSS, many commanders were understandably reluctant to install one of these conversion kits and give up the lethal firepower of a 2.75-inch rocket pod for the incapacitating effects of tear-gas grenades.

Supplies of bulk agent powder were available but the dispersers used to spray it from a helicopter were difficult to work with and only worked effectively when the helicopter was flying slowly just above tree level. This put the ship and crew at extreme risk from enemy small-arms fire. The downdraft from the blades also caused some of the agent to swirl back into the aircraft, forcing the pilots and weapons crew to wear their protective masks during the operation. The cloud also left a coating on the aircraft and made it necessary to decontaminate the helicopter after the mission.

A number of units also used the bulk material to make improvised bombs they dropped from helicopters to contaminate key terrain or deny the enemy access to critical resources. However, the persistent hazard created by these devices made such weapons impractical for perimeter defense or direct support during an attack. For these situations, soldiers use the M7 grenades to fabricate improvised canister cluster bombs. There were different variations but all the devices operated along the lines of the BFOG, an acronym for "box full of grenades." To make one, soldiers pulled the pins from twenty-five grenades and carefully placed each into a plywood box in such a way that the safety levers, or spoons, were held in place. Then they wrapped detonating cord around the box and attached a blasting cap with a short delay fuse. The fuse was ignited just before it was dropped from a helicopter. When the cord exploded, it ruptured the box and scattered the grenades, which allowed the spoons to fly off and caused all of the grenades to function at essentially the same time. The grenades were dispersed in a circle about 150-feet in diameter, generating a cloud covering an area about the size of a football field.[6]

Based on repeated requests from field commanders, the military accelerated efforts to develop new weapon systems capable of rapidly delivering a high concentration of gas over a large area and also on munitions giving a soldier the ability to attack point targets out beyond the range he could throw a hand grenade. To reduce the time between a concept of design and fielding a final product, researchers primarily focused on developing ammunition for weapons already available in Vietnam. To ensure a new munition actually functioned in the jungle as it did during development – and, more importantly, it actually met the needs of the soldiers expected to use it – as soon as prototypes were available they were sent to Vietnam and field tested by combat units during actual operations. Many of these pilot programs were coordinated by the Army Concept Team in Vietnam, which compiled the test results and made a final recommendation as to whether the system should be fielded, modified or abandoned. Based on comments from soldiers who participated in the field tests, the team also made recommendations on any additional training soldiers might need before using one of the new weapons, as well as offering suggestions about potential changes to existing combat doctrine to capitalize on the capabilities of the new system. This process was very successful. Within three years, the army developed, tested and fielded three new helicopter-delivered canister clusters, three cluster munition dispensers for planes and jets, shells for the 105-mm howitzer, 155-mm howitzer and the 4.2-inch mortar, as well as two cartridges for the M79 grenade launcher and two new types of hand grenades.[7]

Through the end of 1966 and the early months of 1967, the logistics system struggled to keep up with the demand for CS munitions. By the middle of the year, however, production had increased, new shipments were arriving in Vietnam, and the stress was easing on the system. Then, on July 24, General Westmoreland issued MACV Directive 525–11, and soon demand for CS weapons once again exceeded supply. In this order Westmoreland delegated the authority to approve using tear gas during combat operations to his corps commanders.[8] Further, he directed the generals to view riot-control munitions as standard combat weapons and to employ the agents as a normal component of available firepower. General Westmoreland also made it clear he wanted all the officers in his command to take every opportunity to encourage their Vietnamese counterparts to use tear gas on the battlefield whenever possible. Ironically, the only specific prohibition included in his order was a ban on using riot-control agents against civilians during a riot. He did not want the United States drawn into a potential political quagmire like the 1963 Buddhist crisis in Hue. During periods of civil unrest, Westmoreland retained sole authority to authorize the US military to use tear gas against civilians.

Corp commanders immediately delegated this authority on down the chain and soon soldiers were using tear gas in a wider variety of tactical situations. Still considered to be one of the best weapons for breaking contact with a larger enemy force, patrols also found it was a very effective way of countering an enemy ambush, disrupting the guerrilla's ability to fire accurately into the kill zone and giving the soldiers a chance to either counterattack or withdraw. In addition to grenades and M79 rounds, soldiers in various mechanized infantry and armor units attached an E8 rocket pack to their vehicles for this purpose. During a helicopter insertion into a potentially hot landing zone, commanders often arranged for an artillery battery to fire a combination of CS and high-explosive rounds into the surrounding jungle. Ideally, the agent was delivered just before the helicopters set down so the enemy did not have a chance to recover. In these instances, both the soldiers and helicopter crew wore their protective masks during the insertion.

Under this new directive, the larger tear-gas weapons became an on-call tactical asset available whenever the situation warranted. This was particularly true for the aerial cluster munitions, which could be used to deliver an instantaneous high concentration of gas on point, linear or area targets. There were two other features making these munitions particularly attractive to infantry commanders. One was the accuracy of the delivery systems, which allowed them to be used safely against targets in very close proximity to friendly forces. The other was, while the battery-sized submunition canister weighed enough to penetrate the jungle canopy, it was not heavy enough to seriously injure a soldier who was struck by one. For these reasons, cluster munitions became a favorite weapon of line commanders during close combat with a determined enemy force.

The following series of engagements occurred shortly after the directive was issued, and illustrate the utility of cluster munitions and also how units relied on them during critical situations. On September 4, as Company B of the 1st Battalion, 5th Marines was moving into position to reinforce another unit that suffered heavy casualties during a firefight, the marines were ambushed by a company of North Vietnamese firing from well-fortified positions hidden in a village. Caught in the open, the marines were instantly pinned down under the withering blanket of fire. Unable to mount a counterattack or withdraw out of range, the company commander requested a CS strike to help suppress the enemy weapons. Within minutes, helicopters flew over the village and dropped several cluster munitions on the enemy. Thousands of submunitions rained down on the village, generating a gas cloud that quickly engulfed the enemy soldiers. Unprepared for the gas attack, the Communists abandoned their positions and fled toward a nearby river. As the volume of fire fell away, the marines attacked, killing twenty-six of the enemy soldiers and securing the village. Since there were still a large number of North Vietnamese and Viet Cong soldiers in the area, the marines, along with the unit they were sent to reinforce, set up a joint perimeter in the village and waited for additional reinforcements.

Several hours later, helicopters deposited two additional companies of marines at a landing zone about two-and-a-half miles east of the village. Shortly after the two companies set out for the village, they ran into a very large North Vietnamese force. The Communist attack succeeded in isolating each of the companies, preventing the marines from setting up a unified defensive perimeter. Although they kept both of the companies pinned down, the guerrillas focused their attack on just one, pounding the marines with mortar rounds and heavy automatic weapons. In desperation, the company commander called in a series of CS strikes on his perimeter when it appeared one of his platoons was going to be overrun. Although the gas forced the guerrillas to break off their assault, the Communists renewed their attack as soon as the cloud thinned and drifted away.

Some of the cluster munitions fell upwind of the Americans and the roiling cloud flowed over the marines as well as the guerrillas. Many of the marines lost or discarded their protective masks during the battle and suffered just as much as the enemy. The battalion chaplain, Lieutenant Vincent Capodanno, was helping the medics with the wounded as the gas cloud came in. Despite the intense irritation of the gas, he calmly handed his mask to a young man near him who was beginning to panic, then went back to comforting the injured. Chaplain Capodanno was killed later that day and awarded the Medal of Honor for his actions during the battle. He was the first Navy Chaplin to die in combat during the war.

Heavy fighting continued throughout the day and into the night. Eventually the North Vietnamese broke off their attack and withdrew back into the jungle.

The marines, battered and bloody, were finally able to continue their movement to the village and link up with the units they were sent out to reinforce.

Two days later, the marines were once again in a pitched battle with a heavily armed enemy force. This time, though, the marines were pressing the North Vietnamese and threatening to overrun enemy positions. As night fell, however, the Americans broke off the assault and took up defensive positions. In the darkness, the tables turned. Now on the offensive, the Communists launched two successive attacks on the marine lines. During the second onslaught, they succeeded in breaching the marine perimeter and the battle degraded into furious hand-to-hand fighting. For over an hour, the North Vietnamese continued to press the attack until the marines once again called in tear gas on their own perimeter and finally drove the Communists away.

At the end of the week, the Americans were still hunting down remnants of the Communist forces they had chased throughout the Que Son Basin. Passing near a village they thought another unit had searched, a platoon of marines was ambushed by a well-entrenched company of North Vietnamese hiding in positions scattered around the huts. The Americans were quickly pinned down by the heavy volume of machine gun and mortar fire. The rest of the company heard the battle and quickly moved up to relieve the platoon. Despite the support of artillery, mortars and helicopter gunships, the marines could not breach the heavily fortified enemy defensive positions and were forced to break off their attack. As close air support jets bombed the enemy bunkers, another marine company moved up and prepared to join in the next assault. Just before the two companies attacked, two A4 Skyhawk jets dropped cluster munitions on the village and saturated the enemy positions with tear gas. This time, the two rifle companies easily overran the enemy positions.[9]

Cluster munitions were also very effective as a means of suppressing enemy anti-aircraft fire. For example, they played a critical role during the resupply operation of the 1968 Battle of Khe Sanh. Surrounded by North Vietnamese, the only way to bring in supplies was by air. While planes could land at the airstrip on the main base, the only way to reach the marines defending the isolated hill outposts was by helicopter. This fact was not lost on the North Vietnamese. With lots of opportunity to practice, the Communists soon became very proficient at shooting down the supply helicopters. On one occasion, the guerrillas shot down three in a single day. Eventually the pilots came up with a strategy, dubbed the Super Gaggle, to give themselves some cover during these missions. Minutes before the cargo helicopters arrived in the air space over Khe Sanh, several A4 Skyhawk jets bombed enemy positions with napalm while others dropped CS cluster munitions on all of the positions where anti-aircraft weapons were located. As the helicopters began their final approach, two of the jets returned and dropped smoke bombs along both sides of the planned flight path. While the helicopters maneuvered between the two smoke screens, the jets continued to patrol the area, engaging any enemy positions still firing at the helicopters. This scenario was repeated up to four times each day for over a month. During that time, the number of helicopters hit by enemy fire was reduced 50 percent; only two were shot down. As one marine captain put it, "you could get in ten helicopter loads on the hill in one minute and get the birds the hell out of there and into smoke where the NVA couldn't see to shoot [them]."[10]

Another critical, but more unusual, use of tear gas as a means of suppressing potential enemy fire occurred during the Mayaguez Incident.[11] The thirty-one-year-old SS Mayaguez was a 480-foot-long freighter routinely transporting cargo between Hong Kong, Singapore and Thailand. On May 12, 1975, as it sailed near two small uninhabited islands about sixty miles off the coast of Cambodia, a Cambodian gunboat approached the vessel and fired several shots over its bow. Before the boarding party could secure the ship, the crew managed to send out a distress call reporting they were fired on, boarded and being forced to proceed to an unknown Cambodian port. Around noon the next day, the Mayaguez arrived at Koh Tang, another small island located twenty-seven miles off the Cambodian mainland.[12]

Within hours of the seizure, the United States was taking diplomatic measures to try to resolve the crisis. Fearful of another Pueblo Incident, however, President Gerald Ford also ordered the military to prepare for a rescue mission.[13] The Pentagon's initial plan called for a contingent of marines to jump from helicopters onto the cargo containers stacked two high on the deck of the ship; then move from container to container until they could work their way down to the main deck. Such an operation against a well-armed enemy force would be extremely risky. The only other alternative was a classic ship-to-ship boarding like the one in the pivotal scene of many pirate movies. In this option, a naval ship would come alongside the captive vessel and marines would swarm over the railings directly onto the main deck of the Mayaguez. Ultimately, the Pentagon decided to use the USS Holt, one of six ships dispatched to the area at the beginning of the crisis, to conduct the first combat ship-to-ship boarding since 1826.

The Americans did not know the size of the Cambodian force on board the Mayaguez because small boats were constantly shuttling back and forth between the ship and Koh Tang Island. However, intelligence analysts expected the marines to face some thirty Cambodians armed with automatic and anti-tank weapons, and expected these defenders to put up a vigorous fight. Another disadvantage for the Americans was they did not know the location of the hostages. Since some or all of the prisoners might still be on board, the marines had to verify the status of each target before firing. Under these conditions, and without any possibility of surprising the defenders, the Americans decided to incapacitate everyone on the ship with tear gas at the beginning of the operation. The planners also hoped the confusion caused by the gas would give any hostages on board some added protection during the confrontation.

Shortly after first light on May 15, the Holt sounded general quarters and began moving toward the Mayaguez, which was about fifteen miles to the east.

On-board was the assault force consisting of fifty-seven combat marines from Company D, 1st Battalion, 4th Marines, two Navy corpsmen, two Air Force explosive ordnance demolition specialists, an army intelligence officer to serve as the interpreter and six Merchant Marine volunteers who would serve as a temporary crew for the Mayaguez until the hostages were recovered. The weather was ideal – it was warm, there were just a few white clouds in the sky, there was a slight breeze blowing from the northwest and the sea was nearly calm.

Ten minutes before the Holt arrived alongside the Mayaguez, two air force A7s used CBU-30s to cover the Mayaguez with CS bomblets. The pilots scored nearly perfect hits and the gas rapidly saturated the ship. With only the light breeze, the cloud was going to linger over the ship for a long time; anyone on-board without a gas mask would be unable to fire effectively at the approaching ship or repel the boarding party.

Unlike the weather, the operational conditions for maneuvering the Holt alongside the Mayaguez were anything but ideal. Normally, if two ships were to be secured together it was a highly coordinated affair with one of the ships moored to a dock to prevent unnecessary movement and sailors on-deck to assist with the mooring lines. The Mayaguez, however, was swinging free at anchor and the personnel on board would be attempting to repel the boarders, not assist them. This meant the first marines landing on the deck not only had to neutralize the enemy defenses, but also had to receive the mooring lines and secure the two ships together. The captain of the Holt was also very concerned Cambodian soldiers on the island, only a thousand yards to the southwest, would fire on his ship while it was moored to the Mayaguez. To minimize the risk, he decided to tie up on the seaward side. Unfortunately, this put the Holt downwind of the Mayaguez and in the slowly drifting gas cloud. Now, in addition to all the other complications, sailors on the Holt had to wear protective masks to avoid being incapacitated by the gas. The masks made it difficult for them to communicate, distorted their vision and affected their depth perception during the tricky maneuvering.

As the Holt pulled alongside the Mayaguez, the masked marines in the assault force prepared to leap from the main deck of one ship onto the main deck of the other. Just after the first two marines leapt onto the Mayaguez, the backwash generated when the two ships came together pushed them back apart. With the rest of the marines unable to jump the twenty-five foot gap, the two marines stood alone on the deck of the hostile ship. Fortunately, no one was trying to repel the attack. Sailors quickly threw over the mooring lines and the marines lashed the ships together. About five minutes later, the remaining members of the boarding party scrambled over the railings and onto the Mayaguez.

The marines quickly secured the critical areas of the ship including the main deck, the bridge and the engine room. Then they began to search for hostiles, hostages and booby traps. Although the gas dissipated out on deck, it lingered inside the ship and the marines had to continue wearing protective masks throughout the search. While they found recently prepared food in the kitchen, it was soon clear the vessel was abandoned. In just over an hour the marines declared the ship clear of hostile forces.

Even though the Mayaguez was apparently undamaged and there were no explosives or other hazards left behind to hamper operation of the vessel, the Holt still had to tow it away from the island because the engineering plant was shut down and completely cold. It would take several hours to light the boilers and reestablish power for the ship. These operations were done with flashlights while wearing protective masks because of the residual tear gas lingering below-deck.

As the two ships moved slowly out to sea, a Thai fishing boat with the entire Mayaguez crew surrendered to the USS Wilson, another of the ships dispatched to the area at the beginning of the crisis. After undergoing quick medical checks, the crew returned to the Mayaguez and began making the ship ready to continue its interrupted voyage. Within a few hours, the Mayaguez was back underway and headed for Singapore.[14]

While tear gas was ultimately an unnecessary precaution that became a signi-ficant hindrance to the Merchant Marines working below-deck to relight the boilers, it is obvious how critical it would have been if any Cambodians had been there to defend the ship when the marines came on-board. Even a small force armed with rocket-propelled grenades, automatic weapons and hand gre-nades would have made the operation extremely costly, if not outright imposs-ible, for the marines and sailors. This is especially true when one considers the difficulties the Americans had mooring the two ships together.

Access to riot-control munitions also added to the safety of artillery missions fired in and around friendly units. Depending on the size and characteristics of the specific munition, the risk of being killed by shell fragments extended out to over 300 feet. The danger of being wounded by shrapnel extended much farther, though, out to almost 2,000 feet. Approximately 50 percent of all artil-lery missions fired during the Vietnam War were targeted very close to friendly positions or into an area virtually surrounded by converging friendly forces.[15] In many instances, there were also civilians in the area and it was not always pos-sible to know their precise location during the battle. In these situations, an off-target shell could be disastrous. General Westmoreland was acutely aware of the danger to non-combatants and instructed his unit commanders that artillery missions fired "in populated areas should be restricted whenever possible to close support missions and to clearly identifiable targets. [Commanders should] frequently impress upon [their] troops the need for prudence and good judg-ment in the employment of firepower."

With a tear-gas shell, the risk to both friendly forces and civilians was greatly reduced. These munitions used a small charge to eject four or five submunition canisters out of the base of the shell, which were either filled with CS powder and used for area contamination, or a pyrotechnic mixture of CS and designed to produce a dense agent cloud for immediate tactical effects. Although the shell could be set to detonate on impact, it was usually set for an air burst at an altitude of 300 to 450 feet to order to maximize the dispersal of the submunition canisters. The size and placement of the expelling charge produced few fragments when it exploded and, like the submunitions from the aerial canister clusters, the pyrotechnic canisters were specifically designed to minimize the risk of serious injury to anyone struck by one after it was ejected from the shell. These features allowed tear-gas munitions to be called in virtually on top of friendly positions during critical situations.

These rounds were also good for counter-battery fire against mortar and rocket attacks. These types of attacks were hard to prevent and difficult to suppress because the guerrillas only fired their weapons for a few minutes before fleeing the area. Often by the time Allied artillery could identify the enemy location, get approval to fire from the appropriate command element and then return fire, the guerillas were gone. Since tear-gas munitions were non-lethal and posed little risk to either friendly troops or civilians in the area, artillery units could arrange for blanket approval to use these shells for counter-battery fire in their sectors, thus greatly reducing their response time to such attacks. And even though the gas did not kill the guerrillas, the cloud quickly permeated throughout the launch area, preventing additional firings and inhibiting escape until fighter aircraft or helicopter gunships arrived and engaged the enemy gunners.[16]

Despite the wide range of successful applications, there were many times when tear gas did not contribute to the success of an operation. In some of these cases it was simply the nature of the mission and nothing the US tried seemed to work. A good example of this was the effort to reduce enemy ground fire against the C123 aircraft flying the Ranch Hand defoliation missions. While spraying, the aircraft would slowly fly long, straight patterns at low altitudes over enemy controlled jungle; planes were routinely hit by enemy small-arms fire. Despite efforts to suppress the gunners with both preemptive and reactive attacks by fighter jets, helicopter gunships and Cobra attack helicopters firing traditional ordnance, the C123s were still hit frequently and several were nearly brought down.

In October 1968, the air force decided to try using tear gas to temporarily blind the enemy gunners while the planes flew over. As the planes sprayed a patch of jungle near Vung Tau, jets flew in just ahead of the planes and dropped CS cluster bombs along their flight path. Because the planes flew at tree-top level while spraying, the flight crews wore protective masks to avoid the effects of the CS. Although the gas greatly reduced the volume and accuracy of enemy ground fire, it did not eliminate it. Since the crews complained bitterly about having to wear the uncomfortable masks while flying and the gas was not 100 percent effective against the enemy gunners, the squadron commander concluded it was not worth the trouble.

Two years later, a new commander resurrected the idea. This time he opted for tear gas in combination with conventional fragmentation bombs, hoping the guerrillas would be not only blinded but also forced to stay under cover until the slow-moving airplanes completed their mission and passed out of range. Even this combination did not eliminate all of the ground fire, however, and many of the aircraft were still hit. After a few sorties, the squadron concluded tear gas, even in combination with antipersonnel munitions, did not make their missions any safer and stopped using it.[17]

Another complicating factor limiting the effectiveness of tear gas was the determination of enemy soldiers to endure the effects and keep fighting. Based on laboratory experiments, the military realized motivated soldiers could ignore the irritation and even build up a tolerance to otherwise incapacitating concentrations. While this tolerance was short-lived and disappeared soon after leaving the agent cloud, it was often enough to get the guerrillas out of a tight situation. An example of this occurred during the effort to recover the Mayaguez. Early in the incident, after reconnaissance planes tracked the vessel to Koh Tang Island, the US stationed jet fighters and fighter-bombers over the Mayaguez to prevent the Cambodians from moving the ship closer to the mainland. As pilots circled the area, they were constantly trying to identify where the Cambodians were holding the hostages. Eventually one of the pilots saw guards herding some of the crew onto the deck of a Thai fishing trawler tied up to the Mayaguez. When the trawler began moving toward the mainland, fighter jets attempted to turn it back toward the island by firing warning shots across its bow. Since the Cambodians knew the Americans would not sink a boat full of hostages, the fishing trawler merely continued toward the mainland. After unsuccessfully firing numerous salvos the pilots changed tactics. Two of the jets got in front of the trawler, dropped down to just a few hundred feet above sea level, then turned and flew head on toward the trawler. As they passed overhead in this obvious act of intimidation, they dropped tear-gas bomblets onto the deck of the ship. The irritation was intense and the Thai crew was desperate to turn around. The Cambodian guards were resolute, however, threatening to shoot if the fishermen altered course. Everyone on the boat, crew and hostages alike, scurried around trying to kick the small bomblets off the deck as fast as they could. After the cloud dissipated and it was clear the boat was not going to change course, the jets came back for a second pass. This time the gas on the small boat was so thick everyone was overcome and vomited. The Mayaguez Third Engineer passed out; since he had a history of heart trouble, his crewmates thought he was dead. Fortunately he woke up about twenty minutes later without any lasting effects. Once again, the guards were undeterred by the gas and refused to allow the trawler's crew to change course. Short of sinking it, the fighter pilots had done everything possible to prevent the fishing trawler from reaching the mainland; they broke off their pursuit and headed back to the Mayaguez.[18]

Perhaps the most fundamental reason chemical agents failed to perform as expected was soldiers and their commanders did not understand the characteristics of gas or the munitions delivering it. For example, all of them had experienced the effects from exposure to CS; many assumed it was a universal response. They did not realize some individuals were less sensitive to the irritation than others. This was also true for animals. A humorous illustration of this occurred in May 1967 as a patrol from the 1st Infantry Division moved along a trail near Phuoc Vinh. The soldiers accidently disturbed a beehive and found themselves immersed in a swirling mass of the stinging insects. Without thinking, one of the soldiers decided to drive the bees away by discharging a CS grenade. While the gas had no effect on the bees, the soldiers suffered the typical effects of exposure. The scene degraded into a comical dance as the Americans tried to put on their masks while fending off their miniature assailants. As one described it, "I grabbed my mask and tried to put it on, but only trapped more bees under the mask. When I took it off to wipe them away, they flew back under the mask again."[19]

A more common problem was that soldiers did not understand that, while they could aim the weapon delivering the munition, they could not control the cloud the munition produced. Once the agent was released into the air, the cloud was influenced by both weather conditions and the terrain of the target area. Such factors as wind speed, atmospheric stability, temperature and humidity affected not only the direction and distance the cloud traveled, but also stability.[20] For example, on three separate occasions during the 1968 siege of Khe Sanh, jets dropped CS on high-traffic infiltration routes to try to flush enemy soldiers out into the open. On each occasion, thick cloud cover prevented the jets from flying during the morning when atmospheric conditions were favorable for a chemical attack. When the cloud cover dissipated in the afternoon, the atmospheric stability changed as well. Despite the unfavorable conditions, the marines were determined to disrupt the nightly attacks and proceeded with their plans to flush the enemy out into the open. On all three occasions, the gas formed a plume going straight up; the cloud did not cover the target and none of the enemy were forced from cover. This scenario was repeated on numerous occasions throughout the war.[21]

Overall, these limitations and failures were minor and the benefits of using tear gas were widely recognized. By the end of the war, almost every type of weapon system available to both the army and the air force had at least one munition capable of delivering riot-control agents. In instances where a suitable munition was not available to meet the requirements of a particular situation, soldiers improvised and fabricated something from materials on hand. Even if American soldiers initially viewed riot-control agents with little more than guarded skepticism, by the end of the war they came to view tear gas as a valuable addition to their arsenal of weapons and it was incorporated into almost every type of military operation.

6

NICHES

As the Americans began incorporating CS into the broader scope of their combat operational plans, they quickly realized its fundamental properties – it was essentially non-lethal; it was effective at low concentrations; the cloud rapidly diffused, spread out over a large area and penetrated into hardened defensive fortifications; and, if delivered properly, the contamination could persist for extended periods – made it the best weapon for a number of tactical situations. Sometimes the decisive advantage obtained by using gas became obvious when a new weapon system was introduced onto the battlefield; at other times it was the result of careful analysis of past combat operations or the suggestion from a combat soldier in the field. Still other times it was pure chance, a discovery made through the impulsive actions of soldiers trying to get out of a tight situation with nothing to lose.

Ironically, the situation that reopened the door for the United States to use riot-control agents in combat and the one these agents were uniquely suited for, that is to say incapacitation of soldiers hiding among civilians, was soon only a minor consideration for American troops. While Washington continued to maintain throughout the war that tear gas was routinely used for this purpose, field commanders told MACV in the spring of 1968 this was in fact not the case. These officers said their units rarely used CS specifically to save civilian lives and doubted it would ever be used routinely for this tactical purpose. The commanders justified their conclusion by pointing out civilians quickly evacuated a battlefield to prevent becoming hostages. While their justification was not entirely accurate, their conclusion was, and tear gas was only rarely used specifically to segregate combatants from civilian hostages. However, there were five other key niche areas where tear gas was universally regarded to be the key asset to resolve tricky situations. The first four of these were: breaking contact, flushing an enemy out of hiding, denying the guerrillas access to either key terrain or critical resources, and search–and–rescue operations.[1]

The ability to break contact, or safely withdraw from battle against a superior force, was a fundamental problems facing Allied patrols. As soldiers moved through the thick jungle, it was not uncommon to suddenly stumble upon the enemy at very close range. In encounters where the patrol was caught in an ambush, outnumbered or out–gunned, the difference between life and death was often decided in the first few seconds. If the soldiers were unable to quickly break contact and withdraw, then they would likely be overrun and killed.

Classically, in order to break contact, the forward element of the patrol began shooting into the enemy positions as rapidly as possible to suppress the enemy fire. As the guerrillas dropped behind cover, the rest of the patrol disengaged and moved away from the fighting. Once the withdrawing soldiers found appropriate cover, they began firing on the enemy positions, allowing the forward element to move even farther away from the guerrillas. This bounding process was repeated until the patrol completely disengaged from the enemy. Although methodical and orderly in concept, the process did not always work out well.

As General Westmoreland recognized early in 1965, tear–gas grenades were a unique and effective weapon that patrols could use to help them break contact in these situations. The gas cloud broke up the initial enemy assault and the effects from exposure prevented any type of coordinated pursuit. In some cases, the effects from exposure to the gas were dramatic, turning the tide of the battle so the patrol could overpower the guerrillas.

The need for this type of tactical capability was particularly acute in small units, such as long–range reconnaissance patrols, operating with limited artillery and close air support. Like everything else, when out on patrol a soldier's supply of tear–gas grenades was limited to what he could carry with him. Each soldier also carried all of his food, water and ammunition, as well as a portion of the common equipment needed for the mission. The longer the patrol, the heavier the basic load on each man. This meant fewer grenades and fewer times the soldiers could use gas to break contact. Eventually, the United States developed a special CS grenade for long–range patrols that was smaller and weighed much less than the standard M7. Although the XM58 did not generate nearly as much gas, the reduced weight and smaller size allowed individual soldiers to carry more of them. This gave them more options on when to use them and how much gas to deploy at any given time. In a typical scenario, team members tossed three or four of the small grenades in front of the enemy line to build up an initial cloud. As the patrol quickly moved away through the jungle, soldiers continued to randomly drop grenades to further disorganize any pursuit. In many instances, the small cloud generated by the XM58 was so localized that there was no need for members of the patrol to don their protective masks.[2]

If helicopters were going to insert the patrol, prior to the operation the helicopter pilots, patrol leader and forward air controllers held a joint briefing to establish take-off times, checkpoints, flight formation and emergency extraction plans. As part of these pre-mission briefings, the patrol leader laid out his plan for using CS to break contact and cover his team's extraction. If gas might blow back into the landing zone, the pilots were warned to have their protective masks available.[3]

Once airborne cluster munitions were widely available, CS became an even more versatile weapon for breaking contact. A cluster bomb was filled with miniature bomblets that pilots could accurately deliver very close to the perimeter of a patrol without any risk of killing or seriously wounding friendly soldiers. Each munition instantaneously generated a massive, dense cloud over a large area – a circle up to 350 feet in diameter when a helicopter released a cluster munition or an ellipse up to 330 feet long by 200 feet wide when released from a plane or jet – often enveloping the entire enemy unit.

It was just such a scenario that led to a major controversy years after the end of the war. On June 7, 1998, the premier edition of *Newsstand: CNN & Time* aired a story entitled "Valley of Death" alleging the United States used nerve gas during Operation Tailwind so an Allied unit could break contact and escape from a much larger Communist force. The producers at CNN did not grasp the effect exposure to the high concentration of agent produced by a cluster munition had on an unprotected individual, and immediately jumped to the conclusion the agent released must have killed the North Vietnamese soldiers.

The operation occurred in September 1970 when a force of sixteen Special Forces soldiers and over 100 Montagnard irregulars secretly crossed the border from South Vietnam into Laos. These soldiers were conducting a reconnaissance in force and providing a diversion for another operation. Following three days of a running battle with a larger North Vietnamese unit, nearly every member of the patrol was wounded. Under heavy fire, exhausted and nearly out of ammunition, the Allies watched helplessly as the Communists massed for a final assault. As the North Vietnamese pressed forward, two A-1 Skyraiders flew over and used CBU-30s to shower the enemy with CS bomblets. As the concentrated cloud of gas rapidly enveloped the enemy positions, the guerrillas were hit by the full effects of the agent. Many of them collapsed; they were blinded, retching and gasping for fresh air. None of the Communists were able to see the helicopters settling down on the landing zone, much less shoot at the patrol making a last desperate dash for safety. Within minutes the patrol was onboard the helicopters and headed back into South Vietnam.[4]

The next major innovative niche was flushing, the tactic pioneered by the 1st Cavalry Division during operation Masher-White Wing and enthusiastically endorsed by the division commander. It was more than just an extension of the classic reconnaissance by fire – the tactic of firing small arms or artillery into an area where enemy soldiers might be hiding, in the hope they would give away their positions by firing back or fleeing to better cover. Flushing was a means of augmenting the effectiveness of conventional weapons, in essence increasing their lethality, by driving soldiers who did not have gas masks into the open where they could be engaged more effectively. It was particularly useful against unprotected guerrillas occupying well-entrenched and heavily fortified positions that proved to be nearly impervious to projectiles and explosives.

Shortly after the conclusion of Operation Masher-White Wing, the 1st Cavalry Division was part of Operation Hawthorne, an attempt to drive the Communists out of the critical Central Highlands. During the second week of the operation, the Americans ran into exceptionally heavy resistance on a ridge north of Kon Tum, where three battalions of the North Vietnamese Army's 24th Regiment occupied an elaborate complex of hardened bunkers and tunnels. Despite 13,000 rounds of artillery and more than 100 sorties by close air support fighter-bombers, the Americans were unable to drive the Communists off the ridge. On June 24, in an attempt to repeat its earlier success in the Kim Song Valley, the 1st Cavalry Division used helicopters to drop 900 CS grenades along the ridgeline and saturated the area with tear gas. As enemy soldiers staggered into the open seeking fresh air, B-52s began pounding their positions. After over forty minutes of continuous bombardment, the B-52s departed for home. Minutes after the last bomb fell, soldiers from the 101st Airborne and 1st Cavalry Divisions assaulted up and onto the ridge. The Americans quickly eliminated what little scattered and uncoordinated resistance they encountered.[5]

This technique, sometimes referred to as "Red Lightning," was used by many units throughout the war and became a standard tactic for assaulting hardened targets. It was so effective that the tactic became a standalone mission. In the early phase, a long-range reconnaissance team shadowed a Communist unit back to the enemy's stronghold deep in the jungle, plotting the location on a map as a future target. Once the mission was approved, at some later date helicopters suddenly appeared over the camp, dropping tear-gas grenades or cluster munitions and saturating the area with CS. After the helicopters cleared the airspace, bombs fell, killing anyone forced into the open by the gas and disrupting any defensive efforts. As the last explosion died away, a second lift of helicopters inserted an assault force; the soldiers overran the camp and eliminated any residual resistance. These highly coordinated operations were very successful and extremely difficult to counter, even by well-trained North Vietnamese Army units.

There were other variations of this strategy that did not involve coordinating a bombardment by B-52s from Guam and even eliminated the infantry assault phase. Such variations allowed for more immediate tactical application of the technique when a momentary target of opportunity was identified. One version involved helicopters working in conjunction with close support jets armed with napalm and rockets. As usual, the helicopters flew in low over the target and saturated the area with CS. As the enemy fled into the open, the jets arrived and delivered their ordnance. Yet another variation minimized the assets involved down to a pack of helicopters working in tandem to investigate and neutralize potential hotspots. One of the helicopters made a pass over a potential target and saturated the area with CS while the others waited a short distance away. If any guerrillas broke cover, all of the gunships moved in with rockets and machine-gun fire. This particular variation was so successful some units required all of its gunships and command-and-control helicopters to carry tear-gas munitions on every flight so the pilots could engage targets of opportunity encountered during routine operations.[6]

Down in the jungle, infantry soldiers also found ways of using tear gas to increase the effectiveness of their weapons. One situation where it proved highly effective was during an ambush; using CS during the initial paroxysm of firepower magnified the disorientation and confusion of the guerrillas caught in the kill zone. It also added to the patrol's safety immediately after executing the ambush, when the soldiers moved forward to search the bodies for intelligence. Any guerrilla not killed in the firefight was unable to refrain from coughing and sneezing, alerting the soldiers someone was still alive. However, if the Americans were careless and used tear gas when the wind was blowing toward them, the cloud would drift back into their positions. When this happened, the soldiers were blinded just like the guerillas, giving any surviving enemy soldiers a chance to get away.

In addition to tear-gas grenades, soldiers often filled old ration bags with CS powder and taped them to the front of a claymore mine. When the patrol initiated the ambush by detonating the mine, the blast filled the target area not only with lethal pellets but also with the irritating powder, incapacitating anyone not immediately killed. When soldiers used these improvised munitions there was a lot of residual contamination, making it necessary for anyone searching the bodies afterward to wear a protective mask. Even protected by a mask, if a soldier moved forward before the cloud dissipated, the powdered agent would severely irritate his skin. If he did not remove the powder, within a short time the irritated skin blistered and became a serious chemical burn.

Always looking for a way to use technology to solve the myriad problems it faced in Vietnam, the United States military began using electronic detectors to track guerrillas hiding in the jungle. In addition to magnetic devices designed to react to the metal in enemy weapons and infrared detectors used to locate enemy campfires, it also used an "artificial nose" capable of detecting volatile biological waste material. In other words, this device "sniffed" out the ammonia in urine; operators identified potential enemy bivouac sites by locating high concentrations of this gas. These devices worked fairly well since the air in the Vietnamese jungles was virtually free of industrial pollutants that caused interference and produce false readings.

Commonly called a "people sniffer," the XM3 was mounted in a helicopter and rapidly surveyed large sections of jungle. When the army first started conducting sniffer missions, a typical operation involved a helicopter outfitted with the XM3 accompanied by several attack helicopters. The sniffing helicopter flew over the jungle at an altitude of just ten to twenty feet above the tree tops and speeds between ninety and one-hundred miles per hour. When the detector identified a hot spot, the helicopter made several passes over the area and attempted to identify the source. If the operator believed the source was an enemy camp, he either call in the attack helicopters or referred the target to an artillery unit on standby for the call. If the operator could not determine if guerrillas or non-combatants were producing the source, he called in ground troops to search the area.

After observing numerous search operations, the Viet Cong realized the detectors reacted to animal as well as to human byproducts. They began to lay false trails for the sniffer patrols with rags soaked with urine from water buffalo. This produced an abundance of false alarms and caused the attack elements to waste their munitions on empty jungle. The Americans countered this tactic by incorporating a flushing technique known as "jitterbugging." Soldiers equipped the sniffer helicopter with E158 canister clusters and dropped them on ambiguous targets. If the gas caused enemy soldiers to reveal themselves, the waiting attack helicopters, artillery or air mobile infantry units engaged them. This phase of the technique became known as "piling on."[7]

Using tear gas as a means of augmenting the effectiveness of conventional weapons caused a serious controversy, second only to the outcry following Peter Arnett's 1965 article. Many began to argue this tactic made tear gas tantamount to a lethal weapon, putting the United States in violation of international law. The Pentagon downplayed the significance of the charges, asserting tear gas was both legitimate and humane, and denying the United States military would ever use lethal chemical weapons in Vietnam. In a perverse twist of logic, Warren Nutter, Assistant Secretary of Defense for International Security Affairs, noted during questioning by the Senate Foreign Relations Committee even in situations when tear gas was used to increase the lethality of other weapons, it was still done for humanitarian purposes. If CS was not used and the Viet Cong remained behind cover, America would have to employ more painful weapons such as napalm bombs and flame-throwers.

Analysts warned the Pentagon that the continued use of riot-control agents in this capacity seriously undermined the concept of humane non-lethal chemicals and could ultimately lead to the prohibition of such weapons. Despite the controversy, the military continued using tear gas to enhance the lethality of traditional weapons until April 1975 when President Ford issued Executive Order 11850, prohibiting the military from using riot-control agents in a war zone except in specially designated defensive situations.[8]

Another niche for riot-control agents was using bulk powdered agent to deny the enemy access to key terrain and critical resources. As early as 1964, experts suggested bulk material sprayed along enemy trails was an effective way to eliminate enemy infiltration routes; forcing the North Vietnamese instead to move through areas where they could be easily observed and engaged by mortars, artillery or air strikes. These proponents also suggested bulk agent could be used tactically as a force multiplier,[9] dispersing the powder on likely routes of escape the enemy might use to evade American forces. As a rapidly deployable but non-lethal *corridor sanitaire*, such contamination zones reduced the number of soldiers needed to prevent the guerrillas from exfiltrating without posing the long-term risks to non-combatants associated with a traditional minefield. In other words, a way to help solve the strategic problem of forcing the elusive guerrillas to stand and fight.

An early example occurred during Operation Crazy Horse, which took place between May 16 and June 5, 1966. Once again, the 1st Cavalry Division was back in Binh Dinh Province pursuing elements of the 2nd Viet Cong Regiment. As the 1st Brigade pressed the attack against the guerrillas northeast of the Vinh Thanh Valley, other units airlifted into landing zones behind the enemy in an effort to block their withdrawal. There were insufficient forces, however, to block all of the possible trails the guerrillas could take out of the area. One of the likeliest escape routes wound through rough, mountainous terrain under dense vegetation offering plenty of cover from aerial observation. Unable to either secure the area or effectively patrol it from the air, they used a helicopter equipped with two M5 dispersers to create a CS barrier 1,000-feet wide and three miles long over a canalizing area anyone using the trail had to cross. Over the course of the operation, they reapplied the barrier only once after intermittent rains washed part of it away. Based on periodic inspections, they determined no enemy soldiers were able to successfully cross the barrier and escape.[10]

Unfortunately, the operational requirements of a disperser forced the helicopters to fly just above the tree-tops at very slow speed, which made them extremely vulnerable to enemy ground fire. Almost immediately, soldiers began to improvise less dangerous ways to quickly apply the agent over a large area. Initially, the Americans used unsophisticated frangible devices filled with CS powder. A container of agent was thrown from a helicopter and simply broke open when it struck the ground. Such munitions were very inefficient and guerrillas could easily pick a way around the hotspots created at each point of impact without aerosolizing the residual dust. Once soldiers began using an explosive charge to rupture the container just before it hit the ground, however, they were able to spread a heavy layer of contamination fairly consistently over a large target. The uniform deposit greatly reduced the chances of a guerrilla tiptoeing through the area without stirring up the agent.[11]

During the summer of 1966, the Chemical Section of the 1st Infantry Division began experimenting with an improvised bomb constructed from the fifty-five-gallon drums used to ship bulk CS to Vietnam. These drums, each containing eighty pounds of powdered agent, were fitted with an improvised burster and fuze system set to detonate at either tree-top level or just as the drum struck the ground. Based on these tests, the Americans found a single drum of agent detonated just as it passed through the jungle canopy effectively contaminated a circle almost 400 feet in diameter.

The 1st Infantry Division used these improvised devices a number of times in January 1967 at the start of Operation Cedar Falls. One such bombing mission occurred on January 16, when thirty drums were dropped on an enemy base camp. In order to achieve maximum coverage on the target, fifteen drums were dropped on each leg of a cross pattern centering on the camp. The dispersal of CS was very effective and kept unprotected enemy troops from reentering the camp area for quite some time.

Since drums of agent were readily available and were exceptionally easy to convert into the improvised bombs, other units soon began using these munitions to contaminate key terrain. For example, during Operation Pershing (February 12, 1967–January 21, 1968), the 1st Cavalry dropped nearly 400 drums on enemy bunkers and tunnels; during the first few months of 1969, the 2nd Brigade, 25th Infantry Division bombed enemy infiltration routes, lines of communication, tunnel and bunker complexes, and suspected rocket launching sites around the western edge of the Iron Triangle; and, during the six-month period between November 1, 1969 and April 30, 1970, the 4th Infantry Division dropped nearly 3,000 improvised bombs on targets in their area of operation.[12]

The army eventually formalized the concept by developing a burster system specifically designed to fit the CS shipping drums. Designated the XM925, the system consisted of a fuse, burster and drum cover. For aircraft safety, it incorporated both a fuze lanyard and arming rotor that had to turn fifteen-to-twenty times before the unit could explode. Although the initial design produced a significant number of misfires, by 1971 the XM925 bursters were more reliable and effective than the improvised burster systems.[13]

Drum bombs were so effective for contaminating critical terrain that, in 1968, the United States Air Force attempted to deploy them from C–123 and C–130 airplanes. Airplanes targeted key North Vietnamese infiltration routes into South Vietnam and set the bursters to detonate at ground level to ensure maximum residual contamination. After several attempts, however, the air force decided the dispersal pattern was too uneven and the enemy could find a way through the residual contamination. It discontinued the project in favor of the BLU–52, a modified fire bomb delivering over 250 pounds of CS.[14]

Large areas could also be contaminated quickly with smaller devices thrown from M113 armored personnel carriers (APCs) as they passed over the target area. The 25th Infantry Division used this method to contaminate a road through the Xom Moi Woods on July 11, 1967. Soldiers constructed the dispersion devices by tying two of the eight-pound shipping bags together with a quarter-pound charge of C4 placed between them. A time fuse and blasting cap were used to set off the explosive charge. As the APCs moved along the road, a soldier standing in the back of each vehicle lit the fuse on one of the munitions and threw it out the ramp door. Using these simple devices, four APCs were able to quickly create a contamination corridor nearly 800 feet wide along the entire length of the critical section of road.[15]

Soldiers of the 1st Cavalry Division developed a grenade-sized contamination device to deal with enemy bunkers, which was one of the most common defensive fortifications built by the insurgents. Individual bunkers were usually well-constructed and typically made with thick logs and hard-packed clay, although in some instances they were made with concrete and steel I-beams. In either case, bunkers could withstand all of the typical organic weapons available to an infantry battalion; it could even withstand an artillery or aerial bombardment unless one of these larger munitions scored a direct hit. Most of a bunker was below ground level; only one or two feet extended above the surface. There were often small firing ports in these low-profile walls allowing the guerrillas to engage attackers without exposing themselves to hostile fire. In larger fighting complexes, the Viet Cong laid out the bunkers with overlapping fields of fire, capable of providing mutual protection from attackers who might attempt to exploit a blind spot in any single bunker. The guerrillas also dug a series of trenches or short tunnels to interconnect the individual bunkers, allowing the defenders to move undetected between the various fighting positions.[16]

The Americans quickly realized CS was an effective way to drive the Viet Cong out of one of these bunkers. Unlike traditional fragmentation grenades that soldiers had to throw into the bunker to be effective, a gas grenade only had to land near the enemy position – upwind so the cloud billowed in through the firing ports. Unfortunately, the gas cloud generated by an M7 pyrotechnic grenade quickly dissipated and did not leave any residue to deter the guerrillas from reoccupying the fighting position. To keep the enemy out of these positions longer, soldiers threw an M25 gas grenade into the bunker along with a standard fragmentation grenade. The M25 was a bursting-type grenade that filled the bunker with a cloud of powdered agent. When the fragmentation grenade exploded seconds later, it blew the CS powder farther into the trench or tunnel connecting the bunker to the other fighting positions. The dust eventually settled onto the floor and walls but was easily re-aerosolized if anyone disturbed it.

At times there were insufficient M25 grenades to meet the demand from the field. During one of these periods, the chemical section of the 1st Cavalry came up with an improvised grenade. Known as the "bunker use restriction bomb," or BURB, it was originally made from the shipping container for the warhead of a 2.75-inch rocket. Soldiers filled it with about one pound of CS and used blasting caps to rupture the container and disperse the agent. These devices contained about eight-times as much agent as the M25 grenade and created a dense cloud that filled the bunker and adjoining tunnel, and also left a thick residual coating preventing anyone not wearing a mask from reentering the structure. Depending on the type of CS used, the agent remained active in the bunker for as long as a month. BURBs were so effective that the army also formalized this concept and began manufacturing the devices in the United States and shipping them to units in Vietnam.[17]

Ultimately, most of the CS used during the war was employed in an attempt to deny the enemy access to key terrain. As in tunnels, one of the primary factors affecting the persistency of the agent was its rate of hydrolysis once it was released into the environment. The more water the finely ground powder was exposed to, the faster it decomposed. Normal CS was only good for a few days under typical conditions. If it rained or the air was very humid, then the time was even shorter. When the United States switched to CS1, the persistency jumped up to between seven and fourteen days. A further improvement occurred when the military began using CS2. This version was so hydrophobic it was easily re-aerosolized even if it landed on water. Anyone wading across a contaminated rice paddy or swamp disturbed the agent floating on the surface and was instantly engulfed in an irritating cloud. CS2 remained effective for up to thirty days under typical conditions in the jungle.[18]

Under some circumstances, the residual contamination was vastly more persistent than expected and haunted subsequent Allied activities. An interesting example occurred at an old fort sitting on the edge of the Mekong Delta. Built by the French in 1910 it was archaic – complete with a moat, towers and revolving steel pillboxes – but solid. Since the South Vietnamese Army was unwilling to expend the resources and effort necessary to raze the fort, when the last unit occupying the fort was ordered to leave, soldiers spread a heavy layer of CS powder throughout the interior as a way to hinder future Communist activities. Years later, a company from the 199th Light Infantry Brigade decided the fort made an excellent base of operations. Unaware of the residual contamination, the Americans moved in and began exploring. In some of the inner rooms deep within the fortress, sealed away and protected from the elements, the agent was still active. When soldiers entered one of those rooms and began rummaging around, they inadvertently aerosolized the powder residue. Carried by air currents, it affected the unlucky trespasser and then drifted out the door, down the hall and into other areas. On a few occasions, so much agent became airborne men were hanging over the tower battlements trying to find some fresh air. Despite their best efforts, the soldiers were never able to fully decontaminate a number of the rooms and had to accept those areas were permanently off-limits.[19]

Selecting the correct version of CS was key to the success of a denial operation. If units intended to reoccupy the area shortly after spreading the contamination, the best choice was CS or possibly CS1. If soldiers wanted the contamination to persist for an extended period, it was CS2. If an incorrect version was inadvertently substituted for the desired one, the mission could be jeopardized. For example, during 1969, the 3rd Marine Regiment was confronted with a steady trickle of North Vietnamese soldiers infiltrating across the Demilitarized Zone and moving south through their area of operation to strengthen local Viet Cong units. Despite intense patrolling, the Americans were unable to eliminate this clandestine migration. Changing their tactics, the marines decided to pull their patrols and use CS to contaminate a large section of mountainous jungle about half-a-mile south of the Demilitarized Zone. The persistent agent would force the insurgents out of the contaminated area and onto specific well-known trails where the marines placed seismic detectors. When the sensors responded to enemy activity, the marines would call in pre-registered artillery and air strikes.

After nearly two weeks without any notable sensor activity, the marines discovered the target area was contaminated with CS1 and not CS2. This meant after only a few days the agent had degraded in the humid environment and the enemy enjoyed unfettered access to all of the trails throughout the region. Realizing the enemy could be anywhere, the marines carefully searched the contaminated area and all of the terrain back up to the Demilitarized Zone. During their search the marines engaged in a number of significant firefights, killing a total of forty-three North Vietnamese insurgents they found hiding in the jungle.[20]

Unfortunately, the very characteristics making CS2 so effective – the ultra-fine particle size and the coatings preventing agglomeration and hydrolysis – also made it the most difficult version of the agent to disseminate uniformly over a large area. All of the air-dropped munitions used to deliver bulk CS2 caused excessive aerosolization when actuated and resulted in inconsistent contamination of the target. The guerrillas were aware of this flaw and sometimes succeeded in snaking their way through a treated area without experiencing excessive discomfort. Throughout the war, the Americans worked on ways to improve on delivery without compromising agent effectiveness. One interesting method involved blending the CS2 powder with a moisture sensitive substance, such as calcium carbide, and pressing the mixture into pellets. Moisture in the air caused the pellet to disintegrate and left a small pile of easily aerosolized agent on the ground. In pellet form, the agent could be scattered in a very uniform pattern directly from a hopper attached to a low-flying aircraft. The desired density of contamination could be obtained by simply changing the air speed or the rate of application. Despite various feasibility studies, this pelletized version of CS never made it into combat.[21]

In addition to denying the guerrillas access to key terrain and limiting their maneuverability during a battle, persistent agents were also used as a means of denying guerrillas access to other resources as well. Since 1962 the Allies used herbicides to kill the enemy's crops, hoping to disrupt Communist operations by stressing the insurgent's logistics system. In concept, the crop-destruction program forced guerrillas to divert tactical units from combat operations to finding food. Unfortunately, the program actually hurt the civilian population much more than it impacted the insurgents, since the guerrillas simply collected foodstuffs, primarily rice, from local farmers as a tax. These taxes were consolidated into caches and hidden in inaccessible or unusual places. For instance, on one occasion, soldiers hastily digging fighting positions in a graveyard uncovered a large rice cache in a false gravesite. It was covered by grass mats, a plastic sheet and sand. On another occasion, a large cache of rice was found in a pigpen covered with a sheet of corrugated tin and under six inches of fresh manure.[22]

Whenever these caches were recovered, every effort was made to ship the food back to a civilian redistribution center. In some situations, however, this was not practical. Sometimes the sheer mass of the stockpile limited the available options for dealing with it. Individual caches ranged in size from several hundred pounds to over 1,000 tons. In many cases, numerous caches were clustered close together so the overall hoard often ran into the hundreds of tons. While evacuation of the rice by helicopter was sometimes possible, for such large quantities helicopters were not a realistic option. The ubiquitous UH–1H helicopter had a limited cargo capacity and its utility for moving large quantities of rice was questionable. Even with the more robust CH–47 cargo helicopters, moving the larger caches required a significant commitment of key limited resources.[23] If a mechanized unit was involved in the recovery, it had access to APCs, but, like the UH–1H, these vehicles had limited cargo capacity. Another option was to turn the rice over to a South Vietnamese unit with access to trucks; however, the Vietnamese commander was not always willing to cooperate and sometimes considerable pressure was required to get even a portion of the rice evacuated. A final option taken whenever possible was to coordinate with the local district or province chief for porters to transport the rice out of the combat area. Their cooperation often depended on the proximity of the cache to a village and the potential for retribution by local Viet Cong once the Americans left the area.[24]

If all of these options failed to materialize and the captured rice could not be removed from the combat area, either because of the volume or because of the tactical situation, then it had to be destroyed or at least rendered inedible. Soldiers tried scattering the rice with explosive charges but soon learned blasting did not damage the individual grains and the Viet Cong simply picked them up. The Americans also tried burning the caches but without much success. Conversely, engineers used bulldozers to push rice into a river, but this option was obviously limited by the proximity of the cache to a river and access to heavy earth-moving equipment. For ethical, legal and strategic reasons, it was not possible to simply mix the rice with poison and leave it for the enemy. However, it was acceptable to render the rice unpalatable by mixing with a noxious but non-toxic substance. An example of such a material was the repellent carried by pilots to ward off sharks when their aircraft went down in the ocean. Although nauseating and very effective, there just was not enough repellent in the logistics system to effectively adulterate one of the multi-ton caches of rice.[25]

A contaminant that was available in large quantities and readily accessible to soldiers in the jungle was powdered CS, which left a taste not only easily detectable but also quite repulsive. Typically, soldiers placed bags of powdered CS on top of the cache – about one pound of CS for every 100 pounds of rice – and then use explosives to scatter both the rice and the agent. This contaminated the rice and also prevented unprotected individuals from entering the area. By the time the CS lost its potency and the Viet Cong reentered the area to recover the rice, the grains were rotten. The 1st Division used this procedure frequently during Operation Cedar Falls. A few months later, the 25th Infantry Division added their own twist to the process, pouring diesel fuel over the cache before scattering the rice with explosives. Then the chemical section detonated several fifty-five-gallon CS drum bombs over the blast zone, saturating the area with the persistent powder.[26]

Soldiers used CS to contaminate other foodstuffs as well. For example, during Operation Malheur, Company A, 2nd Battalion of the 502nd Infantry located an enemy cache of eighty tons of rock salt. Because of the tactical situation, they did not have the time or resources to transport the spice to a redistribution center. To denature the salt, soldiers distributed twenty eight-pound bags of CS throughout the cache, then scattered the stockpile with cratering charges. Seven days later, the concentration of CS was still heavy in the area and the disintegrating salt was untouched.[27]

American long-range patrols operating deep in enemy-controlled jungle sometimes used a scaled-down version of these techniques to ruin small stockpiles of enemy provisions. One example occurred in October 1970 just after a team of army rangers executed an ambush in a remote section of jungle. As the Americans quickly moved out of the area, they stumbled onto a fifty-five-gallon drum full of corn. In a hurry to leave the area before enemy reinforcements arrived, the rangers still took time to drop a white phosphorus grenade – to burn as much of the corn as possible – and a CS grenade – to contaminate the remains – into the drum before they ran down the trail.[28]

CS was also used as a deterrent to enemy salvage operations. The Viet Cong were notorious for their ability to recover and recycle "worthless trash" discarded by American soldiers. For the guerrillas, dumps and abandoned facilities were a treasure trove. To prevent, or at least delay, these salvage operations, Americans often intermixed CS powder with garbage or spread it throughout abandoned facilities. For instance, in 1971 the Americans finally decided to abandon Khe Sanh. After crushing and burning everything they could not remove, the marines saturated the area with CS powder, hoping to delay enemy salvage operations long enough for the weather to finish destroying anything left behind.[29]

Search-and-rescue operations to recover the crew of downed aircraft was the fourth key niche for tear agents. The Communists went to great lengths to capture these individuals and it often came down to a race between the rescuers and the enemy soldiers combing the area. In these situations, tear gas had a telling advantage over traditional weapons since it could be used in very close proximity to the downed crew without endangering them. A good example of this occurred on February 15, 1969. During a rescue operation in the enemy-infested A Shau Valley, the recovery helicopters were unable to get anywhere near the downed F-4 pilot because of the intense anti-aircraft fire coming from enemy positions throughout the valley. The escort planes, only equipped with standard fragmentation and napalm bombs, could not use their weapons without endangering the downed pilot. As the frustrated recovery teams continued to circle overhead, enemy soldiers were closing in on the grounded American. Running out of time, A-1 Skyraiders armed with CBU-19 CS cluster munitions left Pleiku Air Base and raced toward the valley. Maneuvering through the deadly gauntlet of enemy fire, the planes dropped the bomblets onto the enemy positions. As the CS roiled over the enemy gunners, their fire became erratic and disorganized. A helicopter, with the crew wearing protective masks, hastily touched down and pulled the F-4 pilot aboard. Within minutes, the rescued pilot was out of the valley and heading for home.[30]

In some cases, such as when the crew was surrounded or captured, the escort planes dropped the cluster bombs so the crew was engulfed in the cloud along with the enemy soldiers. Anticipating the effects of the gas, the Americans could take advantage of the chaos and escape. This is not to say the crew did not suffer in these situations. As one air force pilot described his experience:

> [t]hey laid it all along the top of the ridge ... [some of] it hit me.... I ran into a tree and was wrapped around the tree urinating, defecating, and retching all at the same instant.... It also made me want to sneeze.... After that every time I'd come up on the air and ask for [more CS], as soon as I'd tell them where, how far and the heading, I'd tell them, "Don't get it close to me."[31]

The gas also had an impact on the crews of the recovery helicopters; the rescuers were forced to wear protective masks, severely hampering both radio and on-board communications. As a case in point, on December 18, 1971 the crew of an F-4D Phantom ejected near the border of North Vietnam and Laos when they ran out of fuel. Because it was getting dark and the weather conditions were deteriorating rapidly, they were forced to spend the night in the jungle. As the rescue helicopter was maneuvering to pick them up the next morning, guerrillas fired at it and struck the right engine. The damage was sufficient to force the crew to abandon the rescue attempt and return to base for repairs. To hamper the enemy soldiers searching the area, an A-1 Skyraider dropped several BLU-52s, leaving a thick layer of CS powder between the Americans and the guerrillas.

When another recovery helicopter arrived on the scene, the crew was warned to wear their protective masks since their rotor wash would probably stir up the CS powder. The masks obscured their vision and made communications difficult, even to the point of creating a situation threatening the aircraft. As Captain Jones, the helicopter pilot, described the operation:

[h]overing was very difficult as corrections and observations given by my crew were distorted and unintelligible with the gas masks on. Once over [the downed pilot], it took five minutes to locate him through the thick jungle canopy.... At one point during the hover my tail rotor got dangerously close to a tree. I was unable to understand the [Pararescue Recovery Specialist] on the aft ramp telling me not to move back. He finally ripped [his] mask off and used his helmet microphone to warn me. He immediately suffered from the effects of the [gas] we were whipping up with our rotor wash.

The whipping cloud of agent also affected the unfortunate F-4 crew waiting on the ground. Without protective masks they immediately began coughing and crying, symptoms of exposure lasting until the helicopter gained altitude and was well away from the agent cloud.

The consequences of the swirling plume of CS were not all bad, however. As the rescue team dragged the crew of the downed Phantom aboard, the strong rotor wash entrained more of the agent and carried it farther out from the pick-up point, until it rolled over the Viet Cong soldiers moving in to disrupt the recovery. The guerrillas were instantly incapacitated and unable to interfere with the operation.[32]

By the end of 1967, at least one A-1 Skyraider on each search-and-recovery operation carrier out in South Vietnam was armed with CS weapons; weapons that were used routinely to enhance the safety of a mission. But this was not true everywhere. On February 2, 1968, the Joint Chiefs of Staff granted the air force authority to use CS during search-and-rescue in the neighboring country of Laos. However, American operations in that country were politically sensitive, and using chemical agents, regardless of their non-lethal effects, would only increase that sensitivity. For this reason, whenever tear gas was used during a rescue mission in Laos, the on-scene rescue commander had to immediately notify the headquarters of both the 7th Air Force and the 3rd Aerospace Search and Recovery Group in Saigon. As a consequence of this bureaucracy, tear gas was rarely used during search-and-recovery operations in Laos until after the South Vietnamese invasion in 1971.[33]

As the war progressed, soldiers realized tear gas was a valuable resource and also that there were a number of scenarios where it was arguably the best option to resolve the situation. This was due to the ability of the agent to permeate and diffuse over a wide area, penetrate into hardened defensive positions and to remain active over prolonged periods. In addition to search-and-rescue, area denial, flushing and breaking contact, there was one other major combat situation where CS played a crucial and indispensable role. In this case, it was a combination of an unfamiliar battlefield, lack of options and the rediscovery of an under-utilized weapon that inspired the marines to try tear gas during the Battle of Hue.

7
URBAN COMBAT

At the beginning of 1968, the fortunes of war appeared to be aligning with the Allies. They had won every major encounter since the battle of Ia Drang in 1965 and had consistently inflicted heavy losses on enemy units while keeping their own casualties to a minimum. Based on American intelligence estimates, the Allies successfully forced the Viet Cong away from most of the population centers throughout the country and blocked the majority of North Vietnamese infiltrators crossing the Demilitarized Zone into South Vietnam. It seemed the war might soon be winding down. Then, in what became known as the Tet Offensive, the Communists launched an inconceivably massive surprise attack that not only stunned the military but also shattered any illusions about ending the war.

Tet is the largest and most important holiday in Vietnam, marking the beginning of the lunar New Year. It officially lasts three days and falls sometime between the last ten days of January and the middle part of February. Derived from ancient religious beliefs involving the full moon and spring planting, it has evolved in modern times into a time to honor friends, family and ancestors, to reflect on the activities of the previous year and to plan for the future. Everyone in Vietnam, regardless of religion, celebrates Tet. During the war, both sides traditionally honored a general ceasefire during the holiday. In 1968, the Allies decided to observe the ceasefire from the evening of January 29 until the morning of January 31. The North Vietnamese declared they would observe a full seven-day truce beginning on January 27 and lasting through the early morning of February 3.

Even during the war, Tet was a time for celebration and the festival in Hue was the most spectacular in all of Vietnam. Homes and shops were decorated, the markets were flooded with goods, and there were nightly fireworks.

Although the holiday only lasted three days, in Hue the gala lasted an entire week and attracted revelers from all over the country. By the end of January there were several thousand visitors clogging the streets in addition to the normal population of nearly 140,000.[1]

In 1968, Hue was the capitol of Thua Thien Province and was the third largest city in South Vietnam, surpassed only by Saigon and Da Nang. It is located in the thinnest section of Vietnam, about six miles inland from the South China Sea and about sixty miles south of what was the Demilitarized Zone. It sits on a bend in the Perfume River, which snakes up from the south. The river passes through the city and divides it into two sections before moving on to eventually empty into the South China Sea. The fortified section of the city north of the river is the Citadel, begun in 1802 by the Emperor Gia Long and modeled on Peking's Forbidden City. In 1968, it occupied approximately three square miles and was surrounded by a thick, earth and stone wall, about thirty feet high and in some places up to ninety feet thick. The sections of the wall not bordering the river were surrounded by a wide moat filled with water up to twelve feet deep. The city defenses also included high ramparts and towers giving ancient defenders a means of protecting the walls and moats. Within the walls was block after block of row houses, parks, villas, shops and various governmental buildings. Located at the south end of the Citadel was the Imperial Palace where the Emperors held court until 1883 when the French took control of Vietnam. A modern addition to the ancient city was a small airfield built within the confines of the protective walls.

On the south side of the river was the newer section of the city. In 1968 it was mostly residential and about half the size of the Citadel. It was roughly shaped like a triangle, bounded on the northern edge by the Perfume River and on the other two sides by the Phu Cam Canal. About one-third of the city's population lived south of the river. The south side of the city also contained the Provincial Capital Building, the US Consulate, the University, the Provincial Treasury Building, the post office, the city's power station and the MACV compound. Hue was considered to be semi-sacred to both North and South Vietnamese because it was the capital back when Vietnam was a unified country. During the previous 100 years of war, Hue had only suffered the ravages of war twice: in 1883 when French warships bombarded it; and in 1945 when Communist guerrillas tried to force the French out of the city. Although the South Vietnamese Army 1st Division maintained its headquarters compound in the northern corner of the Citadel, Hue was traditionally regarded as a neutral, open city and treated with respect by both sides. It was the cultural and intellectual center of Vietnam, a place where most of the city's religious and intellectual leaders advocated strong local autonomy with an emphasis on traditional national values. Hue was regarded as such a safe city that South Vietnamese officers often paid bribes to get stationed there. It was also one of the only cities in South Vietnam where the US did not maintain a protective combat force and only the US advisors to the 1st Division were stationed at the MACV compound.

Hue was a key strategic supply and redistribution hub for the Allies because it lay at the intersection of three main transportation routes. National Highway 1 ran along the western fringe of the city and was a major supply route up to the Demilitarized Zone; a railroad line ran between Hue and Da Nang, allowing the rapid movement of men and supplies to the city and then on up to the Demilitarized Zone; and, finally, the navy brought supplies into the city from the South China Sea via the Perfume River.[2]

Although there were indications that the Communists were planning a spring offensive, neither the US nor the South Vietnamese believed it would interfere with the celebration of Tet. Hanoi, however, saw the Tet holiday as the perfect time to catch the Allies off-guard. Realizing American public sentiment for the war was wavering, and aware that 1968 was going to be an election year in the United States, the Communists decided it was time to escalate the war to the conventional level. In preparation for the campaign, the insurgents conducted a series of probing attacks during the fall of 1967 to test Allied defenses and identify weak points for the main offensive, which would take place during the following February. The North Vietnamese hoped it would be not only a stunning surprise attack, but also a crushing victory since much of the South Vietnamese Army would be home on leave.

The Communists viewed Hue as the weak link in the Allied defensive strategy for the two northern provinces. Capturing the city would sever the supply lines to the units defending the Demilitarized Zone and open the door for a massive invasion. Viet Cong and Communist sympathizers began reconnoitering Hue with an eye toward key targets six months before the attack. Then, in January, as the city prepared for the upcoming holiday, Communist troops masquerading as civilians mingled with the throngs of people who had come for the festival and infiltrated into the city to wait for the main attack to begin. They did not have any difficulty smuggling their weapons and ammunition into the city in wagons, truck beds and other hiding places. Then, on the evening of January 30, approximately 74,000 North Vietnamese invaded South Vietnam and, in conjunction with local Viet Cong units, attacked key populated areas within the I Corps Tactical Zone.[3] The unprecedented scope of the offensive involved assaults on thirty-six provincial capitals, five autonomous cities, sixty-four district capitals and over fifty hamlets.[4] Because of its traditionally neutral status, residents of Hue took little notice of these events.

In the early hours of January 31, two regiments of combined North Vietnamese Army and Viet Cong forces entered Hue virtually unopposed and linked up with the infiltrators.[5] In addition to the assault rifles, machine guns and rocket-propelled grenade launchers carried by typical infantry battalions, the Communists were also equipped with sniper rifles, heavy machine guns and anti-tank weapons. They further augmented this arsenal when they captured the

South Vietnamese 1st Division armory during the initial hours of the occupation. Within a few hours, the Communists seized control of the entire city except for the 1st Division Headquarters in the Citadel and the MACV compound south of the Perfume River. The failure to take these two critical objectives provided the Allied relief forces with footholds within the city and set the stage for one of the bloodiest battles of the war.[6]

Overwhelmed by the size of the Tet Offensive and completely underestimating the enemy strength in Hue, the US initially sent in Company A of the 1st Battalion, 1st Marines (abbreviated 1/1) to relieve the US advisors trapped in the MACV compound on the south side of the city. Along the eight-mile trip up Highway 1 from Phu Bai to Hue, Company A joined forces with four M48 tanks from the Marine 3rd Tank Battalion.[7] Just after the now-reinforced company crossed the Phu Cam canal into the city, it was hit by heavy enemy fire and became bogged down. Lieutenant Colonel Marcus Gravel, the commander of 1/1, hastily organized a reaction force in Phu Bai and raced to the aid of his men. Augmented by the additional marines, Company A was able to fight its way into the MACV compound. Realizing the Communists were in much greater strength and more heavily armed than the marines were led to believe, Lieutenant Colonel Gravel called back for additional reinforcements. By February 3, marine forces in Hue consisted of Company A and the headquarters platoon of 1/1 under command of Lieutenant Colonel Gravel, Companies F, G and H of 2nd Battalion, 5th Marines (abbreviated 2/5), under the command of Lieutenant Colonel Ernest Cheatham Jr., the tanks from 3rd Battalion, and a number of Ontos anti-tank vehicles.[8] Colonel Stanley Hughes, the newly appointed commander of 1st Marine Regiment, was given command of all US Marine forces in Hue.[9]

One of the key tactical objectives for capturing a well-defended city is to seal the perimeter and isolate the defenders. Unable to get supplies and reinforcements, they will eventually succumb through attrition. In this situation, however, Hue was only one of several ongoing simultaneous attacks and the US did not have enough forces available to isolate the eight-mile perimeter around the city. The Communists were able to establish an external resupply system allowing them to bring in guns, ammunition and reinforcements as necessary.[10]

Based on the distribution of Allied forces within the city, the South Vietnamese and US divided operational control of Hue at the Perfume River. The 1st Division, working out of its compound in the Citadel, would handle everything north of the river and the marines, working out of the MACV compound, would clear everything south of the river. For the first thirteen days of the battle, there were two separate and uncoordinated operations ongoing to retake the city.[11]

Combat in cities is often referred to as "military operations on urban terrain," or abbreviated as MOUT. It tends to be one of the most difficult, intense and costly types of military operations and is characterized by close combat, high casualties and a nearly invisible enemy. Units fighting in built-up areas often become isolated, and the larger battle degenerates into a series of myopic, intense firefights. Battalion and company commanders tend to lose their ability to effectively control their units, and coordinating offensive operations becomes complicated and very confusing.

Normal city features such as multistory buildings, stone fences and sewer covers provide cover and concealment, limit fields of observation and fire, and act as barricades slowing and complicating the movement of the attacking force. Buildings, especially ones with thick walls, provide excellent fortified positions. Although streets offer rapid avenues of approach, they also canalize forces into clear, predictable fields of fire, allowing defenders to engage the enemy at extended distances from many directions. MOUT also tends to be more three-dimensional than other combat environments. The defenders can be not only on either side, lurking behind a wall or pile of rubble, but also on a rooftop prepared to fire down on the advancing enemy or in a sewer ready to pop up once the soldiers have passed. These features make urban warfare very vicious and compressed. What would normally be considered an inconsequential advance often becomes a deliberate assault under the most arduous conditions.

When the battle moves inside a building, combat truly becomes three-dimensional. Soldiers have to play cat-and-mouse through an unfamiliar labyrinth of hallways, stairways and rooms on each floor of a building. Each room must be searched and cleared before proceeding. Every door, cabinet, closet, piece of furniture or pile of rubble must be checked not only for hidden soldiers but also for booby traps. Since an enemy soldier could pop through an adjacent doorway or window at any moment and throw a grenade or spray the room with bullets, rooms have to be cleared as rapidly as possible to avoid giving the enemy unnecessary targets. In the urban arena, soldiers require inordinately high morale, steadfast will and patience to endure the stress and grueling physical conditions they face.[12]

During the early 1960s, the possibility of urban warfare was considered so remote that marines only received an overview during basic training. The subject was virtually eliminated from all other training programs. The marines in Hue were unprepared for this type of warfare. Many of them had spent their entire time in uniform patrolling the jungle and never even considered fighting in a city. Through costly experience, they found many successful jungle tactics were suicidal on the streets and they had to learn on-the-job how to fight and survive in this surreal environment.[13]

The North Vietnamese soldiers sent to Hue, on the other hand, received intensive training in urban combat, focusing on tactics, techniques and procedures for defending the city against the inevitable Allied counterattack. The Communists carefully planned and set up their defenses. Captain George Christmas was the commander of Company H, 2/5, and described them this way:[14]

Enemy defenses along Le Loy Street [just south of the Perfume River] were set in strong points several blocks apart. The strong point was normally a three-story building, surrounded by a courtyard, with a stone fence. Snipers were placed in the upper stories (as well as throughout other buildings along the route of advance); automatic weapons in the lower floor. Spider holes surrounded the courtyard. Each spider hole had an NVA soldier equipped with both an AK47 assault rifle and a B40 rocket launcher.... Marine armor was left open to direct rocket and recoilless rifle fire on the long, straight streets ... [t]heir movement was completely canalized; and because enemy fire was from several blocks away, the close-in protection provided by the marine companies had little deterrent effect. The thick, stone walls of the [buildings] were ideal places for the enemy's automatic weapons.[15]

The Communists also had two other key advantages in Hue during the Tet Offensive. First, because of the historic and cultural significance of the city, the South Vietnamese government initially restricted the use of artillery and close air support in order to minimize collateral damage.[16] Removing these key assets was a significant handicap to the marines, especially as they adapted to the alien aspects of urban warfare. The second was the unusually bad weather limiting air traffic; this affected the evacuation of wounded, the influx of supplies and close air support once the initial restrictions were lifted.[17]

The combat was savage and relentless, and advances against the well-armed and entrenched enemy were measured in inches. Small groups of marines moved doggedly from house to house, engaging enemy positions on all sides. Bullets seemed to come from every direction at once. As one private described the situation: "[i]t was like fighting a bee hive. Fire was coming from street level, from windows on the second floor, and from the roof of every building. We had to crawl everywhere."[18]

Without any significant training in urban warfare, and unable to draw on previous battle experience, the marines had to improvise tactics and develop new techniques on the spot. One of their first innovations was to use smoke to make up for the lack of cover and concealment available on the long, open streets. Within hours of arriving in Hue on January 31, the marines were ordered to proceed from the MACV compound in the southern half of the city into the Citadel and relieve the pressure on the South Vietnamese 1st Division. Immediately after they crossed the bridge over the Perfume River and began moving into the Citadel, Company G came under heavy fire from the Communist positions on top of the Citadel wall and from within one of the gates passing through the wall. Several marines were wounded and trapped in front of the main company position with only limited cover. Under cover fire provided by an M60 machine gun and numerous smoke grenades that the M79 gunners rained down on the enemy positions, most of the wounded marines were able to escape the murderous crossfire and withdraw back into the main company position. However, five men were still trapped. While the rest of the company threw smoke grenades and fired more M79 smoke rounds into the enemy positions, several marines commandeered a civilian flatbed truck and used it as a shield during the recovery of the trapped marines. Following several of these hard lessons, it soon became standard practice to use smoke grenades whenever the marines wanted to cross an open area. However, the Communists quickly recognized the ploy and improvised a counter. Whenever the marines used smoke, the guerrillas simply began firing blindly into the cloud with every available weapon. The hail of bullets formed a lethal, impassable wall.[19]

Unable to reach the 1st Division, the marines retreated back to the MACV compound and began operations to clear the south side of the city. Over the next few days, the marines slowly cleared out the North Vietnamese immediately around the MACV perimeter and began to push deeper into the southern half of the city. By February 3, the marines of 2/5 had captured the buildings making up Hue University and sat staring across Ly Thuong Kiet Street at their next objective, a building complex consisting of the public health building, the Provincial Treasury and the post office. The complex was bristling with heavily armed Communists who were looking back across the street at the marines.

The treasury building was the key to the enemy defenses. It was both psychologically and physically imposing, designed to thwart any would-be robbers. It was a two-story building with a loft and a flat roof; the walls were four-to-five-feet thick and made from reinforced concrete. It sat in the middle of an open courtyard surrounded by an eight-foot wall made of masonry and wrought-iron stakes. The marines could only see one gate into the courtyard through this outer wall and it was made of stout wrought-iron bars. To add to their woes, they had no idea of the layout of the interior of the building, how many Communists they were up against or what type of additional defenses the enemy had built. In short, they would essentially be attacking blind.

The marines tried using their heavy weapons to dislodge the defenders. However, rounds from the 106-mm recoilless rifle, 3.5-inch rocket launchers, M72 LAWs and even the 90-mm main gun of the tanks barely dented the walls of the treasury. The only remaining option for the marines was to go in and clear the building room-by-room.[20]

The first obstacle was simply to get across Ly Thuong Kiet Street, a long, open street with very few obstructions to block the view along most of its length. The marines planned to have one company lay down a heavy volume of suppressive fire on the enemy positions while another company scrambled across the street. Once across, the company on the far side could cover the advance of the rest of the battalion. What they did not realize was the North Vietnamese had positions in all the buildings on the western side of the street for at least a block on either side of the treasury. One in particular, the Le Loi Primary School, a block southeast of the treasury building at the intersection of

Ly Thuong Kiet and Tran Cao Van Streets, had a clear field of fire up the length of Ly Thuong Kiet Street. Enemy positions in the school, including at least one 0.51 caliber machine gun in the basement, could fire across the entire marine front.

Following their new standard practice, the marines used smoke grenades and M79 smoke rounds to create a cloud filling the street just prior to the assault. A gentle breeze was in their favor and pushed the smoke into the eyes of the defenders. Unfortunately, the North Vietnamese realized the implications of the smoke and simply began firing all of their weapons blindly into the cloud. The volume of fire was so intense the marines aborted the crossing. Even when tanks were brought up for support, the hail of B40 rockets forced the tanks to keep behind cover.[21] The marines attacked six times over the next eighteen hours, but each time the fierce enemy fusillade drove them back. There were just not enough marines in the three companies to suppress the fire coming from all the enemy positions. The Americans spent the night in defensive positions within the university.[22]

The next morning, the marines adjusted their tactics to compensate for the lessons learned the previous day. First, they placed their M60 machine guns, 3.5-inch rocket launchers and LAWs in elevated positions so these weapons had better fields of fire at the enemy positions along Ly Thuong Kiet Street.[23] Then they relocated the battalion 81-mm mortars so the tubes could provide better support for the attack.[24] Finally, the marines of 1/1 moved into position on their south flank to extend the American front and suppress enemy fire from the positions farther up the street.

Despite the expanded front and all of the well-placed support fire, the marines were once again stopped by the hail of Communist fire. One key problem was that heavy machine gun in the basement of the Le Loi Primary School. A 106-mm recoilless rifle gunner suggested he could drive his 106 mm into the street and fire a round at the machine gun.[25] Even if he was unable to destroy the machine gun position, it would force the enemy gunners to take cover. He also pointed out the back blast would stir up so much dust on the street it would act just like a smoke screen for the assaulting force, but with a couple of advantages. Since the tactic had never been used before, it would be unexpected and, unlike the smoke from grenades that took time to build up to a concentration sufficient to obscure the street, it would be generated instantaneously. The enemy soldiers would not be alerted to the impending assault.

To identify the location of the machine gun for the recoilless rifle gunner, marines threw several smoke grenades into the street simulating the start of an attack. When the machine gun began firing through the cloud, the recoilless rifle moved into the street and destroyed the position. As the street filled with the dust cloud created by the back blast, a marine platoon quickly ran across the street and stormed into one of the buildings adjacent to the treasury. Within minutes the marines killed all of the defenders and cleared the building. Since it was taller than the surrounding buildings and gave a partial view of the treasury courtyard, the Americans were in a good position to support the main attack on the treasury building with suppressive fire on the enemy flank.

Even with this new foothold on the enemy side of the street, the marines could not crack the treasury defenses. Although the marines blew a hole in the courtyard wall surrounding the treasury with a 3.5-inch rocket, as soon as they tried to move through the opening, the North Vietnamese drove them back with intense fire. Nothing the marines did seemed to rattle the defenders and the immensely strong structure seemed impervious to all their weapons. While the marines continued to hammer away at the enemy positions, the officers and sergeants racked their brains for options. Major John Salvati, executive officer of 2/5, suggested tear gas as a possible solution to the strong enemy defenses. All of the 2/5 Marines were issued protective masks prior to deploying to Hue and would be able to move through the gas cloud unaffected. However, it was going to take a lot of tear gas and the agent had to be delivered directly into the enemy positions. Even if the marines could get close enough, simply throwing a few gas grenades into the courtyard would not seriously affect the defenders. Fortunately Major Salvati recalled seeing several E8 launchers back at the MACV compound. The E8 was a disposable, single-use area-saturation weapon firing sixty-four 35-mm rockets in a series of bursts over the span of about one minute. Since they flew in an arcing trajectory, the small rockets would still clear the wall surrounding the treasury building even if the launcher was fired from behind cover. The major quickly drove back to the compound and picked up four launchers. After explaining his plan to Lieutenant Colonel Cheatham, Major Salvati hurried down to Company F and worked out the details with Captain Mike Downs.

Major Salvati carefully set up one of the launchers behind a courtyard wall with a direct line of sight to the treasury. Unfortunately, when he pulled the lanyard to fire the E8 it disintegrated in his hand because it had rotted in the humid Vietnamese climate. Since the E8 could also be fired electronically, he located a crank generator for a field phone and attached the leads to the firing terminals on the launcher. As soon as he began cranking the generator, the rockets began firing. Within seconds, the northeast face of the treasury was enveloped in a CS cloud beginning to permeate into the building through open windows and holes in the wall. Several of the 35-mm rockets even managed to pass through windows and began emitting CS directly in the building.

As soon as the rockets began raining down on the treasury building, marine gunners shot the iron courtyard gate and the front door, blasting both of them off their hinges.[26] Marines wearing protective masks began racing across Ly Thuong Kiet Street, through the gate and up to the hole that was once the front door. At the same time, marines from the building adjacent to the treasury rushed through the opening they previously blasted in the courtyard wall. Some marines went after enemy positions in the courtyard while others ran toward the front door. Racing across the courtyard, the Americans shot several North Vietnamese soldiers who stumbled out of the building seeking fresh air. Knowing the amount of gas permeating into the building might not be sufficient to prevent the defenders from shooting at them as they moved through the doorway, the marines tossed a CS grenade and an M26 fragmentation grenade through the opening before moving inside. As the gas from the grenade filled the room, the fragmentation grenade exploded and the marines dived through the doorway, blindly spraying the room with their M16s on full automatic. They moved quickly to clear the rest of the building, racing down hallways and into each room. Marines threw tear gas and fragmentation grenades through each doorway before entering and spraying the room with bullets. The cloud generated by the profuse use of tear gas grenades was so thick they had to feel their way through some of the rooms. Within minutes of firing the E8, the building was cleared and the battle was over.[27]

New to gas warfare, the marines did not anticipate the breeze from the river would carry the cloud from the treasury courtyard down the street. The marines of 1/1 were in the middle of a very pitched battle with a large North Vietnamese force in the Joan of Arc School and Church complex, another enemy stronghold on Ly Thuong Kiet Street. As wisps of the cloud drifted over the American positions they began to feel mild but unmistakable effects of exposure. When more of the gas arrived, the effects intensified and the surprised marines had to stop their attack. Unlike their brothers in 2/5, the 1/1 Marines did not have protective masks and were just as vulnerable to the gas as the Communists. As he was enjoying his success at the treasury building, Lieutenant Colonel Cheatham received a terse radio transmission from his counterpart in 1st Battalion. However, there was little he could do except offer an apology and assure Lieutenant Colonel Gravel there would be better coordination in the future.

Once the treasury building and Joan of Arc School and Church complex fell, the marines quickly captured the other buildings on the block. Realizing the critical role played by tear gas in capturing the treasury building, Colonel Hughes stressed to his battalion commanders he believed tear gas would be a major asset for them in the urban setting. He particularly emphasized using the E8 launcher since it delivered the gas from a distance and rapidly built up a large, highly concentrated cloud. By the end of the day, Major Salvati acquired a number of additional E8 launchers and distributed them to the fighting companies.[28]

For the individual marine, it was the gas grenades that rapidly became a standard piece of equipment, especially during search-and-clear operations. When a marine only tossed a fragmentation grenade into a bunker before storming in, the enemy soldiers inside were often shielded from the effects of the grenade by sandbags or debris and were still able to fight. A number of marines were injured or killed learning this lesson. When a CS grenade was used, the irritating cloud of gas usually drove the enemy out of the bunker seeking fresh air. Even when the defenders stayed in the bunker, they were unable to see clearly and posed little threat to the marines. This less-lethal technique also gave the marines the opportunity to capture enemy soldiers for interrogation. For example, after fighting all day to take the treasury building and the surrounding complex, the marines of Company F were resting near the post office in what they thought was a protected area. Suddenly, enemy soldiers in a nearby underground bunker began firing at them. The Americans missed the hidden position during the initial search-and-clear operation and the enemy was capitalizing on the mistake. The firefight continued until the marines threw two CS grenades into the bunker. Within seconds, the firing stopped and a North Vietnamese warrant officer crawled out and surrendered. Several other guerrillas ran out a back exit; most of them were killed as they ran toward nearby buildings. Sounds of coughing and gagging could still be heard in the bunker so the marines called for anyone inside to come out and surrender. Unable to convince the Communists to come out, one of the marines fired a LAW rocket through the front entrance of the bunker, setting off a series of powerful secondary explosions when it exploded. When the explosions finally stopped and the smoked died down, several marines donned their protective masks and searched the bunker. They found twenty-four dead Communists along with nine rifles, one lightweight machine gun, five B40 rocket launchers and three satchel charges. In a similar instance the following morning, marines found twelve North Vietnamese soldiers hiding in a shed near the post office. In an effort to take the soldiers prisoner, one of the marines threw a CS grenade into the hut, hoping the gas would drive the enemy out into the open. After enduring the gas for a few seconds the Communists charged out of the shed, firing about blindly until the marines killed them.[29]

Sometimes, however, carrying CS grenades was a liability. While standing near a second-floor window, Private First Class Jim Walsh was struck in the chest by a sniper round. As the horror of being shot settled in, he realized he was unable to breathe and was having trouble seeing. He became convinced the bullet had pierced a lung and he had a sucking chest wound. Luckily for him, the round had in fact glanced off of his flack vest and done little more than bruise his ribs and knock the wind out of him. When it ricocheted off his vest, however, it struck a tear-gas grenade he had attached to his web gear. He was covered in the CS mixture from the grenade and many of the effects he was feeling were due to inhaling the agent. Once his buddies realized he was not seriously hurt, they got him into fresh air and washed off as much of the CS powder as they could. Other than a sore chest and clear sinuses, he was fine.

The marines incorporated tear gas into more of their operations and increasingly turned to it in critical situations. For example, 2/5 surrounded a large building full of North Vietnamese late in the afternoon on February 5. After Companies F and G took up positions blocking the only possible escape routes,

Company H began the assault. The Communists were well dug in and putting up a terrific fight because there was no possibility of escape until after nightfall. Once it was dark, however, most of the guerrillas would be able to slip past the marines and disappear into the city. The significance of the diminishing daylight was not lost on the marines, either. Under increasing pressure to finish the job, an American tank moved up and fired five rounds from its main gun into the building, hoping to dislodge the desperate enemy soldiers. Although the volume of fire slackened for a moment, the Communists did not budge. As the sunlight continued to fade, the marines decide to try one more assault. With the tank and other marines of Company H delivering a high volume of suppressive fire, a platoon wearing protective masks quickly moved up beside the building and began throwing CS grenades in through the windows and doors. As the gas spread and began to have an effect, the platoon moved in and began clearing the building. Using a combination of gas grenades, fragmentation grenades and automatic weapons, they rapidly overran the enemy. The marines recovered the bodies of twelve North Vietnamese along with a large number of weapons and an ample supply of ammunition. Only three marines were wounded during the attack.

It did not take long for the Communists to recognize the impact of tear gas and make modifications to their defensive strategy. For example, on February 6 marines used four CS grenades to cover an attack on the main administration building of the hospital. Once again, the tear gas blinded the North Vietnamese, forcing them to abandon their positions and flee out a back door. Recalling the tactic used earlier in the battle for Hue to counter marine smoke screens, Communist snipers hiding in nearby buildings who were unaffected by the agent fired randomly into the gas cloud. Although the volume of fire was insufficient to disrupt the assault, two marines were wounded.[30]

As the battle for Hue continued, the marines learned at least some of the Communists had gas masks. During an attack on the provincial prison, marines threw CS grenades through a hole blasted into the building with a recoilless rifle. As they waited for the enemy to begin crawling out, the Americans were surprised when the still billowing grenades were thrown back through the hole instead. The marines did not find any masks among the bodies and supplies scattered about the prison, but a few days later they collected several after capturing the Provincial Capitol Building. Fortunately for the Americans, only some of the North Vietnamese officers and senior sergeants had them. If masks were issued to more of the Communist troops, the value of tear gas would have been greatly reduced, and retaking Hue would have cost a great many more American lives.

The marines got another surprise as they searched through the enemy positions in the provincial prison. They found four cases of American-made CS grenades, leading to speculation the grenades coming back out through the hole in the wall were not the ones thrown in. It also raised the possibility that the

North Vietnamese might be able to conduct future gas attacks against the marines. However, as it turned out this was the only incident where the Communists used gas, and these four cases of grenades were the only ones recovered in Hue. The relatively small supply suggests the source of the grenades was the 1st Division Armory, which the Communists captured on the first day of the battle.[31]

The next big hurdle for the marines was the Provincial Capitol Building, which was the heavily fortified command post of the 4th North Vietnamese Army Regiment. The Communist flag flying prominently on the flagstaff was a thorn in the morale of the marines right from the beginning of the battle and many of them became fixated on bringing it down. As with the other strong points the North Vietnamese established along Le Loy Street, the marines would have to begin their assault by crossing an open street in full view of a myriad enemy positions. This time, however, the Communists were armed with at least one recoilless rifle, a weapon that could seriously damage the tanks supporting the marine advance. Further, because of the layout of the adjacent buildings, there were only a limited number of locations from which the marines could make their assault. These were all easily identifiable and well-targeted by the enemy. To make matters even worse, the capitol building sat in the middle of a large courtyard open for about 150 feet in all directions. This meant the final phase of the assault would be without cover and in full view of all of the enemy positions in the building and along the street.

Hoping for a quick repeat of their success at the treasury building, Major Salvati quickly set up and fired an E8 launcher to initiate the attack. Unfortunately, none of the rockets made it into the building and the breeze from the river rapidly dispersed the cloud before it could permeate inside. Unaware the gas was not having an effect, the assault force charged across the street wearing their protective masks and took cover behind the courtyard wall. It only took a moment for them to realize the gas was not having the desired effect on the enemy. However, the marines pressed forward and, despite a withering volume of enemy fire, were able to capture an outbuilding, giving the Americans a foothold across Le Loy Street.

Under the existing weather conditions, any further use of tear gas would actually work against the marines. Since the wind would rapidly dissipate the agent cloud, it would have little effect on the defenders. The marines, however, would still have to wear their protective masks because they would be assaulting through the remnant of the cloud. The masks hampered their ability to communicate, severely limited their vision, and were uncomfortably hot and stifling. These limitations reduced their combat effectiveness and put them at a major disadvantage to the unencumbered enemy who were suffering only minimal effects. Unable to use tear gas, the marines abandoned their assault and began hammering the building and surrounding enemy positions with tanks, recoilless rifles and mortars. The battle became a stalemate as the North Vietnamese responded with automatic weapons, rockets, recoilless rifles and mortars of their own.

In mid-afternoon, a particularly heavy barrage of mortar and recoilless rifle rounds seemed to have an effect on the defenders in the capital building. Since the wind shifted and was coming from a direction tending to blow a gas cloud into the faces of the enemy, the marines decided to attempt another assault. At the signal to initiate the attack, a marine fired one of the remaining E8 launchers.

This time, the cloud filled the courtyard and even drifted back into the street, muffling and diffusing the sounds of the battle. The assaulting marines rushing into the street became confused in the swirling gas cloud and began running in the wrong direction. Fortunately, one of the marines providing cover fire stopped them before they went too far. As the slightly embarrassed platoon returned to the jump-off point, the marines set up and fired another E8 to ensure the tear-gas cloud remained at an effective concentration. This time, the platoon went in the right direction. The marines quickly blasted a hole through the courtyard wall and charged the front door. Even affected by the gas and unable to see clearly, the North Vietnamese put up a fierce fight, firing blindly toward the oncoming marines. After a vicious firefight at the entryway, the marines made it into the building. Once inside, it was the standard search-and-clear operation – gas and fragmentation grenades and automatic weapons. The fleeing Communists continued to fire, even though obviously affected by the gas and unable to see clearly.

As soon as the building was secure, the marines moved outside and cut away the Communist flag. As they hoisted the US flag over the provincial capital, wisps of lingering tear gas drifted by and induced some artificial tears that combined with the emotional ones already flowing. It was a significant victory for more than just morale. Much of the coordinated enemy resistance in the southern half of the city collapsed after the destruction of the regimental command post.[32]

The Americans continued pursuing the remaining enemy units through the southern half of the city, mopping up scattered pockets of resistance. On February 9, the marines received a tip about the location of the North Vietnamese 804th Battalion Command Post. Command-and-control elements were always a principal target, so the Americans called in a massive artillery and mortar barrage on the location late that afternoon. At dawn the next morning, Company A was sent out to search the location, determine if it had indeed been the command post and evaluate the effectiveness of the artillery strike. When they arrived, the marines observed several enemy soldiers moving around in the target area. Since the enemy knew it was common practice to send out a reconnaissance-and-evaluation team after key artillery or bombing missions, the few soldiers the marines saw might be part of an ambush team. Unable to complete the mission without entering the blasted building, and not willing to take any chances, the marines fired an E8 launcher into the structure and saturated the area with CS before attacking. Caught by surprise and overcome by the tear gas, the North Vietnamese were easily overpowered by the marines. After establishing a security perimeter, the masked marines quickly picked through the rubble and confirmed it was the location of the command post. Although they only found a few bodies in the rubble, there were indications of numerous other casualties.[33]

On February 10, the marines received another boost to their firepower. Two 4.2-inch M30 mortars, from 1st Battalion, 11th Marines arrived and set up positions near the LCU boat ramp on the Perfume River.[34] The M30 was the only mortar in the US arsenal capable of firing tear gas as well as high-explosive and illumination rounds. The mortars went to work within hours of setting up their positions, firing a CS mission in support of a marine unit caught in an ambush. The patrol was moving through Hue Stadium toward a supposedly abandoned South Vietnamese Army compound when it came under heavy fire from enemy soldiers occupying positions in the compound's walls. The ambush started when a B40 rocket streaked out of a hole in the wall and struck the lead tank, disabling it and killing the driver. Then machine guns and automatic rifles raked the marines as they scrambled for cover. Under the hail of bullets and rockets, the marines were unable to move across the open terrain and close on the enemy positions. The patrol leader called in the CS mission for the M30s and, within minutes, rounds began impacting in and around the old army compound. As the gas took effect, the volume of fire dropped off and the marines moved in and overran the enemy positions.[35]

By the end of the day on February 10, the fighting on the south side of the river was essentially over. The marines continued to search the city and clear away isolated pockets of resistance they encountered. They also moved into the outskirts of the city in search of other enemy strongholds. Things in the Citadel, however, were not going nearly as well. After ten days of fighting, the South Vietnamese 1st Division was still bottled up inside its own compound while the Communists controlled everything else inside the protective wall surrounding the city. The North Vietnamese took full advantage of this situation and established a line of logistics from outside the city to bring in not only fresh supplies each night, but also replacements who were well-trained, well-fed and well-equipped.

The North Vietnamese also used the time to prepare hundreds of well-fortified and camouflaged bunkers and fighting positions throughout the city. The layout of the buildings and the streets in the Citadel was even better suited to the style of cat-and-mouse tactics the Communists were employing than the southern section of the city was. Within the thick protective walls of the fortress were rows of single-story, thick-walled, masonry houses jammed close together, many with courtyards and their requisite walls. There were large, low-hanging trees in a number of the courtyards as well as thick hedgerows between many of the homes. Many of the streets were narrow and barely wide enough for a tank or an Ontos to drive down, a limitation compounded by the large trees lining some of the streets. With all of these obstructions, it was difficult to see very far in any direction without standing exposed in the middle of a street.[36]

The North Vietnamese constructed their fighting positions to take full advantage of this environment. Some were hidden in the thick-walled buildings, while others were dug into the hedgerows and dense bushy areas between the houses. All of them were thoroughly camouflaged. Each position had overlapping fields of fire with its neighbors and could cover assaults on other positions farther down the street. Even the massive wall surrounding the entire city was riddled with spider holes and fighting positions.[37]

Unable to coordinate a successful counterattack from outside the city, and facing the degenerating morale of the 1st Division soldiers who felt trapped in their own compound, the South Vietnamese requested US assistance in driving the Communists out of the Citadel. On February 11, General Foster LaHue, commander of Task Force X-Ray and in charge of US operations in and around Hue, ordered the 1st Battalion, 5th Marines (abbreviated 1/5) to help the 1st Division clear the Citadel.[38] Major Robert Thompson, who was just recently appointed battalion commander, moved his men into the Citadel on February 12.

The 1/5 Marines were fresh to the Battle of Hue and, just like the other marines who arrived two weeks earlier, all of their previous combat experience involved operations in the jungle. The limited MOUT training they received also occurred during basic training. When the marines learned they would be attacking dug-in enemy positions in an urban environment, they began reviewing everything they could pool together from their collective memories.[39]

On the morning of February 13, the marines set out to relieve a South Vietnamese airborne battalion in the northeast corner of the Citadel. According to information from the 1st Division, the South Vietnamese established positions along the base of the city wall near a prominent tower built centuries before as part of the city's defenses. Just as the Americans approached the "friendly" positions, the enemy began hammering the marines with automatic weapons, B40 rockets and mortars. The North Vietnamese were firing from all of the buildings surrounding the marines and also down on them from the tower on the wall. Due to a coordination error, the South Vietnamese withdrew from the area without waiting for replacements and the Communists had moved in to fill the void. It was ten minutes before the marines could break contact and withdraw. In that time, the Americans suffered thirty-five casualties including most of the lieutenants and a captain.

Since the restrictive rules of engagement were lifted and the marines could once more call for artillery and close air support, the next morning Major Thompson requested artillery units to walk a barrage in front of his troops to cover their advance. He also requested a barrage of CS shells to create a gas blanket to suppress snipers and force the enemy to abandon their fortified positions in the buildings leading up to the objective.[40] In addition to support from naval 5-inch and 8-inch guns, 8-inch and 155-mm howitzers, jets from Da Nang were also on hand to deliver Zuni rockets, 250- and 500-pound bombs, napalm canisters and CS cluster munitions.[41] One of the critical targets for all of this firepower was the tower on the wall; the heavily fortified enemy positions inside the structure gave the Communists a commanding view of the battle and unobstructed fields of fire down onto the marines. By the end of the intense battle, all the faces of the tower were scorched from burning napalm, a full ten feet of its top was missing due to the heavy pounding from bombs and artillery, and so much CS lingered in the air people over a mile away in the southern half of the city were affected. However, despite all the firepower and determined assaults by the marines, the North Vietnamese in the tower not only refused to withdraw but also suffered minimal casualties. The marines were force to call off their attack until the following day.[42]

During these first two days in the Citadel, the 1/5 was operating at reduced strength because Company D was across the Perfume River assisting units there with mop-up operations against scattered pockets of resistance. Realizing military intelligence had vastly underestimated both the size and tenacity of the Communist forces in the Citadel and he would need his full battalion to proceed with the operation, Major Thompson put in a request to have them transferred back to his command.

Early in the afternoon of February 14, Captain Myron Harrington began moving the two platoons making up Company D across the river and into the Citadel.[43] Since all the bridges spanning the river were destroyed by either one side or the other, the company moved down to the navy boat ramp looking to hitch a ride across on one of the LCUs ferrying supplies into the northern side of the city. When the marines arrived, the two LCUs at the ramp were already loaded with supplies and there was not even enough room for all of the men in one of the platoons. Intent on getting across the river as rapidly as possible, Captain Harrington decided to load as many of his men as he could onto the boats and have the rest come across on the next trip. Captain Harrington, his command group and a single squad squeezed onto the LCUs and tried to make themselves comfortable during the passage. When the LCUs reached the midpoint of the river, enemy soldiers on the north shore and on the Citadel wall fired on the boats. The marines took cover behind whatever was on the deck and returned fire. Despite a few tense moments during the passage, no one was hurt.

Unruffled by the snipers, the LCUs returned to the boat ramp. The remainder of the company piled onto one of them and it started back across the river. Once again, the enemy began firing at the boat when it came into range. This time, however, the M30 gunners, who were at the boat ramp and witnessed the first passage, decided to take a hand. The gunners began firing CS and high-explosive rounds at the enemy positions on the Citadel wall. Unfortunately, a sudden wind shift pushed some of the CS cloud back down onto the river and when the LCU reached the midway point it ran into the cloud. Unprepared for the irritating effects of the gas, the crew immediately turned the boat around and moved back to the south side of the river. As it arrived at the ramp, the marines piled out choking and crying, blinded by the gas. Despite pleading and even threats, the LCU commanders refused to run the gauntlet again. Eventually, a Swift boat commander agreed to tow the marines across the river in three commandeered junks.[44] Because the north side of the river was too shallow near the bank for the Swift boat, the junks were cut free a short distance off-shore and the marines rowed them the rest of the way. Once the command staff was reunited with the rest of the company, the marines moved into the Citadel to join up with the rest of 1st Battalion.[45]

Over the next week, progress through the Citadel was measured in inches. Engagements were often at very close quarters and many times involved hand-to-hand combat. Slowly and cautiously, the Americans moved into and around each house. The marines were constantly concerned about being attacked from the rear, so they moved slowly and made sure they did not miss hidden enemy positions. Whenever they ran into a particularly difficult situation, they called on the M48 tanks and Ontos anti-tank vehicles for fire support. Unfortunately the drivers of both types of vehicles found it difficult to maneuver in the narrow streets and tight alleys, a handicap also making it easy for the enemy to attack them with B40 rockets.

The Citadel was a defender's paradise. In addition to the confusing maze of close-packed houses, alleys and streets, the thick walls of the buildings often withstood the explosions of artillery, rockets and bombs. Even shells from the 90-mm main gun of the M48 tanks fired at relatively short range often bounced off the thick building walls and ricocheted back toward the marines. When the tankers ultimately switched to special concrete-piercing shells, it still took at least two and sometimes up to four rounds to breach a wall.[46]

Just like the marines on the south side, the marines in the Citadel used tear gas liberally when attacking difficult enemy positions, and also during the search-and-clear phase of an assault. In addition to grenades and E8 launchers, the marines in the Citadel had access to CS cluster munitions delivered by the close support jets and, more importantly, the two M30 mortars dug in near the LCU boat ramp. The mortars quickly became the preferred weapon for delivering CS; the high angle of the trajectory made it possible to reach most targets in the city and the timed fuze allowed a round to penetrate the tiled roofs found on many of the buildings before detonating. This latter characteristic was key because it meant all of the agent was released inside the target; the relatively large payload of the rounds ensured the building was rapidly saturated with gas. To the mortar crews, it seemed the tubes were constantly firing CS missions and the air was always tainted with residual gas from their operations. The gunners became accustomed to the constant eye irritation and did not put on a protective mask unless a dense cloud blew back across the river.[47]

The marines continued to move block-by-block through the city. The Communists would hold out as long as possible, then fall back to the next line of defensive positions. On February 19, Major Thompson realized his marines were worn down by the relentless, grinding pressure of this type of combat and needed something to boost their morale and re-energize them. He decided to ask for volunteers for a nighttime operation. The goal of the mission was to infiltrate through enemy lines and capture a large two-story building that was providing the enemy with an unobstructed view and clear fields of fire across the entire marine front. Once they had this key vantage point, the marines would be able to turn the tables, using it to direct artillery and mortar fire against all the enemy positions in the area. A more subtle goal was to give the men that morale boost. Many of the young marines in Major Thompson's command believed the North Vietnamese they were fighting had almost superhuman abilities when it came to hiding and infiltrating through the American lines. Major Thompson hoped this operation would prove marines were just as stealthy as the guerrillas and give his men back their edge.

Marines from 2nd Platoon, Company A volunteered for the mission. They left the battalion perimeter at 3.00 a.m. on February 21. They carefully picked their way through the debris-strewn streets and entered the building at 3.30. After a quick search they realized it was empty; the North Vietnamese apparently withdrew for the night to sleep elsewhere.[48] The marines quickly moved in and took up possession of the building. After a moment's hesitation, two groups of marines moved off to either side and took control of the two adjacent buildings as well. The Americans captured not one, but three buildings behind enemy lines without firing a shot. When they relayed the news back to the battalion, the Major got the jump in morale he was hoping for.

From the second floor, 2nd Platoon had a perfect view of the surrounding area, including the Thuong Tu gate, a major resupply line used by the Communists. Just before dawn, the marines saw two North Vietnamese units moving forward to set up for another day of fighting. The guerrillas were too close to buildings where 2nd Platoon was hiding to use high-explosive rounds so the marines called in a CS fire mission to the M30 mortars. As the rounds landed and the gas cloud engulfed the surprised North Vietnamese, 2nd Platoon snipers began shooting the blinded enemy soldiers. In the confusion of the gas barrage, the Communists never realized the bullets were coming from within their own lines. It became a "turkey shoot" for the expert marksmen. After a few moments, the surviving enemy recovered their wits and ran back the way they came. The marines directed the mortars to switch to high-explosive rounds and continue to shell the retreating guerrillas. Despite the success of the night operation and the advantage gained from the forward observation post, the North Vietnamese defended the rest of the block tenaciously and the marines made little progress during the rest of the day.[49]

During the battle in the Citadel, supply could not always keep up with demand, and CS munitions were rationed. Some units were not even aware of the extent that gas was being used in other sections of the city. One such example was Company C, operating on the extreme right flank of 1/5. On February 23, however, that changed and these marines also joined the chemical war. That afternoon, 3rd Platoon received its first replacements since arriving in Hue. Having just completed the Chemical Warfare School in Da Nang, the new marines brought three E8 launchers with them. Unfamiliar with the boxy weapon and unaware of its application in earlier operations, the platoon leader had them describe its capabilities and explain how it operated. Since tear gas was used previously in 3rd Platoon's area, the platoon leader thought the enemy would be susceptible to a gas attack. He ordered the marines to set up one of the E8s and fire it into the enemy positions across the street. Unfortunately, the new marines never actually fired one before and forgot to secure the launcher so the recoil did not shift the point of aim. The recoil from the first volley of rockets tipped the launcher backward so it was pointing straight up. The remaining three volleys went several hundred feet into the air then rained back down on the marines, engulfing them in a bellowing cloud of CS. Despite the error, the lieutenant was impressed with the weapon's capabilities. After the breeze cleared the air, the marines set up the remaining two launchers, remembering to sandbag them in place. Then, just as night fell, they fired both E8s, saturating the block in front of the platoon's positions with gas.

The next morning, the marines crossed the street and began moving cautiously through the enemy positions. Within a few minutes, the marines realized the enemy was gone. Eventually the Americans discovered the North Vietnamese withdrew not only from their immediate front but also for the next three blocks as well. As the marines cleared each building, they still experienced eye irritation caused by residual CS lingering throughout the area. Evidently the daytime breeze died down after sunset and the gas cloud remained in the area throughout the night. The persistent effects caused by the high concentration of agent forced the unprotected North Vietnamese to withdraw. The marines took three entire blocks in less than three hours without a single casualty. By the end of the day, 1/5 cleared the remaining section along the southeast wall of the Citadel.[50]

Once the South Vietnamese captured the Imperial Palace on February 24, the battle for the Citadel was essentially over. On February 26, the marines left the Citadel to search for Communist forces trying to withdraw toward the coast. On March 2, Operation Hue City officially ended and the marines returned to their normal duty stations. Once again, they were back in the jungles and away from the intensity and carnage of urban fighting.[51]

Tear gas was also used in other urban battles during the Tet Offensive, although not as extensively as in Hue. On January 30, at the same time that Communist forces were moving into Hue, the Viet Cong began an attack on

Saigon by blasting a hole in the concrete wall surrounding the American Embassy. The Embassy compound was considered to be the most secure facility in South Vietnam and the breach sent a shockwave through the responding units. An intense battle raged over the next six hours. As it was drawing to a close, one of the Communists sought refuge in the residence of George Jacobson, a senior American diplomat and retired US Army Colonel. Both Jacobson and his aide, Robert Josephson, were in the house at the time. The military police quickly surrounded the house but the Viet Cong soldier began firing through the windows and forced them to remain under cover. Realizing tear gas would be the most effective way to neutralize the intruder while minimizing the risks to the two diplomats, one of the Americans ran to the nearby Vietnamese police station and obtained some of their gas grenades. When he returned, the police threw one of the grenades into the house through the back door, hoping to drive the enemy soldier out of the house. As the gas filled the house, Jacobson leaned out of a second story window and caught the attention of one of the policemen. He and his aide were trapped upstairs because of both the enemy soldier on the ground floor and the rapidly intensifying tear-gas cloud. Since the Americans could not get out of the house, the police threw Jacobson a 0.45-caliber pistol and two protective masks. As Jacobson quickly pulled on the mask, the Viet Cong soldier emerged from the stairwell and stumbled into the upstairs hallway outside of his room. Affected by the tear gas and unable to see clearly, the Viet Cong fired three shots in Jacobson's direction but missed. Jacobson calmly fired the pistol and mortally wounded the enemy soldier.[52]

The situation in Saigon was not nearly as dire for the Allies as it was in Hue. The US began the battle not only with more soldiers in the city, but also with rapid access to reserve forces including mechanized infantry and armor. Further, the stringent rules of engagement hampering initial operations in Hue did not apply to Saigon and the Americans could call in both artillery and close air support to deal with enemy strongholds. Even with these advantages, tear gas played a critical role during some difficult situations. For example, on February 3 South Vietnamese Rangers were in a fierce firefight with a large Viet Cong force occupying a factory complex in the Cholon suburb of Saigon. The rangers attacked several times but were repulsed by the heavy volume of fire delivered by the determined guerrillas. Unable to crack the enemy defenses, the soldiers called in helicopters to drop E158 clusters munitions on the complex and saturate the buildings with CS. As the cloud filled the factory and the enemy fire dwindled, the rangers donned their protective masks and rushed the Viet Cong positions. This time the soldiers successfully overran their heavily armed opponents.[53]

Another critical role played by tear gas was as a means of suppressing Communist rocket and mortar fire in and around Saigon. In order to limit Allied counter-battery fire, the Communists placed their gun and rocket positions as close as possible to areas congested with non-combatants. Unable to use conventional high-explosive rounds because of the potential for civilian casualties, Allied 105-mm batteries fired CS rounds into the enemy gun positions. The tear gas prevented the enemy gunners from effectively operating their weapons and limited their impact on the battle.[54]

During the Tet Offensive, both field commanders and line soldiers came to realize there were significant advantages gained by using tear gas. The marines ultimately expended 4,700 CS grenades and 350 E8 launchers during the twenty-two days of battle within the city of Hue.[55] In many instances, objectives would have been much harder to overrun without tear gas and Allied forces would have incurred significantly greater casualties. Although United States soldiers in Vietnam initially looked on tear gas with little more than guarded skepticism, by the end of the Tet Offensive they came to view it as a valuable addition to their arsenal of weapons, and the use of riot-control agents was incorporated into almost every type of military operation.[56] Unfortunately, those lessons were not fully incorporated into doctrine and made available to all units throughout the country. With the rapid turnover in US personnel, many of them were forgotten or lost.

Only a few months after the end of the Tet Offensive, the Communists launched a second wave of attacks targeting numerous towns, cities and military installations across South Vietnam. Known officially as the May Offensive, it took place just days before the beginning of the Paris Peace talks and was primarily designed to show the world the Communists still held the initiative in the war. As CBS reporter George Severson noted:

> One difference between this fighting and the Tet Offensive seems to be that the enemy this time has no illusion about capturing [the cities]. The object of the exercise … seems to be to cause as much damage and suffering as possible."[57]

Enemy soldiers once again infiltrated various sections of Saigon and established heavily fortified defensive positions. Relying heavily on artillery and air strikes during the hard fighting that followed, US forces destroyed many of the neighborhoods they liberated from the Communists. The US Embassy initiated an official investigation of the 9th Infantry Division after receiving numerous complaints from residents about the excessive use of force and high number of civilian casualties. One of the key questions the residents asked was why the US did not use tear gas to flush out the enemy, especially if the building also contained civilians. Although the Division was ultimately exonerated, the widespread collateral damage did lead to some changes. After assuming command from General Westmoreland, General Creighton Abrams banned the use of supporting arms in Saigon without his personal approval. Assessing their Pyrrhic victory, he told his staff:

I have estimated that we can successfully defend [Saigon] seven more times, and then we're going to be faced with the embarrassment that there's no city left. And I don't know how the hell we're going to explain [our success if there is] no goddamn city!"[58]

Even on the few occasions when tear gas was employed, it did not seem as effective as it was earlier in the year. For instances, in June, at the end of the May Offensive, South Vietnamese Special Forces surrounded the last major enemy stronghold in the Saigon area. After two days of heated battle, the soldiers decided to try a tank assault under cover of tear gas. As the gas spread over the enemy position, the tanks moved forward. Out of options and with nowhere left to run, the Communists held their positions and filled the air with B40 anti-tank rockets. The hail of rockets stopped the assault and drove the tanks back behind cover. The soldiers eventually conducted a night assault, surprising the defenders and bringing the stand-off to a close.[59]

After the May Offensive was over, the US military convened a special panel to study the battle in and around Saigon. The members were charged with developing a list of suggestions to improve defenses against future Communist urban operations. One of the key recommendations was to equip the South Vietnamese Air Force with weapon systems allowing the "maximum use of CS riot control agents." Fearing the Communists might quickly launch a third wave of attacks, the panel also urged MACV to restrict the use of key CS munitions to urban operations until the logistics system could replenish the in-theater reserves to appropriate levels. Both of these recommendations were approved and implemented.[60]

The urban combat of the Tet and May Offensives, unprecedented in the war, forced soldiers to find innovative answers to unique and unfamiliar problems. They quickly found out their usual techniques of fire and maneuver did not work in an urban environment because they could not suppress the myriad multilevel enemy positions. No individual weapon or tactic proved to be the single key to urban combat. Tear gas, tanks, artillery and air support all filled critical niches providing options for the myriad situations the soldiers faced. Of all of these weapons, though, it was the liberal employment of CS in Hue that was credited with saving the lives of many marines, limiting non-combatant casualties and preventing excessive damage to the historic and cultural features of the city, as well as its critical infrastructure.[61]

8
COMMUNIST CHEMICAL OPERATIONS

The Communists also had an active chemical warfare program during the war, although not nearly as developed as the Allies'. Along with a relatively uninspired propaganda program, their initial focus was on defensive preparation to reduce exposure to the "toxic" herbicides used during deforestation operations. Most of the Viet Cong, and many in the North Vietnamese Army, were from rural backgrounds and relatively naive; they were easily frightened by the magic of modern industry. In one instance, shortly after the start of the program, 112 Viet Cong surrendered simply because they heard defoliants would be sprayed in their area. Capitalizing on these fears, the Communists were able to inspire resentment against the South Vietnamese government and its American advisors. They also conducted rudimentary training on the properties and effects of the other common chemical warfare agents stockpiled in the arsenals of both the United States and the Soviet Union. Although the Communist leadership anticipated there might be limited tangible benefit from these programs, the real dividends once again lay in their leverage as a propaganda and recruiting tool. Their focus changed when the United States began supplying South Vietnam with combat munitions filled with riot-control agents.[1]

As with all other aspects of the war, there was a significant difference in the training, equipment and capabilities of the soldiers in the North Vietnamese Army and the Viet Cong guerrillas. Modeled after the Soviet Army, the North Vietnamese had both chemical reconnaissance teams trained to identify and delineate areas of contamination, and decontamination units equipped with large sprayer systems including the ARS-12 tanker truck, ADM-48 decontamination truck, and the ADA motorized shower and decontamination truck. Each apparatus could be filled with either water or a neutralizing solution and used to wash groups of severely contaminated people or clean large areas covered with a persistent agent. Soldiers in these detachments received in-depth training on chemical warfare; in some cases they were sent to either Communist China or the Soviet Union to attend one of their military's chemical warfare programs.

As part of their training, they learned how to identify chemical agents using colorimetric field identification kits. These kits, supplied by both the Soviet Union and Communist China, contained small glass tubes filled with various chemicals designed to identify a specific warfare agent. The operator would break off the ends of the tube, insert one end into a hand pump and draw either contaminated air or a small amount of a suspicious liquid into the tube. If the suspected warfare agent was present, then the contents of the tube turned a specific color. The kits also contained strips of paper impregnated with reagents that, much like the litmus paper used in a chemistry laboratory, changed color when exposed to a particular class of chemical agent. Using the two types of detectors, the operator could relatively quickly identify or at least classify the type of chemical used in an attack. Larger chemical units also maintained a field chemical laboratory stocked with several items that allowed a trained operator to conduct some basic analytical assays. While these systems could detect and identify all of the major classes of toxic agents, neither the colorimetric kits nor the field laboratory had the capability to identify any of the herbicides used by the Allies or the tear agent CS.

Soldiers in chemical units in the North Vietnamese Army were issued protective ensembles so they could safely perform their duties in a contaminated environment. These ensembles, also manufactured by both the Soviets and Chinese, consisted of a mask and rubberized impermeable suits, gloves and boots. A common mask typically used by a lower-ranking soldier was based on the Soviet ShM-1. Since it covered the entire head, including the ears, and did not incorporate a voice emitter, it was almost impossible for the wearer to communicate with his fellow soldiers. As this was an unacceptable limitation for officers, senior sergeants and radio operators, they were issued a mask like the Soviet K style, which incorporated a voice emitter that allowed them to communicate without removing their protective masks. There were two types of protective suits worn over the individual's combat uniform. One version was a one-piece coverall while the other had separate pants and overcoat. Each also came with a protective cape worn over the other garments like a poncho. Both of these ensembles were extremely uncomfortable to wear and individuals rapidly overheated in even moderate temperatures. Also, despite their relatively simple designs, these suits were not easy to don. Even with training, it took about fifteen minutes for soldiers to properly put on all of their protective equipment.

Unlike their colleagues in the chemical units, typical North Vietnamese soldiers received only a limited amount of formal training on surviving in a chemically contaminated environment. These classes were often conducted by a member of one of the chemical reconnaissance teams or an officer who had received additional chemical training. Their protective masks, if they were issued one, were not necessarily equivalent either. In some cases, they received a respirator that only fit over the nose and mouth, with a separate set of goggles for eye protection.[2]

There is ample evidence to indicate that these masks were effective against all of the tear agents used during the war. On a variety of occasions, American pilots flying over areas that had been heavily contaminated with persistent CS powder reported that they saw footprints and vehicle tracks in the residual agent. They noted that, from the pattern of the tracks, it was obvious the North Vietnamese had not made any attempt to avoid the thick contamination and did not appear to have suffered for their exposure.[3]

A more dramatic demonstration occurred on August 21, 1967, when soldiers from the 1st Cavalry Division found a large group of North Vietnamese infiltrators in a cave about eighteen miles south of Bong Son. For three days, they tried to talk the Communists into surrendering, occasionally punctuating their efforts with tear-gas grenades. The stand-off continued until the soldiers began throwing a combination of tear gas and fragmentation grenades into the cave. At that point, fifteen of the enemy soldiers, still wearing their gas masks, moved out into the open and surrendered. At least nine others were killed by the grenades.[4]

In South Vietnam, the quality of chemical training, if it was available at all, varied greatly among the various Viet Cong units, and generally reflected their provincial background. It tended to focus on practical but simplistic and usually ineffective methods of chemical defense. For example, guerrillas were often told that regular eye glasses and a wet towel over their nose and mouth would protect them from a cloud of tear gas. In situations where they had to cross a heavily contaminated area, they were taught to wear raincoats or just soak their clothes with water or vegetable oil to keep the agent off their skin. Unfortunately the damp clothing would have only exacerbated the irritation caused by the agent and might even increase the risk of localized chemical burns. To remove the residual contamination from their clothing, guerrillas were advised to boil it for a couple of hours in a solution made with ashes from a fire and water. To treat exposed individuals, they were given recipes for homemade antidotes that were supposed to alleviate the symptoms. One such concoction consisted of a mixture of two parts rubbing alcohol, two parts ether and one part chloroform. Casualties inhaled the vapors until they felt better. While these last two solvents were used as anesthetics and possibly dulled some of the symptoms, effects from exposure to CS rapidly dissipated once the individual got out of the agent cloud, so an antidote was not necessary. However, having an antidote, even one that was a placebo, was a major boost to morale.

Other ill-advised guidelines included using brooms to sweep the agent out of a base camp after an attack, which would re-aerosolize the powder; and burning contaminated vegetation, which would volatilize much of the residual agent and suspend it in the smoke. Both of these response options would merely exacerbate the problem and create a significant respiratory hazard for the guerrillas involved in the clean-up. However, not all of their training was as misguided as the previous suggestions. Somewhat more practical advice included using water to wash away the agent or using lime to destroy it.[5]

Mimicking their North Vietnamese counterparts, some Viet Cong units established special chemical teams to coordinate local defenses for a chemical attack. These units were usually under the command of a chemical officer who received specialized training from regional North Vietnamese cadre. Members were responsible for preparing a village for a potential chemical attack and organizing decontamination operations after it occurred. Their post-attack responsibilities also included testing food and water supplies to ensure there was no residual contamination. This was accomplished by giving a sample to a dog or other animal and watching for a reaction.[6]

Whenever possible, these units were given rudimentary training on the entire spectrum of chemical agents available in either the Soviet or American arsenals, as well as the hazards associated with various agricultural and industrial chemicals. Teams were taught not only to recognize symptoms caused by the various agents but also to identify Allied chemical weapons by the munition's shape and markings as well as the means of dispersal; that is whether it burned, exploded or simply broke open on impact. If members could not identify the agent, they were trained in how to collect a sample of the material and safely package it for delivery to a North Vietnamese chemical reconnaissance unit for analysis.[7]

The Viet Cong did not have the capabilities to manufacture modern protective masks and only received a limited supply from the North Vietnamese. Whenever possible, guerrillas also recovered masks from Allied casualties or had collaborators steal them from American or South Vietnamese bases. These high-quality masks were usually reserved for Viet Cong officers and higher-ranking non-commissioned officers. The typical guerrilla improvised a mask from readily available local items unless they were participating in some special operation and higher command determined that the added protection was critical for the success of the mission. The initial version of these improvised masks was referred to as a "mouth bandage" and was similar to the first masks used during World War I. It was a small pad made from layers of gauze and cotton soaked with an aqueous solution of 5 percent sodium carbonate just prior to use. The guerrilla either held it over his nose and mouth or used a strip of cloth to secure it to his face. Motorcycle goggles or simple glasses were used to protect the eyes.

In addition to the obvious problem of having to wet it just prior to a chemical attack, the little protection offered by the mask was gone after the solution dried. A more advanced version of this mask omitted the carbonate solution and instead utilized a small bag of charcoal sewn between the layers of gauze. These masks were also fitted with rubber bands to make sure they remained securely attached to the wearer's face.

As demonstrated in the summer of 1966 during Operation El Paso, however, this advanced version of the mouth bandage provided absolutely no protection either. On July 9, the 272nd Viet Cong Regiment attempted to ambush elements of the 1st Infantry Division. The Americans bombed the enemy positions with several improvised CS munitions made from fifty-five-gallon shipping drums. Although the guerrillas were prepared and quickly put on their gauze masks, they were immediately incapacitated by the agent. The better-equipped Americans, however, were not hindered during their counterattack.[8]

Later, the Viet Cong fabricated masks covering the entire head, protecting the eyes as well. One version was made of nylon from a recovered parachute. Eyeholes were cut into the fabric and pieces of clear plastic sewn over the holes. Another hole was cut where the mask would cover the nose and mouth, and a filter was sewn over that opening. Another version was made from a clear plastic bag or shower cap. With these transparent starting materials, the insurgents only had to cut a single hole for the filter element. In either version, a rubber band was used to seal the mask around the neck. All of the needle holes made while sewing the mask were filled with glue so that the wearer could only draw air into the mask through the filter element.

The filter element consisted of an outer layer of lightweight mesh, such as mosquito netting, followed by a layer of absorbent cotton. A small quantity of specially prepared charcoal was spread over the cotton followed by a second layer of absorbent cotton and another layer of the mesh. The charcoal was prepared by filling a pot with small pieces of rice husks, coconut shells or cotton waste; sealing it; and then heating it for eight hours or more in a fire. After cooling, the carbonized bits were removed from the jar and ground into a powder. Sometimes the crude charcoal was also treated with industrial chemicals, like nitric acid, in an effort to further enhance its ability to absorb chemicals. The finished mask, as well as any charcoal that was not immediately used to prepare a filter, was stored in plastic bags to protect it from humidity. The Viet Cong claimed that these filters were effective for up to ten minutes against all classes of chemical agents.

Both versions of this mask distorted the wearer's vision, made it difficult to breathe and were just generally uncomfortable to wear. Needless to say, wearing one for the first time was a novel experience for many of the insurgents, especially the rural ones. Whenever possible, units made new recruits wear masks during training to ensure these guerrillas would not panic while wearing one in combat.[9]

In April 1967, several soldiers from the 1st Infantry Division decided to try out a few of the improvised masks taken from prisoners. After donning the masks, they walked into the edge of a gas cloud about 100 feet downwind from an M7 gas grenade. The men quickly experienced severe eye and respiratory irritation and ran out of the cloud so they could flush out their eyes with water. Based on this experience, they decided that the masks were only slightly better than wearing nothing at all. A more scientific study undertaken at Edgewood Arsenal found that individuals were incapacitated within ten seconds after being exposed to the typical field concentrations generated by an M7 grenade, and remained unable to perform any significant activity for almost three minutes after exiting the agent cloud. At lower concentrations, it took up to three minutes to incapacitate test subjects, although they started to suffer considerable irritation almost immediately after a test began.[10]

For individual decontamination, the Viet Cong initially tried using common folk remedies for skin irritation and wiped themselves with mashed garlic bulbs or boiled onions in an effort to neutralize the agent on their skin. When these proved ineffective, the North Vietnamese provided guidance on how to put together decontamination kits from common household and agricultural items. These kits typically consisted of small packets, usually ten grams or less, of such things as powdered lime, chlorinated lime, vegetable oil, cotton, soap powder and baking soda. They even added copper sulfate and potassium permanganate if these industrial chemicals were available. Some of these items were included to neutralize the effects of a specific toxic chemical agent: powdered lime for nerve agents, chlorinated lime for both nerve and blister agents and copper sulfate to extinguish burning white phosphorus. Unfortunately, other than the powdered soap, none of the contents of these kits were good as a decontaminant for riot-control agents. Some, in fact, aggravated the irritation caused by exposure to the agents. However, since Communist propaganda maintained the US was actually employing toxic agents, these kits helped boost the morale of the individuals carrying them. The other readily available and highly recommended decontaminating agent carried by every soldier was urine. While not as aesthetically pleasing as the assembled ingredients of the decontamination kits, it probably worked better than just about everything in one of the kits except for the powdered soap and water.[11]

For collective protection at one of their base camps, North Vietnam recommended that Viet Cong units build chemical-proof bunkers and eliminate the need for individuals to don their gas masks. The key feature in the design was a "filtering pit" made of alternating eight-inch-thick layers of sand, charcoal and dry lime. When an attack occurred, guerrillas entered their assigned shelter, sealed the entrance and used a bellows system to draw air through the filter into the shelter. Although many of the Communist tunnel and bunker complexes incorporated some fairly elaborate ventilation systems, there is no record that any of these filtering pits were ever found.[12]

The first reported offensive use of chemical agents by the Viet Cong was in the fall of 1965 when a unit of South Vietnamese militiamen were sprayed with a "nausea-inducing" gas. Neither the chemical agent nor the means of delivery were fully disclosed and the attack was never verified by the United States. The

North Vietnamese official press agency immediately denounced the charge as, "a sheer fabrication and a deceitful propaganda stunt," and proclaimed that since the Viet Cong were winning the war, the guerrillas had no reason to resort to chemical warfare. If it was indeed an American propaganda ploy, then it was somewhat successful since a number of reporters in the United States used the incident as a counterpoint to the controversy surrounding Operation Stomp and as justification for American soldiers to continue using riot-control agents in combat.

The first attack on American troops occurred on November 10, 1966 during Operation Attleboro. A small patrol from the 1st Infantry Division established an ambush site along a key trail in a swamp about five miles northwest of Suoi Dau in the Tay Ninh Province. When members of the local Viet Cong contingent discovered the intended ambush, they attacked the soldiers with tear-gas grenades. The grenades were essentially glass bottles fitted with wooden handles to facilitate throwing, and filled with a liquid material that caused intense eye and nose irritation. The bottles broke when they landed around the soldiers and released the volatile liquid. Caught by surprise, the soldiers fumbled about for a few moments before they were able to don their protective masks. The lingering residual effects from exposure to the agent prevented them from firing on the guerrillas running back into the jungle. Although no one was seriously injured, the ambush site was compromised and had to be abandoned.

The Americans had been lucky. The previous day, another patrol scouring the jungle nearby uncovered an enemy arsenal that included a cache of approximately 1,300 Chinese-manufactured tear-gas grenades. In contrast to the crude improvised ones used in the attack, these grenades contained an explosive charge capable of generating an agent cloud about 200 feet in diameter. And unlike American riot-control munitions, the metal body of these grenades would have produced a large number of sizable fragments in the explosion, likely killing everyone close by.

Within days, the attack and the recovered Chinese grenades became a topic of discussion at the 21st Session of the United Nations General Assembly. It began when the Hungarian delegation tabled a proposal to have the use of any chemical or biological weapon denounced as an international crime. Although they worded their proposal broadly, it was clear they were targeting the United States for using riot-control agents and herbicides in Vietnam. Obviously the United States representative strongly opposed the resolution, describing it as a Communist propaganda tool. After reminding the Assembly that the 1925 Geneva Protocol did not clearly define tear gas as a chemical weapon, and that such agents were used by police around the world, he went on to describe the attack on the patrol and the discovery of the cache of Chinese gas grenades, using this as proof that the Communists would also be guilty of an international crime under the Hungarian resolution. Following several rounds of charges and accusations back and forth across the aisle, the United States eventually convinced the Assembly to change the wording in the resolution into what was essentially a reaffirmation of the Geneva Protocol.[13]

In early 1967, there were other minor clashes where the Viet Cong used various types of gas grenades. The first of these occurred in Binh Duong Province on January 16 and involved soldiers from the 3rd Brigade of the 4th Infantry Division. Unable to break contact after being surprised by an American patrol, a platoon of about twenty guerrillas threw several tear-gas grenades at the soldiers, hoping to force the Americans to break off pursuit. The wind was blowing in the wrong direction, however, and pushed the cloud back onto the guerrillas. The Americans did not even need to put on their masks, as they continued to chase the now-blinded Viet Cong through the jungle. Another minor incident occurred on February 11 when Communist forces attacked an outpost manned by troops of the 1st Cavalry Division. After suffering three casualties, the guerrillas used gas grenades to cover their withdrawal.[14]

The first significant use of tear gas occurred on February 28, 1967, during Operation Junction City. As units of the 11th Armored Cavalry Regiment moved into a heavily defended Communist sanctuary about twenty-five miles north of Tay Ninh, they came under fire from guerrillas hiding in the jungle. After a brief but fierce engagement, the guerrillas decided to withdraw. This time, the Viet Cong used a large number of gas grenades and the cloud enveloped the American unit. The Americans had to don their protective masks to keep from being incapacitated by the gas. Although three Communists were killed during the battle, the majority of the guerrillas were able to use the gas cloud to cover their retreat and escape.[15]

Initial attitudes of American commanders concerning these incidents ran the gamut. Many generals and senior field grade officers downplayed the significance and minimized potential problems any guerrilla force equipped with gas might cause. These officers were convinced that the Viet Cong would never be able to acquire a sufficient arsenal to begin using chemicals on a widespread basis. They noted that, in addition to an adequate supply of weapons, the Communists would also have to obtain enough gas masks to issue one to every guerrilla. They further argued that, even if it did become more common, it would have little impact on their units since all of their soldiers were very well trained and each was equipped with an effective protective mask. To these officers, the enemy only had a limited supply of tear-gas grenades and was using these weapons simply to boost the morale of the typical ill-equipped insurgent.

Other officers thought the enemy was acting in desperation. For example, after trumpeting the chemical exploits of his own unit and its ability to deliver massive amounts of CS powder on an enemy target, one officer hypocritically responded to a question of his views on the enemy use of gas by commenting:

> [w]hen a person has his back against the wall he gets desperate. I think Charlie is going to approach that position in the not too distant future,

and conceivably at that time he will use whatever he can possibly get his hands on.

Another group believed such incidents portended an escalation in the war. These officers believed enemy use of tear gas would increase and the Viet Cong arsenal would soon expand from hand grenades to larger stand-off weapons such as mortars and artillery. The most pessimistic of this group believed that there was a real potential for the enemy to escalate the chemical war and begin using lethal chemical agents. Unlike their senior counterparts, company grade officers were particularly concerned about what they believed to be a lack of appropriate training given to new recruits arriving in Vietnam. As one captain put it, once toxic gas was introduced,

> there would be many casualties due to inadequate training. Unfortunately, the majority of casualties from chemical attack[s] have always been due principally to a lack of troop training and indoctrination as opposed to the effectiveness of the agents and skill of enemy employment.[16]

The primary impediment to the expanding Viet Cong offensive capabilities was a source of chemical munitions. Although Communist China did provide grenades, mortar rounds and artillery shells to the North Vietnamese, only a limited number of these trickled down to the Viet Cong. So, just as they had done countless other times, the insurgents would have to make do with materials on hand. Now the key hurdle became a source of suitable chemical agents. One option was to produce improvised agents from ground-up indigenous plants such as hot peppers and horseradish, or steal industrial chemicals with lacrimatory vapors. There were several attacks employing these types of materials. One occurred on April 6, 1967, at the start of Operation Francis Marion in the central highlands about thirty miles southwest of Pleiku City. The Viet Cong attacked the 81-mm Mortar Platoon of Company C, 3rd Battalion, 8th Infantry Regiment four times with some type of improvised material. The guerrillas threw bottles or paper packets filled with a green powder that "oxidized when exposed to air" to produce an irritating aerosol. The fourth attack was the most severe; soldiers were forced to don protective masks when a strong wind blew the agent into their positions. Although causing some eye irritation, there were no casualties reported as a result of the exposure to whatever material the Viet Cong had used. During another series of attacks that occurred in July 1968, the occupants of two South Vietnamese militia posts were not as lucky. In these cases, soldiers were sprayed with a liquid agent that was reported to cause several soldiers to vomit or spit up blood. Once again, the material was never identified.[17]

Another option was to locate old stockpiles of degrading agents abandoned by the French when they left the country. However, this old and degrading material was in limited supply and would not give the insurgents any significant operational capability. In addition, the guerrillas faced a significant technical hurdle using munitions retrofitted to deliver these agents. While it worked in hand grenades and mines, a liquid filling would have severely altered the ballistic characteristics of a modified mortar or artillery shell and made it highly inaccurate. In other words, even if the Viet Cong had manufactured and fired such a shell, it would not have hit the target.

As it turned out, the greatest source of both chemical munitions and bulk agent was the United States military itself. As one guerrilla put it, "[t]he Americans used their weapons to fight us and we used them to fight back." Initially, the Viet Cong simply collected grenades captured during combat operations, but after the Americans began stepping up their chemical operations in early 1966, the insurgents began actively seeking out storage areas so that they could steal munitions, containers of agent and protective equipment. Regional commanders gave strict orders forbidding local units from using any of the items acquired unless specifically authorized to do so. Everything was supposed to be delivered to higher command and stockpiled for future operations. Soon, Allied patrols recovered increasing numbers of the stolen masks and gas grenades from weapons caches found in the jungle.[18]

In January 1967, American units started making improvised bombs from the fifty-five-gallon drums used to ship the agent to Vietnam. They dropped these munitions from helicopters as a way to contaminate enemy base camps and supply lines. These munitions were effective and quickly gained widespread acceptance; some units often dropped thousands in a single month. As with all munitions, but especially with improvised ones, there were a considerable number of duds; a trend that continued even when the military began manufacturing a standard burster system. In many cases these drums remained intact when they hit the ground; even the ones that broke open often contained uncompromised bags of agent. These duds provided the Viet Cong with a ready source of bulk CS powder.[19]

The insurgents also went back and recovered the CS-filled submunitions from malfunctioned canister clusters. Although these munitions were dependable and had a low malfunction rate, they were used so frequently and contained such a large number of submunition (over 200 per cluster) that the number of recoverable duds quickly mounted. Once the Americans realized that the guerrillas were converting these submunitions into miniature gas grenades, they began taking steps to cut down on the number of dud munitions. One field expedient method soldiers used was to attach a standard smoke grenade to each canister cluster and pull its pin just before dropping the unit from a helicopter. If the cluster malfunctioned, then there would only be a single thin smoke plume instead of the large agent cloud. Using the base of the plume as a target, an attack helicopter would move in and destroy the malfunctioning cluster munition with a missile.[20]

The Viet Cong came up with a variety of ways to use the recovered bulk CS powder. One was as a method of initiating an ambush on a mechanized unit or a convoy. They simply spread the bulk powder along a roadway and the vehicles aerosolized the powder when they drove through it. As the unprotected drivers lost control of their vehicles, the guerrillas fired into the confused mass. Soldiers were faced with the prospect of fighting blind or risking additional casualties when they paused to put on their masks.

They also began using it to make a variety of improvised weapons. In some cases, the guerrillas simply rewired the failed burster charge and used the entire drum as a large landmine. However, these were not very efficient unless detonated thirty-to-forty feet above the ground. More often, the Viet Cong would use each individual shipping bag out of a drum or even further subdivide these eight-pound bags into smaller containers. Not only did this create a greater stockpile of weapons, but the smaller bags were easier to transport and emplace. Much like their Allied counterparts, they soon found that several bags used in tandem were a more efficient way of generating an agent cloud than simply detonating an entire drum.

As with the South Vietnamese Army, and even to some extent the Americans, the early chemical activities of the Viet Cong and North Vietnamese were uncoordinated. Because of their lack of experience, their initial operations were sometimes even counterproductive. A common problem was when guerrillas miscalculated the effect the wind would have on the agent cloud generated by their weapons. For example, on two different occasions early in 1968 the Viet Cong planned to initiate an assault on a firebase using a mortar barrage in conjunction with a chemical attack. They hoped the gas would blind and confuse the defenders long enough to allow the first wave of guerrillas to get through the wire and into the main camp. If they were lucky, even the soldiers that kept their heads would not be able to don their masks in time to stop the charge. In preparation for the initial assault, sappers quietly moved to the outer perimeter wire and set up several command-detonated devices, which were made by attaching a small explosive charge to the bottom of one of the recovered eight-pound shipping bags of CS. In both instances, they were able to complete their missions and retreated back into the jungle without being detected by the camp sentries.

As the time for each attack drew near, assault forces massed just behind the improvised gas munitions so they could follow the cloud into camp and have the best chance of getting past the defenders. At the signal, the sappers detonated the devices and the assault forces surge forward. However, in both cases the wind blew the agent away from the camp interior and straight into the charging guerrillas. Despite protection from improvised gas masks, the cloud stopped the assault like a wall. The defenders watched with amusement as the guerrilla forces staggered about running into each other before they scattered back into the jungle.[21]

With experience, along with higher-quality munitions and gas masks, Communist chemical operations became more sophisticated and better coordinated. As always, these improvements manifested themselves in the North Vietnamese Army units long before they appeared in operations conducted by the Viet Cong. For example, in October 1967, the 2nd Battalion of the 4th Marines was acting as the defense force for a key bridge along the vital road that served as the only supply line to Con Thien, a critical firebase located on a small hill just half-a-mile south of the Demilitarized Zone. To facilitate coordination of the overall defensive set-up, each company took up positions in one of the quadrants formed by the intersection of the road and the stream. At 1.25 a.m. on October 14, the North Vietnamese began an attack on the southwest quadrant with a bombardment of rockets, artillery and mortar rounds. Under cover of the barrage, the Communists massed for their assault not more than 150 feet in front of the marine positions. The marines, however, saw the enemy activity and were prepared for the attack. Their heavy volume of fire broke up the assault before the guerrillas could even reach the first row of wire around the outer perimeter.

The surviving North Vietnamese retreated back into the jungle and crossed the stream into the northwest quadrant. At 2.30 a.m. they began their second assault with another barrage of mortars and rocket-propelled grenades, destroying a machine gun emplacement and several key back-up positions in the marine perimeter. This time the guerrillas also preceded their charge with a large number of tear-gas grenades. The ensuing confusion in the marine lines as they sought to put on their protective masks allowed the North Vietnamese to breach the wire and move into the marine perimeter. They quickly overran the company command post, killing the company commander, three platoon leaders and the forward observer. As the hand-to-hand fighting continued, the guerrillas drove even deeper into the marine perimeter and attacked the battalion command post, killing or wounding most of the battalion staff. Although the marines eventually drove off the North Vietnamese and prevented them from destroying the bridge, twenty-one Americans were killed and twenty-three more were wounded. Only twenty-four Communists were killed during the skirmish.[22]

Another example occurred on August 23, 1968 at the Cam Le Bridge across the Song Cau Do River on Highway 1, a major transportation artery from Da Nang to the critical outpost defenses along the Demilitarized Zone. This bridge was also guarded by a contingent of marines whose duty was not only to prevent the enemy from destroying the bridge, but also to cut down the number of infiltrators slipping south into Da Nang. While guard duty was on a rotational basis among various units, each usually set up their command post on the north side of the bridge, placing their machine guns in an observation tower and an old French bunker overlooking the bridge from the south side of the river. Just after 1.00 a.m. the Viet Cong began firing rocket-propelled grenades and mortars at the guards manning the machine guns. As the barrage lifted, guerrillas swarmed the gun positions, forcing the marines to withdraw to the command post on the north side of the bridge.

Within minutes, the marines moved back across the bridge and counterattacked the enemy occupying their old positions. However, the heavy volume of enemy fire brought them up short and they had to take cover on the bridge just shy of the southern river bank. As the marines went to ground, the guerrillas threw tear-gas grenades into the American positions. The marines, not anticipating the North Vietnamese would be equipped with tear gas, did not have their protective masks with them when they assumed guard duty. The intense irritating effects quickly drove the marines away from the southern bank and forced them back to the center of the bridge where some sandbags offered protection from the enemy small-arms fire. Although the gas still occasionally drifted over these new positions, the concentration of agent was not enough to drive the marines back farther along the bridge. Protected by the sandbags, they were able to keep the guerrillas from storming across the bridge and attacking the command post on the northern bank.

While the marines on the bridge were exchanging fire with the guerrillas to the south, another Communist unit that was hiding on the north side of the river launched an attack on the command post. In addition to heavy mortar, rocket and small-arms fire, these guerrillas also threw tear-gas grenades into the marine positions. Like the marines in the middle of the bridge, those defending the command post did not have their protective masks with them. They were forced to endure the effects of the gas, occasionally plunging their faces into the river to get some relief from the severe irritation. After an extended pitched battle that included support from helicopter gunships, an AC-47 gunship,[23] tactical close air support and an assault by five tanks, the marines forced the North Vietnamese to abandon the bridge and retreat back into the jungle.[24]

It was during the 1968 Tet Offensive that the North Vietnamese launched their first tank attack against an American outpost. Lang Vei was located on a hilltop four miles southwest of Khe Sanh and was defended by 400 South Vietnamese and Montagnard irregulars and twenty-four American Special Forces soldiers. The camp was surrounded by three layers of barbed wire and protected by numerous fighting positions and bunkers. The tactical operations center, or TOC, of the heavily fortified camp was built of reinforced concrete and steel plate, and dug into ground so that not much more than the roof extended above the surface.[25]

Just after midnight on February 7, 1968, the North Vietnamese began their attack with an intense mortar and artillery barrage. As the bombardment forced the defenders to keep their head down, twelve Russian-made PT-76 amphibious tanks supported by North Vietnamese infantry attacked the compound.[26] The thought of an enemy tank attack was so inconceivable that the Allied soldiers mistook the sound of the approaching vehicles to be malfunctioning camp generators.

An intense battle ensued. Although the Americans were able to destroy three of the tanks and disable a fourth, the camp was soon overrun. The only remaining stronghold was the TOC, which the North Vietnamese quickly surrounded. When blasts from the main guns of the tanks did little more than destroy the entrance doors, the tankers tried to cave in the structure by driving two of the fourteen-ton monsters up onto the roof. When that failed, enemy soldiers threw a shower of fragmentation and tear-gas grenades down the stairwells, hoping to force the Americans out into the open.

Smoke from small fires started by the grenades combined with tear gas, making breathing difficult for the defenders. Many of them became sick and vomited. With only a few protective masks available, they were forced to lie face-down on the floor, hoping to avoid some of the irritating smoke. Those with masks took a few deep breaths of filtered clean air and then passed the mask on to another soldier so that everyone got a few moments of relief. Unable to ventilate the TOC, the gas continued to nauseate the defenders throughout the long miserable night.

Shortly after dawn, it was clear that the Americans would not be able to hold out for much longer. In a desperate attempt to escape, the commander of the Special Forces detachment called for a series of air strikes directly on the camp. The bombs and rockets drove the enemy soldiers away from the TOC, forcing them to seek cover. The jets then made a series of dummy passes over the compound, swooping low as if to drop additional ordnance. This ruse forced the North Vietnamese to stay under cover and keep their heads down. The surviving defenders took advantage of the confusion to quickly move up the stairs, out one of the blown bunker doors and off into the jungle. As a result of the attack, over 200 of the indigenous troops were killed and seventy-five wounded. Ten of the American advisors were killed and eleven more were wounded.[27]

The greatest boost to Viet Cong chemical operation occurred when they began modifying conventional military munitions and adding CS to their rockets, artillery and mortar rounds. These altered munitions gave the guerrillas the stand-off capability that some American officers had predicted was forthcoming. Initially, due to limited supply of these munitions, the Communists only used them in direct support of combat operations, incorporating a number of them at the end of a preparatory mortar barrage to enhance the defenders' confusion just prior to the ground assault. This tactic was particularly effective in conjunction with human wave attacks, greatly increasing the likelihood that the mass would reach the perimeter of a firebase before they were stopped by the defenders. In some instances, it was only the combined response of attack helicopters, tactical bombers and heavy artillery that saved the outpost.

As the guerrillas only used gas in their preparatory bombardments just prior to an attack, whenever Allied soldiers felt any eye irritation during a mortar attack, or simply thought they did, they donned their protective masks and prepared for the inevitable assault. Realizing this, as the insurgents built up their stockpiles of chemical rounds, they took advantage of this conditioned response. They fired gas rounds into Allied positions without any intention of mounting an attack. Until the Allies caught on to this World War I tactic, these harassment attacks helped demoralize and wear down the defenders of remote outposts since they would don their protective masks, preparing for attacks that never came.[28]

The Viet Cong also mimicked American "flushing" tactics, firing a barrage of gas rounds into Allied positions to drive unmasked soldiers out into the open where the follow-on barrage of high-explosive fragmentation rounds would kill them. At times, the Communists also used gas rounds to suppress Allied mortars, forcing the gunners to interrupt fire missions in order to put on protective masks. In these situations, the insurgents also intermixed fragmentation rounds with the gas munitions, once again hoping to catch disoriented individuals in the open.

In some instances, the Viet Cong used gas rounds to counter an Allied CS attack. For instance, early in September 1967 two battalions of the American 5th Marines were conducting a sweep through the rice paddies and bamboo stands of the Que Son Valley, located about thirty-two miles south of Da Nang. According to intelligence reports, the Communists built a major staging area in the valley with hardened fighting positions, including caves and tunnels, and were growing food in preparation for a major offensive deeper into South Vietnam. Near the hamlet of Vinh Huy, a well-equipped force of over 4,000 Viet Cong and North Vietnamese regulars engaged the marines in heavy fighting. Hoping to avoid a costly assault on the well-prepared positions, the marines called in a series of CS strikes intending to force the guerrillas out into the open. Undaunted by the gas, the North Vietnamese launched a gas attack of their own, raining mortar shells filled with tear gas down on the marines. As the gas bellowed up around the Americans, Communists, wearing new Chinese-made gas masks, rose up and in classic World War I fashion mounted a bayonet charge into the marine lines. The marines hastily donned their own masks and met the charge, engaging in hand-to-hand fighting. Eventually the marines repulsed the attack but the battle continued for four days before the remnants of the Communist force were driven back into the mountains. A total of 114 marines were killed with 283 others wounded. The marines estimated that about 370 enemy soldiers were killed.[29]

One of the most well coordinated and deadly Viet Cong gas attacks was on March 28, 1971. Firebase Mary Ann sat on a ridge between two mountaintops, 4,000 feet above sea level. The primary purpose for constructing the base was to place 4.2-inch mortars and 155-mm artillery in a location that gave these weapons a field of fire providing a protective shield for Da Nang and numerous coastal hamlets. The base also housed the TOC for the 1st Battalion of the 46th Infantry Regiment, 196th Light Infantry Brigade, commanded by Lieutenant Colonel William Doyle. The TOC itself was a solid bunker as much below ground as above. On a rotational basis, one of the companies from the battalion was stationed at the base to provide security. No one, however, really believed that the Communists would waste time on such an insignificant outpost. Since it was built, the firebase had only been mortared a few times and its perimeter defenses never probed. Soldiers became lax about security and treated duty at the base as if they were in the rear area. Under this misperception, the post defenses were allowed to slip. A large number of trip flares, installed within the barbed wire perimeter to give early warning of intruders, had been set off accidentally by soldiers working on the wire or by the prop wash of supply helicopters. These flares had not been replaced. Although manned listening posts were usually established outside of a base perimeter to provide warning of enemy activity, none were deployed around Mary Ann. On many occasions soldiers sent out on patrols to check the area around the base simply moved a short distance into the jungle and sat down for the time they were supposed to be outside the camp. Then they would return to the base with a negative report.

In addition to the lax attitude of the soldiers, the firebase itself had drifted into a state of disrepair because it was going to be turned over to the South Vietnamese Army in May. Unwilling to expend any unnecessary effort or resources before the change of possession, the Americans ignored many maintenance issues and needed improvements, instead leaving these for the future owners to deal with. During February, much of the activity on the base was directed at relocating arms, ammunition and equipment to other American firebases. By the beginning of March, all of the ground radar and night vision scopes, along with most of the mortars and artillery, had already been removed. American control would essentially end by mid-month, when the 1st Battalion would be redeployed north of Da Nang. In order to maintain operational control during the final troop movement, the battalion TOC was scheduled for temporary relocation to an intermediate staging area on March 30.

Early in the morning on March 28, about fifty guerrillas from the 409th Viet Cong Sapper Battalion crept up to the base perimeter and began cutting the outer wire. Covered in black camouflage made from soot and grease, they quietly worked their way through the base perimeter defenses. At 2.30 a.m. a mortar barrage hit the camp. In addition to high-explosive rounds, the Viet Cong mixed in a heavy proportion of CS rounds. Under cover of the gas and exploding shells, the sappers, wearing new military-quality protective masks, charged into the camp throwing hand grenades and firing small arms and rocket-propelled grenades. The attack was well-planned and well-rehearsed. The attackers split up into small teams, attacking key targets and shooting everyone they encountered. Satchel charges, used to destroy the remaining artillery pieces, were also thrown into bunkers as the sappers ran past. Many of these explosive charges were also packed with CS powder and filled the bunkers with an irritating cloud of the agent when they detonated. Anyone surviving the blast was left choking and blinded as they tried to dig out of the debris.

At first, the Americans thought that it was only a mortar barrage intended to harass the post. Then the sound of small-arms fire and shouts of enemy infiltrators began to fill the air. As soldiers moved out of their bunkers to take up defensive positions, they were blinded by the CS from the mortar barrage. They quickly moved back inside to find their protective masks. In many cases, before they could reemerge a sapper tossed in a couple of grenades or a satchel charge. After the explosions, the guerrilla moved in and shot any survivors. Realizing the bunkers were not safe, soldiers sought refuge outside in trenches or any other hiding spot. Many were still unarmed and without masks. As the gas swirled around them, they covered their faces with rags, towels or poncho liners and tried not to cough. Unaware the sappers were wearing gas masks, some assumed a masked figure had to be an American and made the mistake of calling out for assistance. Others played dead, even while being stripped of their watches and valuables by greedy enemy soldiers.

The CS drifted into the TOC and reached the radio operators. None of them had brought their masks on duty with them and they evacuated the building in search of fresh air. In order to keep the soldiers in the TOC from effectively directing a counterattack or calling in air or artillery strikes, the guerrillas threw gas-laden satchel charges into the building. Then sappers raced inside, began using more satchel charges to destroy all of the radios and equipment they could find. The explosion from one of the charges knocked Lieutenant Coeonel Doyle over as he attempted to clear the gas out of his eyes. Now dazed from the blast as well as blinded by the CS, he was trying to find a way out of the building when he was confronted by one of the masked sappers preparing to throw a satchel charge at him. Unable to see clearly, Lieutenant Colonel Doyle still managed to shoot the guerrilla in the chest with his pistol. Unfortunately, the enemy soldier had already armed the explosive before the bullet killed him and it detonated as he fell. The blast momentarily knocked the battalion commander unconscious. When he eventually recovered, he was still disoriented from being battered about by the explosions and blinded by the tear gas. Fortunately, by the time he was able to find his way out of the demolished TOC, most of the gas from the mortar barrage had drifted away and he was able to breathe fresh air. After he recovered, Lieutenant Colonel Doyle began trying to organize the base defenses.

Overall, the attack lasted less than an hour. The sappers rapidly moved through the base, blowing up whatever they could, then running out the other side. At the end of the battle, most of the base was in flames. Thirty Americans were dead and eighty-two others wounded. All twelve officers were either killed or wounded. Only fifteen enemy bodies were found, although there were indications that other casualties were carried off. As a result of the massacre, Lieutenant Colonel Doyle and Colonel William Hathaway, commander of the

196th Light Infantry Brigade, received career-ending letters of reprimand from Robert Froehlke, Secretary of the Army. Major General James Baldwin, commander of the 23rd Infantry Division, received a letter of admonishment and was informally relieved of command. For its part, the South Vietnamese Army decided it no longer wanted the compound and Firebase Mary Ann was closed down on April 24, 1971.[30]

The Communists also used tear gas to support their mechanized operations. After the Tet Offensive, the North Vietnamese Army expanded its use of tanks. Despite the shock value a tank provided, its light armor was still vulnerable to many of the organic infantry weapons used by the Allied forces, and North Vietnamese tank units suffered many losses. So, whenever it was available, the Communists included tear gas in their preparatory bombardments to help suppress the fire and reduce the accuracy of the Allied defenders. For instance, during the 1972 Easter Offensive, North Vietnam poured thousands of men and tanks across the Demilitarized Zone in the largest and most conventional campaign up to that time. On several occasions when the South Vietnamese mounted a particularly staunch defense, such as at the siege of Firebase Bastogne and during the assault on the forward command post of the South Vietnamese 22nd Division at Tan Canh, Communist artillery batteries fired tear-gas shells intermixed with traditional high explosives to disrupt command and control of the Allied defensive operations.

Another example occurring during the Easter Offensive was at the battle for the city of An Loc, located sixty-five miles north of Saigon. On the evening of April 7, as the North Vietnamese prepared for their initial assault on the city proper, forces from the Viet Cong 9th Division attacked the Quan Loi airstrip less than two miles from the city limits. The airstrip was a high-priority target because it was where the South Vietnamese refueled and rearmed their attack helicopters. Under the cover of tear gas, the Communists launched repeated human wave attacks, eventually forcing defenders to abandon their positions, destroy whatever equipment they could and then withdraw back into the city.

The actual assault on the city began six days later. Unable to quickly breach the city defenses, the Communists settled into a siege; continually firing rockets and artillery, mortar and tank rounds into the city. On at least three occasions they saturated the air around the command bunker of the South Vietnamese 5th Division with tear gas trying to disrupt control of the city defenses and generally demoralize the defenders. Despite the intense bombardment, the city defenses held and, by May 11, after over two months of fighting, the Communist offensive was broken. Most of the North Vietnamese tanks and armored vehicles were destroyed during the battle. The crucial defense of this city prevented the North Vietnamese from conducting their planned follow-on attack on the city of Saigon itself.[31]

Ultimately it was the massive American air support, principally the devastating firepower of the B-52 bombers from Guam, that finally broke the back of the Easter Offensive. The combined arms lessons learned during the offensive, however, were not forgotten by the insurgents. After the final American withdrawal, when Communist operations in South Vietnam and Cambodia were no longer threatened by American airpower, the North Vietnamese began an all-out effort to improve movement along the Ho Chi Minh Trail in preparation for their next major offensive. Once again they used combined armor and infantry assaults to clear away any pockets of resistance. These tactics were not sufficient in all cases, though, since some of the local militias were still heavily armed and capable of inflicting significant damage on the medium and light tanks used by the North Vietnamese. Effective gas masks, however, were not very common and tear gas often proved to be the deciding factor in these confrontations. An example of this occurred on April 28, 1974, when a North Vietnamese force of about sixty PT-76 tanks and 3,000 infantry attacked Long Khot, a South Vietnamese outpost defended by nearly 4,300 militia and civilians. The Communists wanted to eliminate this particular base because it was an active staging point for ongoing raids against construction activities across the border in Cambodia. After a fierce firefight lasting most of the day, with heavy casualties on both sides, the North Vietnamese were driven back and forced to break off their assault for the night. They were back the next morning, initiating their second attack with an artillery barrage of high explosives and tear gas. This time the assault quickly routed the defenders. The South Vietnamese were forced to abandon the outpost and withdraw to the south.[32]

Throughout the war, the Communist chemical warfare program was principally limited by their lack of industrial resources. They overcame this deficiency by acquiring some chemical equipment and weapons from other Communist countries, scavenging items from the Americans and improvising from local resources. Even though they eventually learned to modify stand-off munitions to carry a chemical payload, their offensive efforts were always hampered by a shortage of chemical munitions. Despite these limitations, by the end of the war many Communist units had developed a respectable level of gas discipline, which helped reduce the impacts of an Allied tear-gas attack. They had also adopted a number of effective offensive tactics, many learned by studying American operations, which were successfully employed against Allied forces.

9
CONCLUSION

Despite being a superpower and having one of the largest chemical arsenals in the world, in 1965 the United States was not fully prepared to fight a chemical war. This was particularly true when it came to riot-control agents. At that time, the military did not have a workable doctrine for using tear gas or vomiting agents in combat and, outside of a short exposure during basic training designed to build confidence in his protective mask, the typical combat soldier did not have any experience with these agents. Notwithstanding these limitations, advocates began touting the potential these chemicals offered in the type of war going on in Vietnam. These proponents said the physical characteristics of an agent cloud made it an ideal weapon for a jungle environment, and the non-lethal effects of the agents gave commanders flexibility over the level of force to apply in any given situation. Further, they pointed out that in this conflict the United States faced an enemy with limited technical capabilities, without chemical protective equipment and unable to retaliate in kind. They won their case when the Kennedy Administration began sending riot-control munitions to Vietnam in 1962.

Guided by their American advisors, the South Vietnamese were the first to use riot-control agents on the battlefield. The South Vietnamese Army had little success with these weapons, primarily due to its soldiers' discomfort with this new form of warfare. When US forces entered the chemical war, the Americans fared much better, quickly developing new and innovative tactics that capitalized on the physical and physiological properties of the agents. Initially, the principal hindrance to American operations was the limited selection of available weapons and an inadequate stockpile of munitions. As new armaments arrived, chemical weapons lost their specialty status and they eventually became a normal component of available firepower for American units.

Although the gas war was initially one-sided, it did not remain that way for long. Communist forces acquired a limited supply of gas masks and, by the end of the war, not only the North Vietnamese but also the Viet Cong were conducting sporadic offensive chemical operations with both grenades and stand-off weapons. Many of their detachments also mimicked American chemical warfare tactics and employed them successfully during a number of attacks.

But how effective was tear gas in combat situations? Did it offer any tangible advantage over more conventional weapons? One of the best ways to assess this is by looking at battles with multiple attacks on the same objective, some supported by tear gas and some not. Two prime examples occurred during the Battle of Hue. When the marines initially tried to drive the North Vietnamese out of the Provincial Treasury Building, they could not even cross Ly Thuong Kiet Street to assault the building because of the heavy volume of enemy fire. They carried out numerous attacks under cover of smoke screens, tanks providing supporting fire and even innovative gunnery with both the battalion mortars and recoilless rifles. Nothing worked. Then, almost in desperation, they fired an E8 backpack multiple-rocket launcher into the enemy positions across the street. The CS cloud generated by the sixty-four miniature rockets quickly enveloped the treasury building. This time, the marines not only made it across the street but also swept through the enemy defensive positions and captured the treasury building within a matter of minutes.

The second example is when the marines tried to take the Provincial Capitol Building. Hoping for a quick repeat of their success at the treasury building, the marines used an E8 launcher to initiate the attack. This time, however, the wind was coming from a direction that pushed the agent cloud away from the building so it had no affect on the defenders. Without tear gas to cover their assault, the marines quickly moved back behind cover and began hammering the enemy with tanks, recoilless rifles and mortars. After several hours exchanging gunfire, the wind shifted and began coming from a direction that would blow the gas into the enemy positions. When the marines fired the E8 this time, the cloud rolled into the building and blinded the defenders. Once again, as soon as the marines were able to engage the enemy with tear gas, they were able to cross the street and quickly clear their objective.

This is not to say tear gas was a panacea; there are other examples cited in this book when CS did not provide the tactical advantage the Allies expected. In the majority of cases, much like the first assault on the Provincial Capitol Building described above, gas did not reach the enemy positions in sufficient concentration to incapacitate the soldiers. There are also examples when the Communists anticipated the attack and wore masks preventing exposure. In a very small percentage of cases, such as when American jets dropped tear-gas bomblets onto the deck of the Thai fishing trawler during the Mayaguez Incident, the guerrillas simply ignored the intense irritation caused by the agents and continued fighting. Overall, however, whenever delivered on target in high concentration, CS quickly incapacitated enemy soldiers and bolstered an Allied attack.

An alternate way to evaluate the effectiveness of tear gas is to look at the perceived value soldiers placed on these weapons. One way to gauge this value is to look at the diversity of the weapon systems available to deliver the agents onto a target; fewer delivery systems indicate more specialized tactical requirements. By the end of the war, there were a variety of hand grenades, various cartridges for the M79 grenade launcher, a shoulder-fired tactical rocket, the E8 backpack rocket pod, dispersers to spray bulk agent, shells for the 105-mm howitzer, 155-mm howitzer and the 4.2-inch mortar, 2.75-inch rockets for the M3 rocket pods mounted on helicopter gunships, a helicopter dispenser that dropped paper bags filled with agent onto a target, a bomb for both planes and jets that delivered over 250 pounds of agent in a single strike, as well as numerous cluster munitions for helicopters, planes and even jets. Many of these systems were developed because of requests or suggestions from soldiers in the field. Another indication of perceived value is the logistical match-up between supply and demand for tear-gas munitions. In virtually every category of weapon system listed above, demand exceeded available stores, and combat units were rationed based on the priority of their operations. This point is further accentuated by considering the multitude of improvised devices soldiers came up with to overcome these shortages.

Attitudes about using riot-control agents for combat varied greatly over the course of the war. Although chemical weapons were never universally accepted, as American soldiers became more familiar with the agents and used them successfully in difficult situations, attitudes evolved from skepticism – tear gas was a non-lethal weapon – to confidence. Some units, such as the 1st Cavalry Division, the 101st Airborne Division and the 1st Infantry Division, embraced gas warfare and developed novel ways to use tear gas on the battlefield, documenting their innovations in the unit's after action reports. As the war progressed, however, the wording in these reports became more mundane, ultimately falling away to simple statistics on the number and types of munitions expended. Eventually, most soldiers regarded CS as just another weapon, the attitude General Westmoreland wanted when he issued Directive 525–11.

The attitudes of politicians and the public toward riot-control agents hinged on the way events were presented in the press. From the casual attitude over early herbicide operations, through the chaos following Peter Arnett's famous dispatch, and back to a guarded but accepting orientation after Operation Stomp, the press set the tone for the two other groups. Once the press regarded tear gas as a mundane standard weapon and stopped highlighting every use, the public lost interest. Without an active public debate, the pressure eased on the politicians.

As the military began using tear gas more routinely, the Johnson Administration continued monitoring the pulse of the press at home and abroad to gauge the potential political impact. Although Hanoi often complained about the use of "highly toxic chemicals and poison gas as war weapons for mass murder in South Vietnam," the majority of the world media ignored the tirade. Even when top US scientists, including seven Nobel laureates, sent an open letter to President Johnson asking him to stop using chemicals during combat operations, the general reaction in the press was to echo the Administration's response and focus on the humanitarian options the agents gave commanders.

Another key factor in this triangle was television. Reporters using this kind of media focused on the visual aspects of an event: the recoil of an artillery piece, dust plumes in the distance as the artillery barrage landed, a soldier crouching behind a low wall as enemy fire chipped away at his cover, the conflagration of a napalm strike. A smoke cloud was not very photogenic; by nature it obscured the visual. Other than a soldier wearing a mask, there was not much to see.

As television brought the war into the homes of the American public, it also brought in the national domestic problems. Everyone could watch the protests and riots; all of the ugly confrontations over the war, civil rights and poverty. A common feature was the gas-grenade tossing contest. The footage of police throwing tear-gas grenades into a crowd and rioters picking up the billowing canisters then throwing them back was very photogenic. In contrast to the battlefield, the cloud also made a picturesque backdrop for the camera as reporters captured the scene of bystanders fleeing the confrontation. These depictions drove home the non-lethal characteristics of the agents. After all, these events occurred on the streets of America's largest cities and the campuses of its major universities; and, though it was obviously uncomfortable, no one was ever seriously injured simply from exposure to the gas. These images, coupled with the contrasting images of the carnage on the battlefield, carried over and helped desensitize the public to any outcry over soldiers using tear gas in combat.

What about the question of the "slippery slope," that is, the argument over whether the availability and widespread use of tear gas unavoidably weakens the constraints on escalation to unrestricted chemical warfare? The first key question is, did the United States in fact use more aggressive agents during the war? There were numerous allegations that Americans used nerve agents and the incapacitating agent BZ. Many of these were a product of the Communist propaganda campaign, picked up and amplified by sympathetic international figures with access to a wider audience. For example, Hanoi routinely asserted the marines actually used toxic gas during Operation Stomp to kill noncombatants hiding in the caves. During the 1967 International War Crimes Tribunal, the description mutated and took on an even more ominous air when the Sub-Committee on Chemical Warfare in Vietnam reported the marines had "flooded the civilians taking refuge in air raid shelters with forty-eight containers of poison gas, killing thirty-five and wounding nineteen. [Present in the shelters] were twenty-six women and twenty-eight children." In another instance, when speaking at the Conference on Chemical and Biological Warfare held in London in February 1968, M.F. Kahn, a French physician and member of the War Crimes Tribunal, told the other attendees, "[t]here has been a persistent report that BZ was used on at least one occasion in [Bong Son] in March 1966."[1]

Other allegations were started by journalists writing articles that were more editorial than fact. For example, Gerard Van der Leun published an article in *Earth Magazine* accusing the United States of testing the nerve agent VX on a North Vietnamese Army outpost about ten miles over the Cambodia border. According to him, air force jets dropped two fifty-pound canisters of VX on the outpost in the summer of 1968, presumably killing everyone. The article reads like a work of fiction, filled with intimate details and vivid descriptions that capture the reader's attention. However, the author makes no effort to substantiate the piece; omitting even the usual claim to anonymous sources. Other articles, much like the one that sparked the Tailwind controversy, were simply poorly researched.[2]

There is no credible evidence currently available that the United States used lethal or incapacitating agents during the Vietnam War. However, the military and various members of the Johnson Administrations gave the idea serious consideration. Some of the proposals were very cloak-and-dagger; such as the suggestion to use an incapacitating chemical agent, presumably BZ, to knock out a team of clandestine operatives suspected of being "doubled" while working in North Vietnam. Once captured, the operatives would be smuggled back into South Vietnam for questioning. Others proposals were more traditional; as when General Westmoreland suggested to President Johnson during the 1968 siege of Khe Sanh that the United States should be prepared to use either tactical nuclear weapons or lethal chemical agents if the North Vietnamese Army began massing along the Demilitarized Zone.[3]

The Department of Defense was also actively conducting research and development on delivery platforms for chemical agents, specifically focusing on the weapon's performance in a jungle environment. These programs were part of a larger review of the military's chemical and biological warfare capabilities known as Project 112, which began in the early 1960s and continued until 1973. During two of these test projects – *Pin Point* conducted in 1966 and *Cliff Rose* conducted September 1967 through January 1968 – the army gathered data on the performance of six CS delivery systems that were eventually fielded in Vietnam. These were the E8 launcher, XM28 bagged agent dispenser, XM920E2 fuse and burster system, the BLU–52A/B CS chemical bomb, and the CBU–19/A and CBU–30/A aircraft dispensers. There were also four test projects that focused on dispersing nerve or incapacitating agents in a jungle environment: *Big Jack, Phase B* conducted in February through March 1963; *Tall Timber* conducted April through June 1966; *Pine Ridge* conducted May through June 1966; and *Red Oak, Phase I* conducted April through May 1967.

During these tests, the military evaluated a number of delivery systems, assessing such things as the overall effectiveness of the munition, height-of-burst distributions, degree of penetration into a jungle canopy, area coverage below the canopy and time–dosage relationships.[4]

So does the Vietnam War put an end to the "slippery slope" debate? Superficially, since only non-lethal agents were used, it would appear the United States avoided sliding down the hypothetical slope – even though tear gas was used widely in combat, there were advocates for using other classes of agents and there was an active program developing chemical weapons that released lethal agents in a jungle. However, evaluating tactical situations where tear gas was used repeatedly leads to a different conclusion. Army units used CS to synergistically enhance the lethality of traditional weapons by flushing unprotected soldiers from defensive positions. Arguably, when tear gas was specifically used to make bombs and artillery shells deadlier, it was no longer a non-lethal weapon, and by using this tactic the United States escalated the chemical war despite never employing lethal agents. Thus, in the strictest sense, the Vietnam War provides an example of a belligerent effectively limiting the classes of chemical agents used in a conflict, while in a broader and more reflective sense, it exemplifies the opposite – underscoring the necessity to consider the tactical intent along with the technical characteristics of the agents.

As an ancillary question, would the United States' mission have benefited by introducing lethal chemical weapons? There were certainly some situations, such as contamination of tunnels and bunkers, where persistent lethal agents would have been more effective than CS. However, even without considering the political cost or the impact on public opinion, the potential harm from expanding the chemical war was far greater than the potential benefit. Undoubtedly, the United States would have lost its unilateral advantage just as it had with riot-control agents. It is possible, even likely, that other Communist countries would have supplied the North Vietnamese with lethal chemical weapons. However, even without outside assistance, guerillas could have improvised by using toxic industrial and agricultural chemicals. For example, parathion was an organophosphate insecticide commonly sprayed on rice paddies. It was also very toxic to humans, acting on the nervous system in the same manner as a military nerve agent. It was very persistent, effective through any route of exposure and lethal in very low doses. Both the Americans and the Viet Cong were aware of the potential hazards and warned their units to avoid exposure. Available from local farmers or a number of commercial sources, the Viet Cong could have used a number of existing improvised munitions to deliver this material.[5]

From a tactical standpoint, chemical weapons are most effective against large formations of soldiers; something that was favored by the Americans as they moved through the jungle but typically not by the Communist guerrillas. Americans also operated out of outposts and firebases vulnerable to chemical attack. If such an attack involved a persistent material, such as parathion, clean-up would have been difficult and time-consuming, disrupting operation of the base and the missions of the units stationed there. A final tactical advantage for the Viet Cong was lethal chemicals, unlike riot-control agents, would have been an effective component in a number of their booby traps.

The overall conclusion is the same as the one reached by the Institute for Defense Analyses in their study on using tactical nuclear weapons in the war:

> use of [these weapons] in Southeast Asia would offer the US no decisive military advantage if the use remained unilateral, and it would have strongly adverse military effects if the enemy were able to use [these weapons] in reply. The military advantages of unilateral use ... are there-fore heavily outweighed by the disadvantages of eventual bilateral use.[6]

By the end of the Vietnam War, tear gas achieved the status that many thought chemical weapons would after World War I: CS was a tactical weapon used as a normal contingent of firepower on the battlefield. Despite this success, combat chemical operations are a largely forgotten facet of the war, over-shadowed by the controversy over Agent Orange and dioxin. There is a legacy, however. As a direct result of Americans using riot-control agents in combat during the war, President Gerald Ford signed Executive Order 11850 on April 8, 1975, limiting future combat operations with these agents to defensive mis-sions in four specific categories: controlling rioters (including prisoners of war); preventing enemy soldiers from using civilians as shields; protecting convoys in rear echelon areas from civil disturbances, terrorists and paramilitary organiza-tions; and during rescue missions in remote areas. Even these specific exceptions require Presidential approval in advance of the operation, a requirement the Joint Chiefs of Staff fulfilled prior to both the 1991 and 2003 Gulf Wars.

APPENDIX A

Technical agent data

The primary riot-control agents used during the Vietnam War were CN, DM and CS. Under typical battlefield conditions, these agents did not cause permanent injury and their effects quickly subsided once the individual escaped from the agent cloud. Typical effects included irritation to the eyes, mucous membranes and respiratory tract, but in very high concentrations they could also cause skin irritation or even blistering similar to severe sunburn. These effects were aggravated by high temperatures or high humidity, both common in Vietnam. Under such conditions, repeated exposures to even relatively moderate doses could have a cumulative effect and cause more severe injuries than normally anticipated. Also, individuals with high blood pressure, cardiovascular problems, asthma, lung congestion or even a common cold would experience increased effects with longer recovery times.

CN. Its chemical name is chloroacetophenone and it was first synthesized in 1869 by the German chemist Carl Gräbe. It is the material that inspired the term "tear gas" and became the key ingredient in the commercial formulation known as mace. It is a crystalline solid with a sharp, fragrant odor like apple blossoms. It is practically insoluble in water and does not readily decompose when it gets wet. It can be dispersed with explosives or mixed with a fuel to form an incendiary composition that will aerosolize the agent when it is burned. The bulk powder can be sprayed directly from a disperser or it can be dissolved in various solvents and sprayed as a liquid.

Aerosols of CN cause lacrimation at about $0.4\,\mathrm{mg/m^3}$. After escaping from the cloud, the irritant effects quickly dissipate and no first-aid is required, although soldiers often rinse their eyes with water. In some sensitive individuals, CN can cause a severe allergic reaction that would exacerbate the effects. An individual can die from an exposure to a concentration of $7,000\,\mathrm{mg/m^3}$ if they remain in the cloud for over two minutes.

Various CN formulations have been standardized over the years, including CNB (a solution in carbon tetrachloride and benzene), CNC (a solution in chloroform) and CNS (a mixture of CN and chloropicrin in chloroform; this version also produces nausea and vomiting in exposed individuals). During the Vietnam War, it was also dispersed as a micropulverized powder, known as CN1, which was persistent for several days after application.

DM. Also known as adamsite, after Major Roger Adams, the American chemist credited with its discovery, its chemical name is diphenylaminechlorarsine and it is the only vomiting agent ever stockpiled in the American arsenal. It is an odorless crystalline solid. Although the bulk material does not react with water, the fine particles generated in an aerosol cloud are hydrolyzed slowly and form a decomposition product that is very poisonous if ingested.

During the Vietnam War, it was typically mixed with a fuel to form an incendiary composition that would aerosolize the agent when it was burned. The residual dust from such a thermally generated cloud could remain active for more than six hours, depending on the humidity. It was also dispersed explosively as a micropulverized powder known as DM1. This form of the agent could remain active for weeks.

Eye and respiratory irritation appear at about $0.38\,mg/m^3$. Exposure to a concentration of between $11\,mg/m^3$ and $75\,mg/m^3$ for two minutes causes incapacitation. An individual can die from an exposure to a concentration of $5,500\,mg/m^3$ if they remain in the cloud for over two minutes. Initial symptoms are typically delayed for one or two minutes and include irritation of the eyes and mucus membranes. Exposure ultimately causes severe headache; nasal discharge; acute pain in the sinuses, the chest and behind the eyes; and finally nausea and vomiting. Casualties also report feeling depression, weakness and sensory disturbances. Unlike the tear agents, full recovery from exposure to typical battlefield concentrations can take three hours or more.

CN–DM. A standardized blend of the tear agent CN and the vomiting agent DM that took advantage of the immediate effects of CN and the delayed, but more severe, incapacitating effects of DM.

CS. Its chemical name is ortho chlorobenzylmalononitrile. Although it was discovered in 1928 by two American chemists, Ben Corson and Roger Stoughton, it was the British who developed it as a riot-control agent. They used it for the first time during the 1958–1959 civil unrest on Cyprus and achieved spectacular results. This inspired the United States military to adopt CS as its standard riot-control agent in 1959. It is a crystalline solid with a pungent, pepper-like odor. It is only slightly soluble in water or other common organic solvents, and the bulk material is not easily hydrolyzed. It can be dispersed with explosives or mixed with a fuel to form an incendiary composition that will aerosolize the agent when it is burned. The bulk powder can be sprayed directly from a disperser or it can be dissolved in a few solvents and sprayed as a liquid.

Compared by weight, CS is about ten-times more effective than CN. Aerosol concentrations around 0.5 mg/m³ cause extreme burning of the eyes, copious flow of tears, sneezing and minor skin irritation. These symptoms increase in severity with concentration and progress to nose and throat irritation, coughing, profuse runny nose, difficulty breathing with a feeling of chest constriction, inability to open the eyes, and stinging and burning of any moist skin. With continued exposure, or at concentrations above 2 mg/m³, symptoms progress to nausea, vomiting and vertigo. After about sixty seconds' exposure to 2 mg/m³, the casualty is usually incapacitated. As with CN, the irritant effects quickly dissipate after escaping from the cloud, and no first-aid is required, although soldiers often rinsed their eyes with water. In some sensitive individuals, CS can cause a severe allergic reaction that would exacerbate the effects. An individual can die from an exposure to a concentration around 30,000 mg/m³ if they remain in the cloud for over two minutes.

Various CS formulations were standardized during the Vietnam War. CS1 was a micropulverized (average particle size, less than ten microns) free-flowing powder consisting of 95 percent CS with 5 percent silica aerogel, a powdered desiccating agent. The aerogel prevented coagulation, increased fluidity and decreased the rate of agent hydrolysis. Unlike the untreated agent, CS1 caused persistent contamination that would re-aerosolize when disturbed, causing respiratory and eye irritation. It could remain effective for up to seven days in the open environment and up to fourteen days in a dry, enclosed space like a tunnel or bunker.

CS2 was the same micropulverized powdered agent in CS1 that was also treated with hexamethyldisilazane. This additive made the agent even more resistant to hydrolysis than CS1, and under ideal conditions it remained effective for almost thirty days. It was so resistant to wetting that even when the aerosol settled on a body of water, any agitation, such as someone wading or swimming, would regenerate an effective aerosol.

Resources

Brophy, Leo, Wyndham Miles and Rexmond Cohrane, *The Chemical Warfare Service: From Laboratory to Field*. Washington, DC: Government Printing Office, 1968, 71–74.

Compton, James, *Military Chemical and Biological Agents: Chemical and Toxicological Properties*. Caldwell, New Jersey: The Telford Press, 1987, 215–230, 237–244.

Davison, Neil, *The Early History of "Non-Lethal" Weapons*. Bradford Non-Lethal Weapons Research Project Occasional Paper Number 1. Department of Peace Studies, University of Bradford, United Kingdom, December 2006, 7–8.

Ellison, D. Hank, *Handbook of Chemical and Biological Warfare Agents*. 2nd Edition. Boca Raton, Florida: CRC Press, 2008, 416, 419, 435–436.

Sidell, Fredrick, "Riot Control Agents," *Medical Aspects of Chemical and Biological Warfare*. Washington, DC: Office of the Surgeon General, Department of the Army, 1997.

Swearengen, Thomas, *Tear Gas Munitions: An Analysis of Commercial Riot Gas Guns, Tear Gas Projectiles, Grenades, Small Arms Ammunition, and Related Tear Gas Devices.* Springfield, Illinois: Charles C. Thomas, Publisher, 1966, 21–25, 29–33, 526.

United States Army Headquarters, *Employment of Riot Control Agents, Flame, Smoke, and Herbicides in Counterguerrilla Operations, Training Circular No. 3–16.* Washington, DC: Government Printing Office, July 11, 1966, 32.

United States Army Headquarters, "Riot Control Agent," *Flame, Riot Control Agents and Herbicide Operations, Field Manual No. 3–11.* Washington, DC: Government Printing Office, August 19, 1996.

APPENDIX B

US munitions and weapon systems

This Appendix contains descriptions of many of the common US munitions and weapon systems that were in use or under development during the war. Listings are grouped together by general categories and arranged alphabetically by their military designation. If the designation is proceeded by an "X," then the military considered it an experimental item when it was initially sent to Vietnam. In a number of cases, these munitions ultimately became a standard item in the US arsenal and the "X" was dropped. In this Appendix, they are only listed with the experimental designation.

There were three basic methods of dispersing riot-control agents used during the war: spraying them, bursting the container that held them or using hot gases from a burning fuel to aerosolize them. Sprayers used either compressed air or a high-velocity fan system to blow the agent onto the target. The agent was fed into the air stream from a storage hopper that held the bulk material.

The simplest bursting munitions ruptured on impact without an explosive charge. These frangible munitions used thin-walled containers such as paper bags, cardboard boxes or shipping containers, and were usually dropped from helicopters. Although they were the easiest to make, they were also the least effective at producing uniform contamination on the target. Other bursting munitions used a relatively small explosive charge to rupture the container and disperse the contents. The size and placement of the charge in relation to the container of agent determined not only the radius of the agent cloud, but whether it scattered it universally or forced it out of the container in a specific direction. These non-lethal munitions could still pose a fragmentation hazard to individuals who were nearby, depending on the nature of the container and the size of the explosive charge.

Pyrotechnic munitions used an incendiary fuel to produce hot gases that would volatilize the agent and carry it out of the munition. The agent vapors would rapidly coalesce to form tiny, solid particles that traveled downwind along with the smoke produced by the fuel. Some munitions used a small explosive charge to launch pyrotechnic submunitions away from the primary casing and increase the area coverage.

Munitions containing riot-control agents were painted gray with the agent name or military agent symbol marked in red letters on the side. Prior to 1960, the descriptive word "GAS" was also inscribed in red on the body of the munition. After that year, the military began using "RIOT" instead. Munitions were also marked with one red band to indicate that it contained a non-persistent agent formulation or two red bands to indicate the agent was persistent.

The terms "persistent" and "non-persistent" were qualitative expressions of the length of time a chemical agent was expected to remain effective after it was dispersed, and were not used in a technical sense to classify agents. Under typical battlefield conditions, non-persistent agents were expected to lose their effectiveness ten-to-fifteen minutes after being released. If the munition was used in an enclosed or confined area such as a bunker or a tunnel, the persistency was greatly increased. In addition to the chemical characteristics of an agent, its persistence was dependent on the weather, method of dissemination and terrain features of the target.

After 1960, the military also added another colored band to some munitions that used an explosive charge to disperse the agent or scatter the submunitions. A yellow band indicated a high-order explosive charge that might also produce some collateral damage, while a dark red band indicated a low-order charge that was just sufficient to expel the agent or submunition.

Dispersers

Dispersers were sprayer systems developed to deliver a high concentration of powdered agent on either point targets or over a wide area. They could deliver a very large volume of agent within a short time and the concentration of agent within the cloud could easily reach lethal levels. For example, one pound of CS, the equivalent of about five bursting-type M25 grenades, could typically be sprayed out in less than three seconds.

Buffalo Turbine. Initially used to spray herbicides. It was an 800-pound, commercially available sprayer-duster that was mounted on a trailer. A UH-1 helicopter was used to transport the Buffalo Turbine into the jungle. Powered by a four-cycle eighteen-horsepower gasoline engine, it had a turbine blower capable of moving 8,500 cubic feet of air per minute. It could hold up to 100 gallons of bulk powdered agent in the attached hopper and, under favorable conditions, it could spray a cone of agent over 200 feet wide. It used a fourteen-inch diameter polyethylene hose to spray the agent into the entrance of a tunnel.

M2 disperser. A 500-pound, modified commercial crop duster that was mounted on skids and typically transported on a truck or trailer. It was almost five feet long, three feet wide and just over 5.5 feet tall. Powered by a four-cycle 8.5 horsepower gasoline engine, it had a turbine blower capable of moving 5,000 cubic feet of air per minute. It had an attached hopper capable of holding forty pounds of powdered agent, which it could disperse in about two minutes through an eight-inch-diameter rotating nozzle. Crew members used a hand wheel to point the nozzle at the target. A minimum of two attendants were needed to properly operate the M2.

M3 disperser. A backpack unit built around the M2A1 flame-thrower and used with the M9 disperser gun. It was mounted on a tubular frame equipped with shoulder straps. It had twin agent tanks, a pressure tank with regulator and a hose that attached to the M9. Each agent tank could hold up to ten pounds of powdered agent that could be delivered in bursts or in a single continuous stream lasting up to thirty seconds. It was usually discharged a minimum of fifty feet away from the target to prevent the rapid build-up of hazardous concentrations or cause excessive dermal injury. The unit weighed about sixty pounds when full.

M4 disperser. A 160-pound system that was mounted in a helicopter, jeep or truck. It consisted of a pressure tank, regulator and cone-shaped hopper mounted on a tubular framework. It was about 2.5 feet long, two feet wide and four feet tall. The hopper held about 100 pounds of CS1 or 120 pounds of either CN1 or DM1. If the M4 was mounted in a jeep or truck, it only took a single individual using the M9 disperser gun to operate the unit. He could disperse the entire hopper of agent in about two minutes. When mounted in a helicopter, it took a two-man crew in addition to the pilots. The agent was delivered through a hose assembly attached to the landing strut and spread by the rotor wash. In this configuration, it only took about twenty seconds to discharge the entire hopper of agent. At least one of the pilots had to wear a protective mask whenever they were spraying because air currents would sometimes carry agent back into the aircraft.

M5 disperser. A 174-pound system that was mounted in a helicopter, jeep or truck. It consisted of two compressed gas tanks charged to a pressure of about 2,000 pounds per square inch, a regulator and a hopper mounted on a tubular framework. It was about two feet long, two feet wide and four feet tall. The hopper held about fifty pounds of CS. If the M5 was mounted in a jeep or truck, it only took a single individual using the M9 disperser gun to operate the unit. He could disperse the entire hopper of agent in about two minutes. When mounted in a helicopter, it took a two-man crew in addition to the pilots. The agent was delivered through a hose assembly attached to the landing strut and spread by the rotor wash. In this configuration, it only took about twenty seconds to discharge the entire hopper of agent. At least one of the pilots had to wear a protective mask whenever they were spraying because air currents would sometimes carry agent back into the aircraft.

M9 portable irritant disperser gun. A delivery nozzle with two hand grips; the pressure release trigger was part of the rear hand grip. The hose from the disperser unit was attached to the rear end of the gun. Depending on the pressure in the tank of the disperser, the M9 had a range of about forty feet in still air and gave the operator the ability to closely regulate the volume of agent released.

M106 disperser (also known as the "Mity Mite"). A twenty-five-pound, commercially available agricultural backpack sprayer-duster used to force smoke and riot-control agents into enemy tunnel systems. It had a 3.5-horsepower two-cycle gasoline engine capable of moving approximately 450 cubic feet of air per minute at a speed of up to 185 miles per hour. It could hold about ten pounds of powdered agent in the attached polyethylene hopper, which it could disperse in about three minutes. It came with two sections of 3.5-inch-diameter flexible tubing. The shorter two-foot section was used when spraying agents directly from the hopper, while the six-foot section was used to force the tear gas or smoke from grenades deeper into a tunnel. Under optimal conditions, the blower pushed the gas cloud through a tunnel at about fifty feet per minute. Once the tunnel was clear, the longer hose was also used to blow fresh air into the tunnel so that Tunnel Rats could begin searching the system. The M106 was relatively simple to use and only took two hours to train a team on the operation, use and maintenance of the unit.

Mars generator. A 175-pound, modified gas turbine engine capable of moving 4,000 cubic feet of air per minute. Operators used a ten-foot length of flexible metal tubing to direct the air flow into a tunnel. It did not have an attached hopper. Instead, tear agents were drawn into the tube by a system of vacuum feeds attached to external containers of agent. Unlike other blowers used to clear tunnels, the products of combustion from the engine were also exhausted through the flexible metal tubing into the tunnel at a temperature approaching 1,000 degrees Fahrenheit. The extreme heat and toxic byproducts of combustion prevented Tunnel Rats from using the Mars generator to flush a tunnel with fresh air prior to searching the system.

Grenades

Both pyrotechnic and bursting tear-gas grenades were used during the war. A pyrotechnic grenade would lay down a continuous cloud for a short period, usually no more than a couple of minutes, and was more effective in blanketing an area with an aerosol than a bursting-type grenade. However, a bursting grenade was better for creating more intense effects on a point target. For example, in a six-miles-per-hour wind, a typical pyrotechnic grenade would create a cloud about thirty-three feet in diameter that would travel downwind for about eighty feet – whereas a bursting-type grenade would create a denser cloud that was only about fifteen feet wide and would only travel downwind for about fifty feet. An experienced soldier could throw either type of grenade nearly 150 feet. Both types employed time-delay fuses that allowed the grenade to reach its target before it actuated, typically from one-to-five seconds. For certain special application, some grenades contained a longer fuse that would burn for up to fifteen seconds.

The M6 series were pyrotechnic hand grenades filled with a mixture of CN and DM. The agent cloud produced by the M6 caused the immediate lacrimating effects of exposure to CN followed in one or two minutes by the more brutal and long-lasting effects of DM. Not only could these grenades be thrown at a target, they could also be fired from a rifle using an M2A1 grenade adapter. This gave them a significantly greater stand-off range and increased their utility. Grenades were gray with a single red band and red markings.

M6. 2.5 inches in diameter and 4.5 inches tall without the fuze. It weighed about 1.1 pounds and contained approximately 10.25 ounces of pyrotechnic mixture; a blend of equal parts of CN and DM mixed with smokeless powder and a magnesium oxide stabilizer. It had a two-to-three-second delay fuse and burned for up to sixty seconds, with a typical burn time of about thirty-five seconds. When functioning, it produced a yellowish, dirty-white smoke. One disadvantage to this agent blend was that the CN tended to interact chemically with the DM and the agents deteriorated during long storage.

M6A1. Modifications to the M6 consisted of isolating the two agents to prevent their chemical interaction. Each agent was blended with an incendiary fuel and isolated in a metal cup within the grenade body. The CN cup contained about 1.4 ounces of agent intermixed with about 3.5 ounces of incendiary fuel and was placed into the grenade first. The DM cup contained about 2.4 ounces of agent intermixed with about 2.2 ounces of incendiary fuel and was placed on top of the CN cup. The total weight of pyrotechnic mixtures was 9.5 ounces, bringing the gross grenade weight to 1.25 pounds. It also had a one-to-two-second delay fuse and burned for up to sixty seconds, with a typical burn time of about thirty-five seconds.

The M7 series. Pyrotechnic hand grenades filled with either CN or CS. The original M7 was one of the first munitions developed by the Chemical Warfare Service (forerunner of the Chemical Corp) after World War I. Not only could these grenades be thrown at a target, they could also be fired from a rifle using an M2A1 grenade adapter. This gave them a significantly greater stand-off range and increased their utility. Grenades were gray with a single red band and red markings.

M7. First issued around 1935 and was the standard tear-gas grenade until after World War II. It was 2.5 inches in diameter and 4.5 inches tall without the fuse. It weighed seventeen ounces and contained about 10.25 ounces of pyrotechnic mixture: a blend of CN, smokeless powder and magnesium oxide stabilizer. It had a two-to-three-second delay fuse and burned for up to sixty seconds, with a typical burn time of about thirty-five seconds. When functioning, flames would emit from the gas ports and tended to ignite nearby combustible materials. On occasion, it was prone to excessive flaming and even to explode.

M7A1. Modifications to the M7 consisted primarily of changes in the number and locations of the gas ports, and changes in the composition of the pyrotechnic mixture. The incendiary fuel was changed from smokeless powder to a mixture of potassium chlorate, sugar, potassium bicarbonate and diatomaceous earth. The A1 had a two-to-three-second delay fuse and burned for up to sixty seconds, with a typical burn time of about thirty-five seconds. This version was filled with either CN or CS; the fill was identified in red letters on the body of the grenade. The CN version weighed 18.5 ounces and contained about 3.6 ounces of CN intermixed with about 8.9 ounces of incendiary fuel. This modification almost doubled the concentration of CN in the cloud generated by the grenade. The CS version weighed sixteen ounces and contained about 9.7 ounces of pyrotechnic mixture. One disadvantage with this particular formulation was that it deteriorated during long storage, which resulted in excessive flaming when it was used. This defect eventually led to the development of the M7A2.

M7A2. Designed to overcome the decomposition problems of the pyrotechnic mixture in the M7A1. Approximately four ounces of CS was sealed in gelatin capsules and placed in alternating layers with 5.3 ounces of incendiary fuel. It had a two-to-three-second delay fuse and burned for up to sixty seconds, with a typical burn time of thirty-five seconds.

M7A3. Modifications consisted primarily of changes in the pyrotechnic mixture. The A3 contained about four ounces of CS pellets intermixed with about 6.5 ounces of incendiary fuel.

The M25 series. Bursting hand grenades. Various versions were filled with micropulverized CN, DM or CS. The micropulverized contents were identified by adding the number "1" after the standard military code for the agent. The M25 was developed toward the end of World War II for guards at large prisoner-of-war camps, and was the first grenade to employ a micropulverized powdered agent filler. The M26 series grenades were spherical and about 2.9 inches in diameter, approximately the size of a baseball. They had a plastic body so that the fragmentation hazard was minimal. The bursting radius was about fifteen feet. They had a two-second time delay and the maximum effect was achieved if the explosion was timed to occur about three feet above the ground. These grenades were designed for point contamination and not meant for area coverage. The primary differences between the various versions were modifications to the fuze and to the design of the plastic body. The M25 and M25A1 were not painted or marked with any coding system; the M25A2 was gray with a single red band and red markings.

M25. Weighed eight ounces and was filled with about three ounces of CN1 and about 0.3 ounces of a magnesium oxide stabilizer.

M25A1. Modifications to the M25 consisted primarily of changes to the fuze. Although it still weighed about eight ounces, the agent payload was increased to about 3.2 ounces of CN1 with about 0.3 ounces of a magnesium oxide stabilizer.

M25A2. Weighed about 7.25 ounces. Modifications consisted of fuze improvements, changes in the plastic body and changes to the agent fill. The CS1 version was filled with about 1.8 ounces of agent blended with 0.1 ounces of silica aerogel to prevent agglomeration. The DM1 version was filled with about 2.1 ounces of agent blended with 0.18 ounces of silica aerogel.

XM47. A special-purpose pyrotechnic grenade. It contained about 4.2 ounces of CS intermixed with about ten ounces of incendiary fuel. It had a two-to-three-second delay fuse and burned for up to twenty seconds. The discharging exhaust gas caused the grenade to move randomly across the ground preventing anyone from picking it up and throwing it back. The grenade had a rubber body that eliminated fragmentation effects and minimized secondary fire hazards. Under ideal conditions, the initial cloud from the grenade would be about forty-five feet in diameter. Grenades were gray with a single red band and red markings.

XM54. A modified M7A3 grenade equipped with an eight-to-twelve-second delay fuse. The extended delay allowed aircraft utilizing the XM27 dispenser to operate at higher altitudes, up to 1,500 feet. When dropped from this maximum altitude, the grenade began to emit a cloud of CS at about 100 feet above the ground. It could also be fired from a rifle using the M2A1 adapter. Grenades were gray with a single red band and red markings.

XM58. A small grenade developed as a way to avoid the bulk and weight associated with larger, conventional CS grenades. It was 3.6 inches long, 1.3 inches in diameter and weighed only 4.2 ounces. This smaller size and weight allowed individual soldiers to carry a number of the grenades in the pockets of their fatigues. Each grenade only contained about 0.7 ounces of CS intermixed with about 0.8 ounces of incendiary fuel. It had a one-to-three-second delay fuse and burned for up to twenty seconds. The smaller cloud generated by this mixture often eliminated the need for friendly forces to don their protective masks as they broke contact. Its greatest drawback was the single exhaust port located on the bottom of the grenade. If it was submerged in a pool of water or got stuck in the mud, the pyrotechnic mixture would go out. Grenades were gray with a single red band and red markings.

Cartridges

Cartridges for individual weapons gave soldiers the ability to disperse agents on targets with increased accuracy and at ranges beyond the distance they could throw a grenade or even launch one using the M2A1 rifle adaptor. They were especially effective when fired into enclosed areas such as bunkers or caves. Due to their high velocity, they would cause serious injury or even death if someone was struck by one at close range.

XM651E1. A 40-mm tactical round for the M79 grenade launcher. It was slightly longer than a standard M79 round with a flat nose. It contained about

0.74 ounces of CS blended with about 1.1 ounces of incendiary fuel. Upon impact, the pyrotechnic mixture was ignited and a cloud of CS was emitted for approximately twenty-five seconds. Under ideal conditions, the initial gas cloud would be about forty-five feet in diameter. It was accurate out to a range of 650 feet, but area targets could be engaged out to 1,300 feet. It would penetrate three-quarters-of-an-inch of plywood at 650 feet and release its CS payload after penetration. The projectile was gray with one red band and red markings.

XM674 (also known as the "Handy Andy"). A multipurpose munition that could be fired from an M8 flare gun, the M79 grenade launcher (using a plastic adapter) or even by holding it in one hand and striking the base with the other. It looked like an aluminum tube, 8.8 inches long and 1.6 inches in diameter, with a firing cap at one end. It weighed twelve ounces and contained a rubber projectile filled with about 1.8 ounces of CS blended with about 1.8 ounces of incendiary fuel. After the projectile was fired, there was a three-second delay before the pyrotechnic mixture ignited and began emitting CS. It continued to burn for approximately thirty-six seconds and, under ideal conditions, produced an initial gas cloud that was about forty feet in diameter. The distance the weapon shot the projectile was unreliable, but usually on the order of about 230 feet. Coupled with a lack of precision, the XM674 was considered a much less effective munition than the XM651. The tube had one red band and red markings. There was another dark red band on the tube to indicate the small propellant charge used to eject the projectile.

Rockets

E8 launcher. A single-use multiple-rocket launcher designed for use against small area targets. Consisting of a box-like launcher module with an attached firing platform, it was about the size of a backpack and weighed thirty-four pounds. It had padded shoulder straps so that a soldier could carry the unit into combat on his back. The launcher consisted of sixteen tubes, each containing four 35-mm E23 rockets, with a total CS pyrotechnic-mixture payload of about 2.1 pounds. When the weapon was fired, all sixty-four rockets were discharged within one minute in a series of four five-second bursts (sixteen rockets per burst). If the target was in an open area, it took about thirty seconds to build up an incapacitating concentration of tear gas. The launcher could be fired either electrically or manually, and was effective out to a range of 820 feet. The range was adjusted by locking the firing platform into one of six preset firing positions (0°, 27.5°, 40°, 55°, 75° or 90°). The size of the impact area varied with range. Because of the large number of rockets impacting in the same area, the size of the initial cloud was relatively independent of meteorological conditions. The launcher had a label on the backpack located between the two shoulder harnesses with a single red band and red markings.

E23. The projectile fired from the E8 launcher. They were preloaded in the launcher and were not available as individual munitions. Each cartridge consisted of a rubber-covered aluminum canister, a propellant cup and a fuse train. Each contained about 0.5 ounces of CS intermixed with about 0.8 ounces of incendiary fuel. Each cartridge had a five-to-six-second delay fuse that was ignited by the expelling charge. The pyrotechnic mix in each cartridge burned for about fifteen seconds after ignition. These munitions were not marked since they were not available for use outside of the E8 projector.

XM96. A shoulder-fired, fin-stabilized 66-mm tactical rocket. It was twenty-one inches long and had a gross weight of about 3.1 pounds. It contained about 0.5 pounds of CS2 that was dispersed as a particulate cloud when the rocket detonated. The warhead was gray with two red bands and red markings. There was an additional yellow band indicating the high-explosive charge.

XM99. A 2.75-inch rocket fired from the M3 rocket pods mounted on helicopter gunships. It was twenty-seven inches long, had a gross weight of about 7.1 pounds and was filled with submunitions containing a total payload of 2.6 pounds of CS pyrotechnic mixture. When the rocket exploded, the submunitions were ignited and scattered over the target. The warhead was gray with one red band and red markings. There was an additional dark red band indicating the low explosive charge.

Artillery and mortars

XM629. Fired from a 105-mm howitzer. The entire cartridge was thirty inches long and weighed forty-two pounds; the projectile itself weighed thirty-two pounds. It was equipped with a variable time fuze that could be set for impact or a time delay. A small charge ejected four canisters filled with a pyrotechnic mixture out of the base of the projectile; each canister contained about 5.2 ounces of CS intermixed with about eight ounces of incendiary fuel. The pyrotechnic mix burned for about sixty seconds and, under ideal conditions, produced an initial gas cloud that was about sixty-five feet in diameter. It had a maximum range of 8.5 miles with an optimum air-burst height of between 300 and 500 feet. The projectile was gray with one red band and red markings.

XM630. Fired from a 4.2-inch mortar. It was equipped with a variable time fuze that could be set for impact, a time delay, or preset altitude of 360 feet above ground level. A small charge ejected four canisters filled with a pyrotechnic mixture out of the base of the round; each canister contained about 6.4 ounces of CS intermixed with about 9.6 ounces of incendiary fuel. The pyrotechnic mixture would burn for about sixty seconds, and under ideal conditions produced an initial gas cloud that was about sixty-five feet in diameter. It had the same ballistic characteristics as a standard high-explosive round used by the mortar. It had a maximum range of 3.5 miles with an optimum air-burst height of between 300 and 500 feet. With the proper fuze settings, it was capable of penetrating a triple canopy jungle. The projectile was gray with one red band and red markings.

XM631. Fired from a 155-mm howitzer. It was two feet long and weighed ninety-seven pounds. It was equipped with a variable time fuze that could be set for impact or a time delay. A small charge ejected four canisters filled with a pyrotechnic mixture out of the base of the projectile; each canister contained about twelve ounces of CS intermixed with about seventeen ounces of incendiary fuel. The pyrotechnic mix burned for about ninety seconds. It had the same ballistic characteristics as a standard high-explosive round used by the gun. It had a maximum range of just over nine miles with an optimum air-burst height of between 300 and 500 feet. The projectile was gray with one red band and red markings.

Bombs and aerial delivery systems

BLU–39 bomblet. The standard submunition for a number of air force cluster bombs. They were preloaded in the dispensers and were not available as individual munitions. These bomblets were approximately the size of a D-cell battery (2.49 inches long and 1.25 inches in diameter) and weighed about two ounces. They contained about 1.3 ounces of a pyrotechnic CS mixture consisting of 0.5 ounces of CS intermixed with 0.8 ounces of incendiary fuel. Each bomblet had a five-to-six-second delay fuse that was ignited by the expelling charge. The pyrotechnic mix in each cartridge burned for about twenty seconds after ignition. The discharging exhaust gas was forced out of the bomblet through an off-center port that caused the canister to move randomly across the ground. This action further dispersed the bomblets throughout the target area and made it difficult for anyone to pick them up or kick them away. Bomblets had a single red band and red markings.

BLU–52B chemical bomb. A modified 750-pound class fire bomb (BLU–1C/B series) casing filled with 260 pounds of CS1. It could be forcibly ejected from high-speed aircraft flying at low levels. The casing was twelve feet long, nearly nineteen inches in diameter and made of thin-skinned aluminum. It did not have a bursting charge but simply ruptured on impact. It had a red band on a gray background at the center of the bomb as well as on each end. When the bomb was filled with CS2 instead of CS1, the designation was changed to BLU–52A/B.

CBU–19/A aircraft dispenser. A modified XM165 canister cluster designed to be dropped by planes flying at altitudes of less than 600 feet. For aerodynamic reasons, high-speed jets could not carry this munition.

CBU–30/A aircraft dispenser. A non-expendable multi-component system consisting of an SUU–13/A disperser, forty CDU–12 submunitions and 1,280 BLU–39 bomblets. The gross weight of the entire system was 750 pounds. The SUU–13/A was a downward-ejecting disperser that remained attached to the aircraft. It held the CDU–12 submunitions, which were cylinders about 9.4 inches long and 4.6 inches in diameter. Each of these submunitions was filled with thirty-two BLU–39 bomblets. When triggered, an electrical firing system ejected the submunitions from the dispenser and ignited the timing train for both the submunitions and the bomblets. The submunitions exploded before they hit the ground, scattering the bomblets over a wide area. The dispensers were particularly effective against linear targets. For example, the typical delivery pattern from a jet flying at about 50 miles per hour at an altitude of 600 feet covered an area 200 feet wide and 3,300 feet long. Because of the accuracy of this delivery system, these dispensers were often used against targets in very close proximity to friendly forces. It could be mounted on both planes and jets, and could be used at speeds approaching 600 miles per hour. The primary limitation on the system was that it could not be used at altitudes greater than 600 feet or the bomblets would burn out before they reached the ground. It had a single red band and red markings.

E49. The submunition contained in the E158 series canister clusters. They were preloaded into the clusters and were not available as individual munitions. The E49 was approximately the size of a D-cell battery (2.49 inches long and 1.25 inches in diameter) and contained about 0.7 ounces of pyrotechnic CS mixture. Each submunition had a five-to-six-second delay fuse that was ignited by the expelling charge. In addition to the expelling charge that scattered the submunitions over the target area, the initial discharge of exhaust gas generated when the fuse ignited the pyrotechnic mixture propelled the submunition an additional forty feet, aiding in the dispersal of the submunitions. After this initial bound, the discharging exhaust gas continued to cause the E49s to move erratically across the ground, further dispersing them throughout the target area and making it difficult for anyone to pick them up or kick them away. The pyrotechnic mix in each cartridge burned for up to nineteen seconds after ignition. The E49 submunitions were heavy enough to penetrate a jungle canopy and disperse their contents at ground level, but not heavy enough to seriously injure a soldier if they were struck by one as it fell. They had a single red band and red markings.

E158 canister cluster. 2.5 feet long, weighed fifty pounds and could be mounted to either planes or helicopters. They could be dropped from any altitudes between 700 and 3,000 feet, and at speeds up to 400 miles per hour. The cluster consisted of eight tubular modules that were heat-sealed together to form a single unit. Each module contained thirty-three E49 submunitions for a total of 264 units per cluster, which was equivalent to over eleven pounds of CS pyrotechnic mixture. Operators used either an altimeter or a time delay initiator to activate an explosive train that ruptured the cluster and scattered the submunitions in a roughly circular pattern. Under ideal conditions, the initial cloud from a canister cluster would cover approximately 7,000 square feet, a circle approximately 300 feet in diameter. The recommended load for a UH–1 helicopter was eight canister clusters; one unit on each side of the aircraft with six replacements. In addition to the pilots, helicopter operations required a crew of three to efficiently arm, release and reload the canister units. Many considered the E158 the best system for aerial delivery of CS used during the Vietnam War. It had a single red band at the center of the cluster and red markings.

E158R2 canister cluster. 2.5 feet long, weighed forty-seven pounds and functioned the same as the E158 canister cluster except that it could be dropped from altitudes as high as 4,000 feet. It had a single red band at the center of the cluster and red markings.

E159. 5.2 feet long, weighed 130 pounds and could be mounted to either planes or helicopters. It consisted of a frame that fit over and clamped together either two E158 or two E158R2 canister clusters. When the pilot activated the unit, an explosive bolt assembly opened clamps allowing the canister clusters to fall free of the frame. The E159 could also be operated manually by simply pushing the unit out the door of a helicopter. In this mode, an arming wire attached to the explosive bolt pulled the firing pin as the frame fell away from the aircraft. Although the E49 submunitions in the canister clusters would not seriously injure a soldier if they were struck by them, if the E159 was released manually, the falling frame, which weighed about thirty pounds, posed a serious risk to friendly forces on the ground. Under ideal conditions, the initial gas cloud generated by the submunitions would cover approximately 97,000 square feet, a circle approximately 350 feet in diameter.

Troop landing smoke screen system (TLSS). An adapter kit for the M3 rocket pods mounted on helicopter gunships, which enabled them to eject pyrotechnic riot-control grenades (M6, M7 series or XM54). First the rocket pods had to be reversed in their mounts so that they would discharge the grenades backward along the helicopter's flight path. Then a conversion plate was clamped over the end of the pod that inserted a spring ejector and an electrically controlled release gate into every launcher tube. Once installed, each of the twenty-four launcher tubes was loaded with seven grenades, for a total capacity of 168 grenades. When they were fired, operators had the option of ejecting the contents of one of the tubes or having the system automatically release the contents of the entire rocket pod. In the automatic mode, it took about ten seconds for the system to sequentially eject all twenty-four launcher tubes. Once expended, it would take two men approximately one hour to reload a pod. The type of grenade dictated the maximum operating altitude for the system; for M6 and M7 grenades, it was 500 feet, whereas the XM54 grenades could be released up to 1,500 feet above a target. In either case, the maximum speed for the aircraft was limited to 115 miles per hour. When it was no longer needed, the adapter kit was easy to remove and the rocket pod could be quickly restored to its original configuration.

XM15 canister cluster. Similar to the E158R2 canister cluster except that the mechanical time fuze, which could be set for up to a ten-second delay, was permanently attached to the unit. It had a single red band at the center of the cluster and red markings.

XM27 dispenser system. An SUU–14/A dispenser filled with seventy-two XM54 grenades. It was 6.75 feet long and weighed 122 pounds full (fifty pounds empty). The SUU–14/A was a rearward-ejecting disperser that remained attached to the aircraft. It consisted of a frame supporting six 2.75-inch diameter aluminum tubes. Each tube contained twelve grenades that had been loaded with their pins removed. The diameter of the tube kept the safety levers, or spoons, of the grenades in place. When the pilot activated the weapon, a piston in each tube pushed the grenades out the rear of the dispenser. Once free of the constraints of the tube, the spoon would fly free and the grenade fuse would be ignited. The optimal operating altitude of 1,500 feet was based on the time delay of the grenade fuse. This dispenser could be mounted on both planes and helicopters, and could be used at speeds up to 350 miles per hour. They were particularly effective against linear targets. For example, an aircraft flying at 100 miles per hour at an altitude of 1,500 feet would deposit a line of grenades approximately 900 feet long. This meant that a grenade would land every thirteen feet along the flight path and create dense overlapping clouds. The XM27 could not be reloaded in the field and had to be retuned through channels to be rearmed.

XM28 bagged agent dispenser. A rectangular aluminum alloy container fitted with a stabilizing tail fin and carried under a UH–1 series helicopter. The body of the container consisted of nineteen compartments, each equipped with an electronically operated trapdoor. Every compartment held approximately 110 paper bags, each filled with about eight ounces of micropulverized CS2 powder. When a trapdoor was opened, the bags fell to the ground and burst on impact, creating a significant dust cloud and leaving a high level of residual contamination. The operator could elect to open a single trapdoor or all nineteen at once. If an operator opened all nineteen trapdoors at once while traveling at eighty miles per hour at an altitude of 1,500 feet, the deluge of bags would contaminate an area about 100 feet wide and 700 feet long.

XM54 smoke generating system. A pump system that injected fog oil from a fifty-gallon reservoir into the engine exhaust of a helicopter to produce a dense screening smoke. Some units added tear agent CNB (a mixture of 10 percent CN in a fifty/fifty solution of carbon tetrachloride and benzene) to the oil in the reservoir to produce a tear-gas cloud.

XM165. A frame that fit over and clamped together two XM15 canister clusters. It was similar in appearance and operation to the E159 canister cluster except it had an improved fuze.

XM920E2 fuze and burster system. An earlier version of the XM925. Problems with the design of the fuze caused the drum to burst at erratic heights.

XM925 fuze and burster system. commercially manufactured fuze and burster for the improvised CS drum munition (see "Drum bomb" under "Improvised munitions"). It consisted of an impact fuze, burster assembly and drum cover that fit over the standard fifty-five-gallon drum used to ship bulk

CS to Vietnam. A lanyard attached to the fuze armed the system when the drum was dropped from a helicopter. Another safety feature incorporated into the commercial system was a vane assembly that had to rotate a minimum of twenty times before the unit could detonate. Along with improved safety, the XM925 also had a significantly lower malfunction rate than the units that soldiers fabricated in the field.

Improvised munitions

A wide variety of field-expedient munitions were created by soldiers during the war. They ranged in size from items that could be thrown, to devices that had to be rolled out the back of a helicopter. Some were exceptionally rudimentary and could be fabricated in a matter of minutes, while others required a considerable amount of preparation. The devices included in this section are examples of various popular designs. In some cases, they were so effective that the military adopted them on a broader scale and had them manufactured commercially in the United States, then shipped to Vietnam.

Bag charge. Made from two eight-pound shipping bags of CS tied or taped together. A quarter-pound of C4 plastic explosive, equipped with a blasting cap and time fuse, was placed between the bags and secured with tape. It was used as an area contamination weapon.

BFOG (box full of grenades). An air-dropped weapon developed by the 4th Infantry Division to supplement the short supply of canister cluster munitions (e.g. the E158). It consisted of a plywood box filled with twenty-five M7A3 grenades arranged so that the safety levers, or spoons, were held in place. Then the pins were pulled from the grenades. The box was sealed and wrapped with detonating cord. A short delay fuse was ignited just before it was dropped from a helicopter. When the cord exploded, it ruptured the box, scattering the grenades and allowing the spoons to fly off. The grenades landed in a roughly circular pattern about 150 feet in diameter and generated a gas cloud that would cover an area about the size of a football field. Another version of this device eliminated the detonating cord, simply scattering the grenades when the box hit the ground and broke apart. This design delivered a much more concentrated gas cloud on a point target.

BR1A (big red 1 alpha). An air-dropped weapon developed by the 1st Infantry Division to supplement the short supply of canister cluster munitions (e.g. the E158). It consisted of two modules, each filled with nineteen M7A3 grenades. The grenades were positioned on a precut plywood base and wrapped with nylon line so that the safety levers, or spoons, were secured in place. The nylon line was also threaded through an M22 line cutter with a time-delay fuse. Once the spoons were secure, the pins were pulled from the grenades. One of the modules was stacked on the other and a plywood top completed the device. A lanyard pulled the igniter on the two line cutters when the BR1A was thrown from a helicopter. The optimum height to deploy a BR1A with a ten-second delay fuse was about 1,900 feet. The fall scattered the grenades and the resulting gas cloud covered an area nearly equal to that generated by the standard M158 canister cluster.

BURB (bunker use restriction bomb). Developed in 1969 by the 1st Cavalry Division as a way to contaminate a bunker complex or tunnel entrance. In the original design, the cardboard shipping container for a 2.75-inch rocket warhead was filled with about one pound of CS powder. The explosion from a standard blasting cap was sufficient to rupture the container and disperse the agent. Although a very effective design, the shipping containers were somewhat bulky and this limited the number of devices a soldier could carry with him into the jungle. A variation that could be carried in greater numbers was made from a free-fall water bag – a heavy-duty container made from eight individual plastic bags nested within each other that was simply dropped from a hovering helicopter to resupply troops in the field with fresh water. After a single inner-layer of the bag was pulled free, dried and filled approximately half-full with CS powder, the top was folded over and tied in a knot. Unfortunately, the knot was not always tied properly and the agent would leak out. When the soldier opened his backpack, he paid the price for his error. The army eventually contracted with a supplier to manufacture this variation of the BURB. These prefabricated munitions were made from aluminized-cloth and consisted of two CS2-filled packets separated by a heat seam. The seam gave soldiers the option of cutting the BURB into two smaller munitions. About 2,300 of the prefabricated BURBs were ultimately shipped to Vietnam.

Can bombs. A simple frangible device made by cutting small cans in half, taping them back together and then filling them with CS. They were dropped from a helicopter and split open when they hit the ground, creating a small zone of very heavy contamination. These devices were typically used on high-traffic areas or enemy base camps. Depending on the type of CS used, the contamination could persist for days or even weeks.

Drum bombs. Constructed from fifty-five-gallon CS shipping drums, each of which contained ten eight-pound bags of bulk CS powder. There were two common arming systems that soldiers used to rupture the container and disperse the agent. One method involved tapping a length of detonation cord around the ends and down the sides of the drum. When the drum was rolled out the open back door of a Chinook helicopter, a lanyard pulled the pin on a fused blasting cap that detonated the cord as the drums fell to the ground. The other method was to place a fused M10 destructor – a high-explosive adapter used to destroy deteriorated or abandoned artillery ammunition – into the drum. Soldiers ignited a time-delay fuse just before rolling the drum out of the helicopter. Ideally the drums exploded just above the jungle canopy, distributing the agent over a wide area. These improvised bombs allowed soldiers to quickly and accurately place a large volume of powdered agent on an enemy position.

Depending on the weather and type of CS used, the contamination would persist for days or even weeks. The army eventually formalized this weapon by developing a burster system specifically designed to fit the shipping drum. The XM925 bursters were more reliable and effective than either of the improvised arming systems.

Tunnel contamination bombs. Used by Tunnel Rats and the Army Corp of Engineers to prevent the enemy from reoccupying a tunnel. Different units developed a number of variations on the same basic principal. For example, the 1st Infantry Division simply ran detonating cord throughout the tunnel system and then placed the eight-pound shipping bags of CS on top of the cord at various intervals. The 173rd Airborne Brigade, on the other hand, transferred the agent into smaller three-pound bags and pre-wrapped them with detonating cord before carrying them into a tunnel. They felt that these were easier to handle in the confines of the narrow passageways. The Australian Tunnel Ferrets preferred to fill old ration cans with CS and used a quarter-pound stick of TNT primed with an electric blasting cap. All of these configurations were very effective at contaminating tunnels and, for at least a short time, preventing the enemy from reentering the systems.

Resources

Hay, John H., Jr., *Tactical and Materiel Innovations*. Washington, DC: Government Printing Office, 1974, 37–38.

Headquarters, United States Military Assistance Command, Vietnam, *Vietnam Lessons Learned Number 77: Fire Support Coordination in the Republic of Vietnam*. May 20, 1970, C57–C60.

Hedden, E.M. and D.C. Hawkins, *CBU-30/A Incapacitating Munitions System, AFATL-TR-67–178*. Air Force Armament Laboratory, Eglin Air Force Base, Florida, October 1967.

Lindberg, Kip, "The Use of Riot Control Agents During the Vietnam War." *Army Chemical Review* (January–June 2007), 51–55.

Parsch, Andreas, *Designations of U.S. Aeronautical and Support Equipment*. June 23, 2006. www.designation-systems.net/usmilav/aerosupport.html#_ASETDS_Component_Listings_Alpha. January 22, 2008.

Robinson, Julian Perry, *The Rise of CB Weapons*. Stockholm: Almqvist & Wiksell, 1971, 192–193.

Swearengen, Thomas F., *Tear Gas Munitions: An Analysis of Commercial Riot Gas Guns, Tear Gas Projectiles, Grenades, Small Arms Ammunition, and Related Tear Gas Devices*. Springfield, Illinois: Charles C Thomas, Publisher, 1966.

Tolson, John J., *Airmobility: 1961–1971*. Washington, DC: Government Printing Office, 1973, 141.

United States Army Headquarters, *Military Chemistry and Chemical Agents, Training Manual No. 3–215*. With changes 1 and 2. Washington, DC: Government Printing Office, December 1963, 6.

United States Army Headquarters, "Riot Control Agents, Equipment, and Munitions," in *Employment of Riot Control Agents, Flame, Smoke, and Herbicides in Counterguerrilla*

Operations, Training Circular No. 3–16. Washington, DC: Government Printing Office, July 11, 1966.

United States Army Headquarters, *Chemical Reference Handbook, Field Manual No. 3–8.* With changes 1–5. Washington, DC: Government Printing Office, January 1967, 21, 23.

United States Army Headquarters, "Riot Control Agents, Equipment, and Munitions," in *Employment of Riot Control Agents, Flame, Smoke, Antiplant Agents and Personnel Detectors in Counterguerrilla Operations, Training Circular No. 3–16.* Washington, DC: Government Printing Office, April 9, 1969; Reprint, Stockholm: Swedish Medical Aid Committee for Vietnam, 1970.

United States Army Headquarters, "Riot Control Agents," in *Civil Disturbances, Field Manual No. 19–15.* Washington, DC: Government Printing Office, November 25, 1985.

United States Army Headquarters, *Army Ammunition Data Sheets for Grenades, Technical Manual No. 43–0001–29.* With Change 1. Washington, DC: Government Printing Office, June 30, 1994.

United States Army Headquarters, "Ammunition Color Codes," Appendix A in *Unexploded Ordnance (UXO) Procedures, Field Manual No. 21–16.* Washington, DC: Government Printing Office, August 30, 1994.

United States Army Headquarters, "Riot Control Agent Munitions and Delivery Systems," Appendix B in *Flame, Riot Control Agents and Herbicide Operations, Field Manual No. 3–11.* Washington, DC: Government Printing Office, August 19, 1996.

United States Army Headquarters, "Obsolete Hand Grenades," Appendix E in *Grenades and Pyrotechnic Signals, Field Manual No. 23–30.* Washington, DC: Government Printing Office, September 1, 2000.

APPENDIX C

Viet Cong improvised munitions

In addition to the limited stockpile of chemical munitions that trickled down from North Vietnam, the Viet Cong fabricated a variety of improvised devices. Some were simply modifications to existing ammunition such as replacing a portion of the high-explosive charge with CS powder. Others were more original. This appendix contains descriptions of some of the more common items encountered by American forces.

Frangible grenade. Essentially glass bottles fitted with wooden handles to facilitate throwing and filled with a liquid material that caused intense eye and nose irritation.

Bursting grenade. Made from a can about three inches long, 2.6 inches in diameter and filled with CS powder. A grooved wooden handle was attached to one end to facilitate throwing. It weighed just over three-quarters of a pound. A pull-style fuse igniter would light a short piece of fuse leading to a blasting cap inserted into a TNT charge. When the grenade detonated, it had a bursting radius of about twenty feet. The grenade was painted green and had a red band. The characters "CS-1" or "HI" were painted in either red or white on the side of the grenade.

Land mine. Made by placing an explosive charge in a burlap bag filled with ten-to-fifteen pounds of CS powder. The mines could be either command detonated or rigged as a booby trap.

Flying mine. A directional device made by placing a box or drum filled with agent and a burster charge in a hole that was dug so it pointed in the general direction of the target. A small propelling charge in the bottom of the hole launched the container at the target and a time-delay fuze mechanism, much like the one used in a hand grenade, set off the burster charge. As the container flew out of the hole, a wire that ran from the pin in the fuze to a sturdy object near the mouth of the hole was stretched tight and eventually pulled the pin. The burster charge detonated after a short delay and dispersed the CS powder. Some of these devices had a range of over 800 feet.

CS projectile. A fin-stabilized munition somewhat resembling a mortar round. It was made from galvanized tin and was about twelve inches long and 2.5 inches in diameter. The inside and outside of the body were coated with wax to retard moisture. Inside the body of the projectile were three bags of CS containing a total payload of about a quarter-pound of agent. It was fired from some form of tube launcher system.

Modified rocket-propelled grenade (RPG) mine. Made by removing the grenade fuze and cutting off the rocket shaft just behind the warhead. A hole was drilled into the stand-off space in the nose of the warhead and it was filled with about one-third of a pound of CS powder. A blasting cap was used to detonate the existing explosive charge contained in the warhead and scatter the agent. The mine could be either command detonated or rigged as a booby trap.

Modified 82-mm mortar round. Made from a standard 82-mm high-explosive round. The guerrillas removed about 60 percent of the explosive and replaced it with CS powder. The steel body of the round still produced a significant number of hazardous fragments when the remaining high explosives detonated. Since modifying the bursting charge reduced the overall weight of the munition and changed its ballistic properties, the Viet Cong also added weights to the round so they could continue using the standard firing tables for the mortar. To identify these modified rounds, they painted the characters "CS-1" on the side and a red strip near the top.

Modified LPO-50 flame-thrower. Instead of thickened fuel, the cylinders were filled with an irritating fluid. This flame-thrower resembled a rifle with a hose running from the stock of the weapon to three tanks worn on the back of the gunner. Each cylinder held nearly a gallon of agent. Unlike American flame-throwers that used a separate compressed-air cylinder, it used an explosive propellant charge to generate the pressure, over 400 pounds per square inch, to push the liquid out of the barrel of the weapon to a range of about 200 feet.

Resources

Headquarters 2nd Brigade, 25th Infantry Division, *Operational Report – Lessons Learned For Period 1 November 1970 to 28 February 1971*, 24. March 16, 1971, http://25thaviation.org/history/id732.htm, October 10, 2008.

Headquarters, United States Military Assistance Command, Vietnam, "Technical Intelligence Bulletin, First Edition," dated May 22, 1966, in *Records of the Military Assistance Command Vietnam, Part 2. Classified Studies from the Combined Intelligence Center Vietnam, 1965–1973*, edited by Robert Lester (Central Michigan University Library, Frederick, Maryland: University Publications of America, 1988), microfilm, Reel 29, F290–F294.

Headquarters, United States Military Assistance Command, Vietnam, "VC/NVA CBR (First Update)," dated February 16, 1969, in *Records of the Military Assistance Command Vietnam, Part 2. Classified Studies from the Combined Intelligence Center Vietnam, 1965–1973*, edited by Robert Lester (Central Michigan University Library, Frederick, Maryland: University Publications of America, 1988), microfilm, Reel 22, F821–F871.

Headquarters, United States Military Assistance Command, Vietnam, "VC/NVA CBR Equipment Identification Guide," dated April 1, 1971, in *Records of the Military Assistance Command Vietnam, Part 2. Classified Studies from the Combined Intelligence Center Vietnam, 1965–1973*, edited by Robert Lester (Central Michigan University Library, Frederick, Maryland: University Publications of America, 1988), microfilm, Reel 30, F272–F355.

APPENDIX D

Protective masks

Masks used by the United States

Listings are arranged alphabetically by their military designation. If the designation is proceeded by an "X," then the military considered it an experimental item when it was sent to Vietnam.

M14 series tank mask. First adopted in 1953. It had a molded black rubber facepiece with a single plastic lens, a cable that connected a microphone in the mask to the tank communication system, and a corrugated hose that allowed the wearer to use either a filter canister or to connect to the collective air purification system in the tank. A redesigned facepiece along with other improvements resulted in the army adopting the M14A1 in 1960 and the M14A2 in 1961.

M17 series mask. First adopted in 1959 and the primary mask used by soldiers during the Vietnam War. It had a black rubber facepiece with twin rounded semi-triangular eye pieces that could be fitted with optical inserts to accommodate soldiers who wore glasses and a voice emitter in the front to improve communication. It came with a detachable hood that provided extra protection to the head and neck. This attachment was rarely worn by soldiers during the war. A key innovation over earlier designs was the twin filter elements that were mounted inside the cheeks of the mask that eliminated the need to produce both a left-handed and right-handed version. Unfortunately, this feature also made it difficult and somewhat time-consuming to change the filters. In 1966, the army adopted the M17A1. This version had a drinking tube so that soldiers did not have to remove their masks to drink from their canteens. Another change was the addition of a resuscitation tube that allowed a soldier to give "mouth-to-mouth" to a fellow soldier in a contaminated environment.

When not in use, the mask was stored in the M15 carrier, which was usually worn on the left hip.

M24 aircraft mask. First adopted in 1962. It was a modified version of the M14 tank mask that incorporated several special features necessary for pilots, including an antiglare cover for the eye lens, a communication cable configured for aviation systems, and a corrugated hose that allowed the wearer to use either a filter canister or to connect to the aircraft oxygen supply. It could be fitted with optical inserts to accommodate individuals who wore glasses.

M25 series tank mask. A further evolution of the M14 mask series that was adopted in 1963. The primary modifications were a newer microphone system and the ability to attach optical inserts to accommodate individuals who wore glasses. The M25A1 incorporated minor changes in the facepiece and harness assembly.

XM28 riot-control agent protective mask. Available from 1968. It was lightweight and constructed of silicon rubber, which made it fit the contours of the face better than the natural rubber used in the M17 mask. Like the M17, the filters were mounted in the cheeks of the mask. However, the filter elements did not provide universal protection; they were only effective against riot-control agents. Two key shortcomings of this mask were an inability to attach optical inserts that would have allowed soldiers who wore glasses to see better while wearing the mask and the lack of a voice emitter. This caused the mask to muffle the wearer's voice and made verbal communication a problem.

Masks used by the North Vietnamese Army and the Viet Cong

The North Vietnamese primarily used masks supplied by other Communist countries, while the Viet Cong typically relied on captured American masks or those that they improvised from readily available local items. The North Vietnamese used variations of the same mask that were manufactured in both the former Soviet Union and Communist China. Only the Soviet nomenclature is used in this appendix.

Soviet ShM-1-style mask. A helmet-style protective mask made of rubber and fitted with two circular glass eyepieces. It had a combined headpiece and facepiece that covered the entire head. Since it covered the ears and did not incorporate a voice emitter, it was almost impossible for the wearer to communicate with other soldiers. The filter canister could be either attached directly to the mask or to the mask via a corrugated tube so that the filter could be worn on the belt.

Soviet K-style mask. This consisted of a facepiece made of soft, flexible rubber that was held on the head by a harness system. Since it did not cover the ears and incorporated a voice emitter it was much easier for the wearer to communicate with others. This mask was usually issued to officers, senior non-commissioned officers and radio operators.

Chinese PK-1-style mask. This consisted of a quarter-face respirator with a filter canister that screwed directly into the base of the mask. The wearer was also issued a separate pair of goggles for eye protection.

Pneumatic mask. A flat rubber sheet fitted with two circular eyepieces that was held on the head by a harness system. After donning the mask, the user would inflate it to insure a proper fit. A charcoal filter canister was attached to the mask in front of the nose. The country of origin is not known.

North Vietnamese KT-69 mask. This consisted of a cloth facepiece, a gauze filter and two plastic eyepieces. Instead of attempting to filter the agents from the air, the gauze filter was soaked with ether just prior to use to counter the effects of the tear gas. The mask was issued with twelve ampoules of the anesthetic. This mask is significant in that it was the first mask to be given a numerical designation by the North Vietnamese Army.

Mouth bandage. An improvised mask used by the Viet Cong that consisted of layers of gauze and cotton soaked with a sodium carbonate solution just prior to use. A more advanced version incorporated a small bag of activated charcoal sewn between the layers of gauze. These masks were held on with rubber bands.

Field-fabricated mask. An improvised mask used by the Viet Cong that was constructed from either a transparent plastic bag or parachute fabric with eyepieces made from clear plastic. In either case a filter element, consisting of a layer of activated charcoal sewn between sheets of fabric, was sewn over an opening cut into the mask where it fit over the nose and mouth. All of the holes made while sewing the mask were filled with glue so that the wearer could only draw air into the mask through the filter element. A rubber band or a drawstring was used to seal the mask around the neck.

Resources

Carey, Christopher T., "New Departures in Design: The 1960s and 1970s," in *U.S. Chemical and Biological Defense Respirators: An Illustrated History*. Atglen, PA: Schiffer Publishing Ltd., 1998.

Headquarters, United States Military Assistance Command, Vietnam, "Technical Intelligence Bulletin, First Edition," dated May 22, 1966, in *Records of the Military Assistance Command Vietnam, Part 2. Classified Studies from the Combined Intelligence Center Vietnam, 1965–1973*, edited by Robert Lester (Central Michigan University Library, Frederick, Maryland: University Publications of America, 1988), microfilm, Reel 29, F295–F297.

Headquarters, United States Military Assistance Command, Vietnam, "VC/NVA CBR Capability in the Republic of Vietnam (First Update)," dated February 16, 1969, in *Records of the Military Assistance Command Vietnam, Part 2. Classified Studies from the Combined Intelligence Center Vietnam, 1965–1973*, edited by Robert Lester (Central Michigan University Library, Frederick, Maryland: University Publications of America, 1988), microfilm, Reel 22, F839–F843.

Headquarters, United States Military Assistance Command, Vietnam, "VC/NVA CBR

Equipment Identification Guide," dated April 1, 1971, in *Records of the Military Assistance Command Vietnam, Part 2. Classified Studies from the Combined Intelligence Center Vietnam, 1965–1973*, edited by Robert Lester (Central Michigan University Library, Frederick, Maryland: University Publications of America, 1988), microfilm, Reel 30, F278–F293.

Robinson, Julian Perry, *The Rise of CB Weapons*. Stockholm: Almqvist & Wiksell, 1971, 191.

Smart, Jeffery K., *History of the Army's Protective Mask*. NBC Defense Systems, Aberdeen Proving Ground, Maryland, undated (circa 2000).

United States Army Headquarters, *Employment of Riot Control Agents, Flame, Smoke, Antiplant Agents and Personnel Detectors in Counterguerrilla Operations, Training Circular No. 3–16*. Washington, DC: Government Printing Office, April 9, 1969; Reprint, Stockholm: Swedish Medical Aid Committee for Vietnam, 1970, 17.

NOTES

1 Introduction

1 Brad Knickerbocker, "The Fuzzy Ethics of Nonlethal Weapons," *The Christian Science Monitor*, February 14, 2003, 2; Brad Knickerbocker, "Can New Arms Cut Casualties?" *The Christian Science Monitor*, March 11, 2003, 1; Kerry Boyd, "Rumsfeld Wants to Use Riot Control Agents in Combat," *Arms Control Today* 33 (March 2003). Online version on August 19, 2008 at www.armscontrol.org/act/2003_03/nonlethal_mar03; Dave Eberhart, "The US's Tear Gas Quandary in Iraq," *NewsMax.com*, April 4, 2003. Online version on July 7, 2007 at www.newsmax.com/archives/articles/2003/4/3/214326.shtml.

2 United States Army Headquarters, *Potential Military Chemical/Biological Agents and Compounds,* Field Manual No. 3–9 (Washington, DC: Government Printing Office, December 1990), 47–66; Fredrick R. Sidell, Ernest T. Takafuji and David R. Franz, eds., *Medical Aspects of Chemical and Biological Warfare* (Washington, DC: Office of the Surgeon General, Department of the Army, 1997), 288–294, 308–324.

3 Good sources of information on the history of chemical warfare from World War I through the Vietnam War are: Julian Perry Robinson, *The Rise of CB Weapons* (Stockholm: Almqvist & Wiksell, 1971); Ludwig Fritz Haber, *The Poisonous Cloud: Chemical Warfare in the First World War* (Oxford: Clarendon Press, 1986); Donald Richter, *Chemical Soldiers: British Gas Warfare in World War I* (Lawrence, Kansas: University Press of Kansas, 1992); Sebastian Balfour, *Deadly Embrace: Morocco and the Road to the Spanish Civil War* (Oxford: Oxford University Press, 2002); Peter Williams and David Wallace, *Unit 731: Japan's Secret Biological Warfare in World War II* (New York: Free Press, 1989); Sheldon H. Harris, *Factories of Death: Japanese Biological Warfare, 1932–45, and the American Cover-up* (London: Routledge, 1994); Thomas F. Swearengen, *Tear Gas Munitions: An Analysis of Commercial Riot Gas Guns, Tear Gas Projectiles, Grenades, Small Arms Ammunition, and Related Tear Gas Devices* (Springfield, Illinois: Charles C. Thomas, Publisher, 1966).

2 Prelude

1 Burkhard Luber, *When Trees Become the Enemy: Military Use of Defoliants* (Hildesheim, Germany: Georg Olms Verlag, 1990), 19–20; Paul Frederick Cecil, *Herbicidal*

Warfare: The RANCH HAND Project in Vietnam (New York: Praeger, 1986), 17–19, 22–23; William A. Buckingham Jr., *OPERATION RANCH HAND: The Air Force and Herbicides in Southeast Asia 1961–1971* (Washington, DC: Government Printing Office, 1982), 4–6; Robinson, *CB Weapons*, 163n.

2 It is clear that President Diem did not know what kind of material he was asking for and only that it would effectively destroy the enemy crops. He was most likely referring to a biological agent that would cause disease in rice. Two biological agents for the destruction of rice that the United States was investigating as part its biological warfare program were the fungi *Helminthosporium oryzae* and *Pyricularia grisea*. *H. oryzae*, designated by the military as "agent E," causes the disease known as Rice Brown Spot. This fungus infects the first seedling leaves, eventually causing leaf spots to appear as the plants grow. Infected plants produce lightweight or chalky kernels. In cases of severe infection, the fungus destroys the kernels. *P. grisea*, designated by the military as "agent IE," causes the disease known as Rice Blast. This fungus causes lesions on the leaves and rice heads. The rice grains do not develop properly and, in severe cases, the stems break and the heads drop off. Crop loss from this disease can reach 90 percent. Both agents were stored as spores (i.e. a powder). D. Hank Ellison, *Handbook of Chemical and Biological Warfare Agents*, 2nd edn. (Boca Raton, Florida: CRC Press, 2008), 609, 612.

3 Buckingham, *OPERATION RANCH HAND*, 13, 208 (n. 12).

4 Starving an enemy into submission is an ancient military tactic and has been employed by the United States military on various occasions in previous wars. Examples include General Sherman's march to the sea during the American Civil War, efforts to starve the plains Indians into submission by wholesale slaughter of buffalo herds and General Franklin Bell's efforts in 1900 to destroy the food stocks of the belligerents during the Philippine Insurrection. Using herbicides to destroy food crops as a means of starving an enemy was a novel variation of the tactic pioneered by the British during the insurgency in Malaya.

5 Memorandum from Paul Neilson, the Assistant Director, Far East, to Edward Murrow, the Director of the United States Information Agency, "Use of Defoliants in Viet-Nam," November 17, 1961, Document 265, Ronald D. Landa and Charles S. Sampson, eds., *Foreign Relations of the United States, 1961–1963, Volume I: Vietnam, 1961* (Washington, DC: Government Printing Office, 1988), 641–642; telegram from Frederick Nolting, Ambassador to Vietnam, to the Department of State, August 16, 1962, Document 256; Memorandum from Worth Bagley, Naval Aide to the President's Military Representative, to General Maxwell Taylor, "Forrestal View on Defoliants," April 26, 1962, Document 170, David M. Baehler and Charles S. Sampson, eds., *Foreign Relations of the United States, 1961–1963, Volume II: Vietnam, 1962* (Washington, DC: Government Printing Office, 1990), 570.

6 Memorandum from Robert Johnson of the National Security Council Staff to Walt Rostow, the President's Deputy Special Assistant for National Security Affairs, "Use of Defoliants in Viet Nam," November 17, 1961, Document 264, Landa *et al.*, eds., *Foreign Relations 1961–1963, Volume I*, 639–641; Note 1 to the Memorandum from Dean Rusk, Secretary of State, to President Kennedy, "Defoliant Operations in Viet-Nam," November 24, 1961, Document 275, ibid., 663–664; Memorandum from Paul Neilson, the Assistant Director, Far East, to Edward Murrow, the Director of the United States Information Agency, "Use of Defoliants in Viet-Nam," November 17, 1961, Document 265, ibid., 641–642.

7 The North Koreans also made claims that the US used chemical weapons during the war, but these accusations were easily disproved and the Communists quickly dropped this aspect of their propaganda campaign.

8 Stephen Loyon Endicott and Edward Hagerman, *The United States and Biological Warfare: Secrets from the Early Cold War and Korea* (Bloomington: Indiana University

Press, 1998), 13, 15, 18; Kathryn Weathersby, "Deceiving the Deceivers: Moscow, Beijing, Pyongyang, and the Allegations of Bacteriological Weapons Use in Korea," *Cold War International History Project Bulletin* 11 (Winter 1998), 176–185; Milton Leitenberg, "New Russian Evidence on the Korean War Biological Warfare Allegations: Background and Analysis," ibid., 185–199; Harris, *Factories of Death*, 230–232. Arguments surrounding this controversy still continue. See, for example, John Ellis van Courtland Moon, "Dubious Allegations," *The Bulletin of the Atomic Scientists* 55 (May/June 1999), 70–72; Stephen Endicott and Edward Hagerman, Letters to the Editor. "Germ Warfare Was Used," ibid. (July/August 1999), 3–5; Mary Rolicka, Letters to the Editor. "Propaganda Value of Allegations of Biological Warfare in the Korean War," *Journal of the American Medical Association* (1998), 274; Edward Hagerman and Stephen Endicott, Letters to the Editor. *The Journal of American History* 88 (June 2001), 324; Ruth Rogaski, "Nature, Annihilation, and Modernity: China's Korean War Germ-Warfare Experience Reconsidered," *The Journal of Asian Studies* 61 (May 2002), 381–415.

9 Memorandum from General Lyman Lemnitzer, Chairman or the Joint Chiefs of Staff, to Secretary of Defense Robert McNamara, "Chemical Crop Destruction, South Vietnam (S)," July 28, 1962, Document 251; Memorandum from Secretary of Defense Robert McNamara to President Kennedy, "Chemical Crop Destruction, South Vietnam," August 8, 1962, Document 262, Baehler *et al.*, eds., *Foreign Relations 1961–1963, Volume II*, 562–564.

10 Memorandum from Edward Murrow, Director of the United States Information Agency, to McGeorge Bundy, the President's Assistant for National Security Affairs, "Defoliation," August 16, 1962, Document 266, ibid., 590–591.

11 Memorandum from Secretary of Defense Robert McNamara to President Kennedy, "Chemical Crop Destruction, South Vietnam," August 8, 1962, Document 262; Memorandum from Secretary of State Dean Rusk to President Kennedy, "Viet-Nam: Project for Crop Destruction," August 23, 1962, Document 270; Memorandum from Secretary of Defense Robert McNamara to President Kennedy, "Defoliant/Herbicide Program in South Vietnam," November 16, 1962, Document 317, ibid., 584–586, 606–609, 732–734; Memorandum Prepared in the Department of State, "Chemical Defoliation and Crop Destruction in South Vietnam," April 18, 1963, Document 96, Edward C. Keefer and Louis J. Smith, eds., *Foreign Relations of the United States, 1961–1963, Volume III: Vietnam, January–August 1963* (Washington, DC: Government Printing Office, 1991), 237–243.

12 Jack Raymond, "Decision on Gas Not President's, White House Says," *New York Times*, March 24, 1965, 1; John W. Finney, "Rusk Defends Use of Nonlethal Gas in War in Vietnam," *New York Times*, March 25, 1965, 1; Headquarters, United States Military Assistance Command, Vietnam, *Vietnam Lessons Learned Number 51: Operational Employment of Riot Control Munitions.* April 24, 1965, 1; Robinson, *CB Weapons*, 185; Kip Lindberg, "The Use of Riot Control Agents During the Vietnam War," *Army Chemical Review* (January–June 2007), 52.

13 When the French left Vietnam in 1954, about 78 percent of the population were Buddhists and only about 11 percent were Catholics.

14 Telegram from John Helble, the US Consul in Hue, to the Department of State, May 9, 1963, Document 112; telegram from John Helble, the Consul in Hue, to the Department of State, May 10, 1963, Document 116; telegram from Ambassador Nolting at the Embassy in Vietnam (Saigon) to the Department of State, 1050. CINCPAC for POLAD. Deptel 1117, May 22, 1963, Document 131; telegram from William Trueheart, the Minister-Counselor and Deputy Chief of Mission in Vietnam at the Embassy in Vietnam (Saigon) to the Department of State, 1136. CINCPAC for POLAD, June 9, 1963, Document 160; telegram from William Trueheart, Minister-Counselor and Deputy Chief of Mission in Vietnam, to the Department of

State, "1193. CINCPAC for POLAD," June 16, 1963, Document 177, Keefer *et al.*, eds., *Foreign Relations 1961–1963, Volume III*, 277–278, 284–285, 314, 366–369, 396–397; Charles A. Joiner, "South Vietnam's Buddhist Crisis: Organization for Charity, Dissidence, and Unity," *Asian Survey* 4 (July 1964), 915–928.

15 Telegram from William Trueheart, Minister-Counselor and Deputy Chief of Mission in Vietnam, to the Department of State, 1093. CINCPAC for POLAD, June 3, 1963, Document 144; Current Intelligence Memorandum Prepared in the Office of Current Intelligence, Central Intelligence Agency, "Buddhist Demonstrations in South Vietnam," OCI No. 1561/63, June 3, 1963, Document 145; telegram from William Trueheart to the Department of State, 1101. CINCPAC for POLAD, June 4, 1963, Document 146; Telegram from Secretary of State Dean Rusk to the Embassy in Vietnam, "1171," June 3, 1963, Document 147; telegram from William Trueheart, the Minister-Counselor and Deputy Chief of Mission in Vietnam, to the Department of State, 1100. CINCPAC for POLAD, June 4, 1963, Document 149, Keefer *et al.*, eds., *Foreign Relations 1961–1963, Volume III*, 343–348, 349–351; "Vietnam Buddhists Say Troops Cut Off Temple," *New York Times*, June 6, 1963, 15; David Halberstam, "The Buddhist Crisis in Vietnam: A Collision of Religion, World Politics and Pride," *New York Times*, September 11, 1963, 14.

16 Ellison, *Handbook*, 143–156; Charles E. Heller, *Chemical Warfare in World War I: The American Experience, 1917–1918* (Washington, DC: Government Printing Office, September 1984), 13–14; Augustin M. Prentiss, *Chemicals in War: A Treatise on Chemical Warfare* (New York: McGraw-Hill Book Company, Inc., 1937), 48, 178–180; Mario F. Sartori, *The War Gases: Chemistry and Analysis*, translated by L.W. Marrison (London: J. & A. Churchill, Ltd., 1939), 217–228.

17 Telegram from Secretary of State Dean Rusk to the Embassy in Vietnam, 1173, June 3, 1963, Document 148, Keefer *et al.*, eds., *Foreign Relations 1961–1963, Volume III*, 349.

18 Telegram from William Trueheart, the Minister-Counselor and Deputy Chief of Mission in Vietnam, to the Department of State, 1100. CINCPAC for POLAD, June 4, 1963, Document 149; telegram from William Trueheart, to the Department of State, 1102. CINCPAC for POLAD, June 4, 1963, Document 150; telegram from the Embassy in Vietnam to the Department of State, 1104. CINCPAC for POLAD. Embtel 1100, June 4, 1963, Document 151, Keefer *et al.*, eds., *Foreign Relations 1961–1963, Volume III*, 349–351.

19 William M. Hammond, *Public Affairs: The Military and The Media, 1962–1968* (Washington, DC: Government Printing Office, 1988), 43; Halberstam, "The Buddhist Crisis in Vietnam"; "Martial Law In Vietnam, *The Lima News*, Lima, Ohio, June 5, 1963, 11. For examples of the limited impact in the press, see "Blister Gas Routs Vietnam Buddhist Mob," *The Fresno Bee*, Fresno, California, June 4, 1963, 1; "US Planes Ferry Troops to Battle Against Buddhists," *Galveston Daily News*, Galveston, Texas, June 5, 1963, 6; "Buddhists Say Main Temple Surrounded," *Galveston Daily News*, Galveston, Texas, June 6, 1963, 8.

20 The French military was so fond of using tear gas against the Viet Minh that ammunition resupply points in the territories were almost always suffering from shortages of MK II tear-gas grenades. *The RAND Corporation Memorandum RM-5271-PR – A Translation from the French: Lessons of the War in Indochina*, Vol. 2, May 1967, Item Number 12050110001, Folder 10, Box 01, Vladimir Lehovich Collection, The Vietnam Archive, Texas Tech University. Online version on March 25, 2009, available through the online catalog at www.virtualarchive.vietnam.ttu.edu/virtualarchive/. Also, on a number of occasions police in Saigon and other major cities had used tear gas to disband rioting civilians. Some of these situations were so severe that they had to call on the assistance of the military. See, for example, "Saigon Rioters Protest US Destroyers in Harbor," *Valley Morning Star*, Harlingen, Texas, March 20,

1950, 1; "Violence Hits Vietnam; Troops Are Called Out," *Daily Review*, Hayward, California, May 7, 1955, 1; "Viet Minh Begins Haiphong Entry," *New York Times*, May 10, 1955, 11; John Roderick, "Anti-Reds In Saigon Stage Riot," *Sheboygan Press*, Sheboygan, Wisconsin, July 20, 1955, 1.

21 Editorial comments in Document 151, Keefer *et al.*, eds., *Foreign Relations 1961–1963, Volume III*, 352–353.

22 Prentiss, *Chemicals in War*, 140, 142, 440–442; Swearengen, *Tear Gas Munitions*, 20; Sidell *et al.*, eds., *Medical Aspects*, 312–314; James A.F. Compton, *Military Chemical and Biological Agents: Chemical and Toxicological Properties* (Caldwell, New Jersey: Telford Press, 1987), 209–214.

23 Finney, "Rusk Defends Use of Nonlethal Gas"; "Excerpts From Transcript of Rusk News Parley on Use of Gas in Vietnam," *New York Times*, March 25, 1965, 13; "The Great Gas Flap," *Time*, April 2, 1965.

24 Tom Mangold and John Penycate, *The Tunnels of Cu Chi* (New York: Berkley Books, 1986), 89.

25 Buckingham, *OPERATION RANCH HAND*, 109–111.

26 The TLSS was an adapter kit that modified a helicopter's 2.75-inch rocket pod so that it could drop 168 pyrotechnic CS grenades.

27 *Riot Control Munitions*, no date, Item Number 3670812011, Folder 12, Box 08, George J. Veith Collection, The Vietnam Archive, Texas Tech University. Online version on December 9, 2008, available through the online catalog at www.virtualarchive.vietnam.ttu.edu/virtualarchive/; John H. Hay Jr., *Tactical and Materiel Innovations* (Washington, DC: Government Printing Office, 1974), 34; Robinson, *CB Weapons*, 186; Hammond, *Public Affairs*, 153.

28 *Riot Control Munitions*; "The Great Gas Flap."

29 "The Great Gas Flap"; United States Army Headquarters, *Employment of Riot Control Agents, Flame, Smoke, and Herbicides in Counterguerrilla Operations, Training Circular No. 3–16* (Washington, DC: Government Printing Office, July 11, 1966), 34.

30 Nick Rowe was a 1st Lieutenant at the time he was captured. The army continued to promote him while he was missing in action.

31 Ernest J. Sylvester, diary entry dated January 29, 1965, in *Through the Silent Diary*, March 9, 1964, Item Number 10850101001, Folder 01, Box 01, Ernie Sylvester Collection, The Vietnam Archive, Texas Tech University. Online version on November 6, 2008, available through the online catalog at www.virtualarchive.vietnam.ttu.edu/virtualarchive/; James N. Rowe, *Five Years to Freedom* (Boston: Little Brown and Company, 1971), 141–151.

32 *Riot Control Munitions*; *Additional Information on Use of Napalm and Gas in SEA*, March 23, 1965, Item Number 3670812013, Folder 12, Box 08, George J. Veith Collection, The Vietnam Archive, Texas Tech University. Online version on December 9, 2008, available through the online catalog at www.virtualarchive.vietnam.ttu.edu/virtualarchive/; MACV, *Vietnam Lessons Learned Number 51*, 2–4.

33 Hammond, *Public Affairs*, 155; R.W. Apple Jr., "Marine Officer Uses Tear Gas In Vietnam, Setting Off Inquiry," *New York Times*, September 8, 1965, 1.

34 Walter L. Miller Jr., "Fight Guerrillas With Chemicals, Says This Expert, And Save Lives," *The Marine Corps Gazette* (July 1964), 37–39; "FAS Opposes Biological & Chemical Warfare," *FAS Newsletter* 17 (June 1964), 1; and see, for example, Joiner, "South Vietnam's Buddhist Crisis," 916.

35 Hay, *Tactical and Materiel Innovations*, 34; Robinson, *CB Weapons*, 187; Hammond, *Public Affairs*, 157.

36 At that time, reporters could attach themselves to units moving anywhere in the country as long as the local commander gave his permission. The reporter did not need to justify his interest in the operation or to coordinate his investigation with MACV.

37 Hammond, *Public Affairs*, 153–154; William M. Hammond, *Reporting Vietnam: Media and Military at War* (Lawrence, Kansas: University of Kansas Press, 1998), 46–47; "The Great Gas Flap."

38 Editorial comments in Document 210, David C. Humphrey, Ronald D. Landa and Louis J. Smith, eds., *Foreign Relations of the United States, 1964–1968, Volume II: Vietnam, January–June 1965* (Washington, DC: Government Printing Office, 1996), 470.

39 "Viets Use 'Tear Gas' on Reds," *The Pacific Stars and Stripes*, March 24, 1965, 1; Michael Malloy, "Discloses Use of Gas," *The Vidette-Messenger*, Valparaiso, Indiana, March 22, 1965, 1; "Viets Start Gas Warfare Against Communist Foes," *Press-Telegram*, Long Beach, California, March 22, 1965, 1; "Non-Lethal Gas Sprayed on Reds," *The Oneonta Star*, Oneonta, New York, March 23, 1965, 1; Hammond, *Public Affairs*, 155.

40 See, for example, Max Frankel, "US Reveals Use of Nonlethal Gas Against Vietcong," *New York Times*, March 23, 1965, 1; Malloy, "Discloses Use of Gas"; "Viet Cong Hit with Nausea Gas," *The Holland Evening Sentinel*, Holland, Michigan, March 22, 1965, 1; Fred S. Hoffman, "Compound Not Secret Nerve Gas, US Says," *The Portsmouth Times*, Portsmouth, Ohio, March 23, 1965, 2; John G. Norris, "McNamara Defends Use of Riot Gas in Viet-Nam," *Washington Post*, March 24, 1965, A1; John G. Norris, "Non-Lethal Gases Secretly Developed For 'Humane' War," *Washington Post*, March 25, 1965, A8.

41 "Asian Reds Make Gas a Top Issue," *New York Times*, March 25, 1965, 14; "Reds Continue Blasts At Gas Use In S. Viet.," *Chicago Tribune*, March 25, 1965, section 1, 4; "Use of Lethal Gas Charged," *New York Times*, April 6, 1965, 9.

42 Norris, "McNamara Defends Use of Riot Gas"; Raymond, "Decision on Gas Not President's"; Finney, "Rusk Defends Use of Nonlethal Gas"; "Transcript of Rusk News Parley."

43 Raymond, "Decision on Gas Not President's"; "Nixon is Critical of Johnson on Gas," *New York Times*, April 3, 1965, 5; letter from Senator Mike Mansfield to President Johnson, March 24, 1965, Document 215, Humphrey *et al.*, eds., *Foreign Relations 1964–1968, Volume II*, 477–481.

44 Letter from President Johnson to Senator Mike Mansfield, April 12, 1965, Document 248, Humphrey *et al.*, eds., *Foreign Relations 1964–1968, Volume II*, 547–548.

45 "Gas (Nonlethal) in Vietnam," *New York Times*, March 24, 1965, 42.

46 Editorials, "Opinion: At Home and Abroad," *New York Times*, March 28, 1965, E11.

47 As quoted in David Hoffman, "Firm War-Gas Stand Urged Upon Doctors," *Washington Post*, January 28, 1966, A2; Steve Hale, "It's Not So Bad, Reporter Gasps," *The Pacific Stars and Stripes*, March 29, 1965, 4.

48 "Scientists Denounce US Use of Gas Weapons," *FAS Newsletter*, 18 (March 1965), 4.

49 "Mail To Senators Asks Peace Talks," *New York Times*, April 4, 1965, 3.

50 Norris, "McNamara Defends Use of Riot Gas."

51 Central Intelligence Agency, *Activities Affecting the United Nations: Attitude of Permanent United Nations Representatives to the Vietnam Crisis,* Intelligence Information Cable. March 26, 1965.

52 Raymond Daniell, "US Scored in UN by Soviet on Gas," *New York Times*, April 6, 1965, 9.

53 Diary entry by David K.E. Bruce, the Ambassador to the United Kingdom, March 23, 1965, Document 211, David C. Humphrey *et al.*, eds., *Foreign Relations 1964–1968, Volume II*, 471–472; and Raymond, "Decision on Gas Not President's."

54 Memorandum from McGeorge Bundy, the President's Special Assistant for National Security Affairs, to President Johnson, "Your Meeting with Foreign Secretary

Michael Stewart of Great Britain, Tuesday, 23 March 11:30 A.M.," March 22, 1965, Document 209; Editorial Note, Document 216, Humphrey *et al.*, eds., *Foreign Relations 1964–1968, Volume II*, 468–469, 481–482.

55 Joseph Cerutti, "Wilson Rejects Plea to Condemn Gas Use," *Chicago Tribune*, March 24, 1965, section 1, 7; Clyde H. Farnsworth, "War-Gas Debate Stirs Commons," *New York Times*, March 24, 1965, 6; "British Reaction Softens," *New York Times*, March 25, 1965, 14; "Riot Gases Used by British 124 Times in Last 5 Years," April 2, 1965, 5.

56 Memorandum from McGeorge Bundy, the President's Special Assistant for National Security Affairs, to President Johnson, "The British and Vietnam," June 3, 1965, Document 330, Humphrey *et al.*, eds., *Foreign Relations 1964–1968, Volume II*, 716–717.

57 "Transcript of the President's News Conference on Foreign and Domestic Matters," *New York Times*, April 2, 1965, 18.

58 Summary Notes of the 550th Meeting of the National Security Council, "Vietnam," March 26, 1965, Document 217, Humphrey *et al.*, eds., *Foreign Relations 1964–1968, Volume II*, 482–486.

59 "The Great Gas Flap."

60 Jack Raymond, "It's a Dirty War for Correspondents," *New York Times Magazine*, February 13, 1966, 219; Hammond, *Public Affairs*, 155.

61 Summary Notes of the 550th Meeting of the National Security Council, "Vietnam," March 26, 1965, Document 217, Humphrey *et al.*, eds., *Foreign Relations 1964–1968, Volume II*, 482–486; Hammond, *Reporting Vietnam*, 47; Hammond, *Public Affairs*, 157–158.

3 Operation Stomp

1 Alex Lee, *Utter's Battalion: 2/7 Marines in Vietnam, 1965–66* (New York: Ballantine Publishing Group, 2000), 20–69; Jack Shulimson and Charles M. Johnson, *U.S. Marines in Vietnam: The Landing and the Buildup 1965* (Washington, DC: Government Printing Office, 1978), 88.

2 Lee, *Utter's Battalion*, 98–122.

3 Allen D. Reece, *A Historical Analysis of Tunnel Warfare and The Contemporary Perspective*, December 1997, 12; Thomas M. Huber, "Lethality in Motion: Tactics," *Japan's Battle of Okinawa, April–June 1945* (Washington, DC: Government Printing Office, 1990); Lee, *Utter's Battalion*, 141; Steve J. Illes, "Combat in Caves," *The Marine Corps Gazette* (July 1966), 39; John G. Miller, "From A Company Commander's Note Book," *The Marine Corps Gazette* (August 1966), 29.

4 The suggestion to use tear-gas grenades is also credited to Captain Alvin Doublet. Shulimson and Johnson, *Landing and the Buildup*, 91.

5 Lee, *Utter's Battalion*, 139–143; Shulimson and Johnson, *Landing and the Buildup*, 90–91.

6 Shulimson and Johnson, *Landing and the Buildup*, 88–91; Lee, *Utter's Battalion*, 133, 141.

7 Shulimson and Johnson, *Landing and the Buildup*, 87–88.

8 "Marine Officer Uses Tear Gas In Vietnam"; "Tear Gas Used To Clear Tunnels Despite US Ban," *The Pacific Stars and Stripes*, September 9, 1965, 3; "Westmoreland Seeking Right to Use Tear Gas," *New York Times*, September 23, 1965, 1; Hammond, *Public Affairs*, 202; Hammond, *Reporting Vietnam*, 64.

9 Lee, *Utter's Battalion*, 145; Shulimson and Johnson, *Landing and the Buildup*, 92; "Hanoi Protests to Group on the Use of 'Toxic Gas'," *New York Times*, September 8, 1965, 3; "Tear Gas Dropped on Vietcong Base," *New York Times*, May 10, 1966, 1.

10 "Marine Officer Uses Tear Gas In Vietnam"; Shulimson and Johnson, *Landing and the Buildup*, 92; Lee, *Utter's Battalion*, 145.
11 Miller, "Fight Guerrillas With Chemicals," 38; Headquarters, United States Continental Army Command, *Education and Training: Operations – Lessons Learned, USCONARC Pamphlet No. 350–30–2* (Washington, DC: Government Printing Office, December 15, 1965), 32.
12 Shulimson and Johnson, *Landing and the Buildup*, 87–88.
13 Lee, *Utter's Battalion*, 144, 146; Shulimson and Johnson, *Landing and the Buildup*, 92.
14 "Westmoreland Seeking Right to Use Tear Gas"; "Tears or Death," *Time*, September 17, 1965; Shulimson and Johnson, *Landing and the Buildup*, 88–91.
15 "US Held Preparing Opinion," *New York Times*, September 23, 1965, 2; "Westmoreland Seeking Right to Use Tear Gas"; "Confirm Tear Gas Can Be Used in Viet.," *Chicago Tribune*, September 23, 1965, section 1, 6; John G. Norris, "Westmoreland Held Seeking Tear Gas Use," *Washington Post*, September 23, 1965, A12.
16 Memorandum from Secretary of Defense McNamara to President Johnson, September 22, 1965, Document 147, David C. Humphrey, Edward C. Keefer and Louis J. Smith, eds., *Foreign Relations of the United States, 1964–1968, Volume III: Vietnam, June–December 1965* (Washington, DC: Government Printing Office, 1996), 402.
17 As quoted in Hammond, *Public Affairs*, 203.
18 Memorandum from McGeorge Bundy, the President's Special Assistant for National Security Affairs, to President Johnson, "Tear Gas in Vietnam," September 23, 1965, 3 p.m., Document 150, Humphrey *et al.*, *Foreign Relations 1964–1968, Volume III*, 413.
19 "General Must OK Use of Tear Gas on VC," *The Pacific Stars and Stripes*, September 25, 1965, 6; "GI's In Vietnam Can Use Tear Gas," *New York Times*, October 6, 1965, 1.
20 Memorandum for the Record, "Luncheon Meeting with the President, Ball, McNamara, McGeorge Bundy, Raborn, Moyers, and Califano," September 29, 1965, Document 155, Humphrey *et al.*, *Foreign Relations 1964–1968, Volume III*, 419–421.
21 "Colonel Cleared in Gas Use," *The Pacific Stars and Stripes*, September 27, 1965, 6; Shulimson and Johnson, *Landing and the Buildup*, 91; William C. Westmoreland, "Report on Operations in South Vietnam: January 1964–June 1968." Section II in *Report on the War In Vietnam (As of 30 June 1968)*. United States Military Assistance Command Headquarters, Vietnam, 110.
22 George L. MacGarrigle, *Combat Operations: Taking the Offensive, October 1966 to October 1967* (Washington, DC: Government Printing Office, 1998), 180.

4 Tunnels

1 Memorandum for the Record, "Luncheon Meeting with the President, Ball, McNamara, McGeorge Bundy, Raborn, Moyers, and Califano," September 29, 1965, Document 155, Humphrey *et al.*, *Foreign Relations 1964–1968, Volume III*, 419–421.
2 For example, at the Battle of Vicksburg, during the summer of 1863, Union soldiers tunneled under Confederate defenses and packed the mine with 220 pounds of black powder. The explosion destroyed the Confederate lines, creating a huge crater. The following summer, during the Siege of Pittsburg, Union soldiers again dug a long mine shaft underneath the Confederate lines and planted 8,000 pounds of gunpowder directly under the middle of the Confederate First Corps line. The explosion created a crater 170 feet long, up to eighty feet wide and thirty feet deep. Hundreds of Confederate soldiers were killed by the blast. This was the beginning of what became known as the Battle of the Crater.
3 Jasper Copping, "First World War Tunnels To Yield Their Secrets," *Sunday Telegraph*, August 26, 2007, www.telegraph.co.uk/news/main.jhtml?xml=/news/2007/

08/26/ntunnel126.xml (August 26, 2007); Reece, *Analysis of Tunnel Warfare* 13, 14; Huber, *Lethality in Motion.*

4 Memorandum for the Record, "Meeting Held at Gia Long Palace, Saigon, Vietnam, 7 Sep 62," September 10, 1962, Document 277, Baehler *et al.*, eds., *Foreign Relations 1961–1963, Volume II*, 622–633.

5 "Base is Overrun by Saigon Force," *New York Times*, November 21, 1964, 1; Hay, *Tactical and Materiel Innovations*, 34; Bernard William Rogers, *Cedar Falls–Junction City: A Turning Point* (Washington, DC: Government Printing Office, 1974), 66; Tom Mangold and John Penycate, *Tunnel Warfare* (Toronto: Bantam Books, 1987), 32; Reece, *Analysis of Tunnel Warfare*, 15–16.

6 "Vast Tunnel System Found," *New York Times*, January 10, 1966, 3; Rogers, *Cedar Falls–Junction City*, 17; Headquarters, United States Military Assistance Command, Vietnam, *Vietnam Lessons Learned Number 56: Operations Against Tunnel Complexes*, April 18, 1966, passim; United States Army Corps of Engineers, *Did You Know: How Army Engineers Cleared Viet Cong Tunnels?*, Number 62. US Army Corps of Engineers Office of History, undated; Mangold and Penycate, *Tunnels of Cu Chi*, 17–20, 24–25, 158–160; Reece, *Analysis of Tunnel Warfare*, 16.

7 US Army, *Employment of Riot Control Agents*, July 1966, 8–16; MACV, *Vietnam Lessons Learned Number 56*, passim; Corps of Engineers, *How Engineers Cleared Tunnels*; Mangold and Penycate, *Tunnels of Cu Chi*, 15, 20, 55–82; Robert R. Ploger, *US Army Engineers 1965–1970* (Washington, DC: Government Printing Office, 2000), 94; Horst Faas, "Huge VC Tunnel Network Found Near Saigon," *The Pacific Stars and Stripes*, January 11, 1966, 6; "The Tunnel Rats," *Time*, March 4, 1966; Tom Tiede, "'Mole Patrols' Love Daylight," *The Pacific Stars and Stripes*, May 8, 1966, 2.

8 MACV, *Vietnam Lessons Learned Number 56*, 4.

9 "Vietnam Troops Blast Tunnels, Burying Reds," *New York Times*, December 18, 1964, 3; Headquarters, United States Military Assistance Command, Vietnam, *Vietnam Lessons Learned Number 45: Viet Cong Tunnels*, February 12, 1965, passim; Mangold and Penycate, *Tunnels of Cu Chi*, 89.

10 When fighting the Viet Minh, the French found that tear-gas grenades were very effective against insurgents hiding underground, but only in tunnels less than seventy feet long. RAND, *Lessons of the War in Indochina*, 92.

11 "Experiences Gained from Operations Against Viet Cong Subterranean Warfare," presentation at the Gia Long Palace on September 20, 1963, as cited in Mangold and Penycate, *Tunnels of Cu Chi*, 89; "Reds' Tunnel Network Is Found Near Saigon," *New York Times*, July 5, 1963, 2; MACV, *Vietnam Lessons Learned Number 51*, 3–4.

12 Diary entry by David K.E. Bruce, the Ambassador to the United Kingdom, March 23, 1965, Document 211, Humphrey *et al.*, eds., *Foreign Relations 1964–1968, Volume II*, 471–472.

13 Charles L. Mohr, "Tear Gas Used by US in Search for Vietcong," *New York Times*, October 9, 1965, 1; John Maffre, "US Publicizes Tear Gas Attack in Vietnam," *Washington Post*, October 9, 1965, A9; "US Paratroopers, Aussies Storm Viet Cong Stronghold," *The Pacific Stars and Stripes*, October 10, 1965, 1; "78 VC Killed in Airmobile's Valley Mop-Up," *The Pacific Stars and Stripes*, October 15, 1965, 6; "More Shooters," *Time*, October 15, 1965.

14 Headquarters, United States Military Assistance Command, Vietnam, *Vietnam Lessons Learned Number 52: Operational Employment of the Mity Mite Portable Blower*, November 22, 1965, passim.

15 "Vast Tunnel System Found"; Charles Mohr, "Viet Cong Fleeing Big Allied Force In Record Sweep," *New York Times*, January 10, 1966, 1; Faas, "Huge VC Tunnel Network Found Near Saigon"; "The Curious Passivity," *Time*, January 21, 1966; "The Tunnel Rats"; *Department of the Army Operations Report 1–66: Lessons Learned,*

22 March 1966, Item number 1070307003, Folder 07, Box 03, Glenn Helm Collection, The Vietnam Archive, Texas Tech University. Online version on March 25, 2009, available through the online catalog at www.virtualarchive.vietnam.ttu.edu/ virtualarchive/; John J. Tolson, *Airmobility: 1961–1971* (Washington, DC: Government Printing Office, 1973), 89; Mangold and Penycate, *Tunnels of Cu Chi,* 59.

16 In some cases, soldiers encountered biting ants that appeared to be a half-inch long. When their nest was disturbed, the ants would emerge into the tunnel and attack the soldiers. There were so many of the ants that soldiers said the walls of the tunnel appeared to be moving. Other soldiers told stories of crawling into chambers so full of spiders that the walls and ceiling were a continuous black mass of moving bodies. These encounters became so common that many soldiers began carrying aerosol insecticides. Descriptions of encounters with animals and insects while exploring tunnels can be found in Tiede, "Mole Patrols"; "The Tunnel Rats"; Mangold and Penycate, "Animals," in *Tunnels of Cu Chi.*

17 MACV, *Vietnam Lessons Learned Number 56,* 11–12; Joseph Galloway, "The 'Tunnel Rats' are Brave Little Moles," *The Pacific Stars and Stripes,* April 19, 1966, 11; Mangold and Penycate, *Tunnels of Cu Chi,* 5–8, 134.

18 MACV, *Vietnam Lessons Learned Number 52,* passim.

19 Galloway, "The 'Tunnel Rats' are Brave Little Moles."

20 For example, in June 1864, Union soldiers secretly began digging a 500-foot tunnel to reach the lines of the Confederates defending Petersburg, Virginia. Working only with hand tools and unable to dig ventilations holes since that would give away the operation, the strain on the miners increased dramatically as they moved away from the entrance and their only source of fresh air. To overcome this problem, Lieutenant Colonel Henry Pleasants had the miners build a wooden duct along the length of the mine. The duct was connected to a sealed chimney at the entrance where soldiers kept a large fire burning. The hot air from the fire rose up the chimney and created a vacuum in the duct, drawing fresh air down the tunnel to miners at the far end of the shaft. On July 17, they reached the Confederate lines and began digging the side tunnels that they would eventually pack with 8,000 pounds of gunpowder. The blast opened a significant breach in the Confederate lines and led to what became known as the Battle of the Crater.

21 "Gas Kills an Australian," *New York Times,* January 13, 1966, 3; Mangold and Penycate, *Tunnels of Cu Chi,* 41, 54–56; Steven Rose, ed., *CBW: Chemical and Biological Warfare* (London: George G. Harrap & Co. LTD, 1968), 91; J.B. Neilands, "Vietnam: Progress of the Chemical War," *Asian Survey* 10, 3 (1970), 217.

22 In some instances, soldiers actually used the reduction of oxygen and production of carbon monoxide as a means of killing Viet Cong who were known to be hiding in a tunnel. Once they had blocked all of the exits they could find, they would throw in smoke grenades and flares to asphyxiate or poison the occupants. For larger systems, they would use twenty-pound HC smoke pots. Operations Critique, 173d Airborne Brigade, Operations Critique, January 8–14, 1966, in *Lessons Learned (Vietnam),* United States Army Infantry School, Fort Benning, Georgia, 1968, V-6; Mangold and Penycate, *Tunnels of Cu Chi,* 104.

23 MACV, *Vietnam Lessons Learned Number 56,* 11–12; Illes, *Combat in Caves,* 39–40; Headquarters, United States Military Assistance Command, Vietnam, *Counterinsurgency Lessons Learned Number 61: Salient Lessons Learned,* January 27, 1967, 19; United States Army Headquarters, *Employment of Riot Control Agents, Flame, Smoke, Antiplant Agents and Personnel Detectors in Counterguerrilla Operations, Training Circular No. 3–16* (Washington, DC: Government Printing Office, April 9, 1969; Reprint, Stockholm: Swedish Medical Aid Committee for Vietnam, 1970), 32.

24 MACV, *Vietnam Lessons Learned Number 56,* 10; Galloway, "The 'Tunnel Rats' are Brave Little Moles"; US Army, *Employment of Riot Control Agents,* April 1969, 9.

25 Corps of Engineers, *How Engineers Cleared Tunnels*; Ploger, *Army Engineers*, 92–95; Reece, *Analysis of Tunnel Warfare*, 33; Mangold and Penycate, *Tunnels of Cu Chi*, 171, 207.

26 "Vast Tunnel System Found"; "The Curious Passivity"; "The Tunnel Rats."

27 Engineers chose acetylene gas for these operations because it was uniquely suitable to this type of operation. In order for an explosion to occur, a flammable gas must be in a confined area and in the right proportion to the ambient air. The ratio of gas to air that will explode has an upper and lower limit and is known as the "flammable range." If the mixture is outside of this range, either too high or too low, then the gas will neither burn nor explode. Unlike many other flammable gases that were readily available, the flammable range for acetylene gas is so wide that it was easy to establish an explosive atmosphere in a tunnel. Also, acetylene gas could easily be generated on the spot from solid calcium carbide, eliminating the hazard associated with bringing compressed cylinders of the gas into a combat zone. Acetylene was generated when the carbide was combined with water. Five pounds of carbide could produce enough gas to destroy nearly ninety feet of tunnel. Reece, *Analysis of Tunnel Warfare*, 32–33; Corps of Engineers, *How Engineers Cleared Tunnels*.

28 Illes, *Combat in Caves*, 40; Corps of Engineers, *How Engineers Cleared Tunnels*.

29 "The Tunnel Rats"; MACV, *Vietnam Lessons Learned Number 56*, 9–10, 13; Mangold and Penycate, *Tunnels of Cu Chi*, 59.

30 173d Airborne Brigade letter JRATA, subject "Tunnel Contamination, Chemical Agent," February 3, 1966, in *Lessons Learned (Vietnam)*, V-6.

31 James L. Schwendeman and Ival O. Salyer, "Composition and Method for Generating Stabilized Lacrimating Foam for Tunnel Denial," United States Patent 3814808, June 4, 1974; Hay, *Tactical and Materiel Innovations*, 37; Reece, *Analysis of Tunnel Warfare*, 33.

32 The high exhaust temperature also prevented Army Engineers from using the Mars generator to blow the explosive acetylene gas down into a tunnel since the gas would be incinerated before it could reach the necessary concentration to form an explosive atmosphere.

33 Army Concept Team in Vietnam, "Letter Report of Evaluation – Large Capacity Tunnel Flushers," November 25, 1966; "1,000° Air Blasts Shot at Viet Cong: New Device is Used to Clear Tunnels North of Saigon," *New York Times*, April 7, 1967, 3; Peter Arnett, "'Tunnel Rats' Use New Technique," *The European Stars and Stripes*, April 10, 1967, 8.

34 Mangold and Penycate, *Tunnels of Cu Chi*, 46; MACV, *Vietnam Lessons Learned Number 45*, passim; MACV, *Vietnam Lessons Learned Number 56*, 5.

35 MACV, *Vietnam Lessons Learned Number 56*, 13.

36 Memorandum from Theodore Heavner, Officer in Charge of Vietnam Affairs, to Frederick Nolting, Ambassador to Vietnam, "Observations in Five Provinces," April 27, 1962, Document 173, Baehler *et al.*, eds., *Foreign Relations 1961–1963, Volume II*, 353–364; Mangold and Penycate, *Tunnels of Cu Chi*, 22; George Donelson Moss, *Vietnam: An American Ordeal*, 3rd edn. (Upper Saddle River, New Jersey: Prentice Hall, 1998), 58.

37 To dowse, a marine would hold a thin brass rod in each hand. Each rod was bent in the shape of an "L" and held such that the long end pointed out in front of the individual as he walked along. According to those that believed in the technique, when the marine walked over a tunnel, the rods would either cross or spread apart, pointing in the direction that the tunnel traveled.

38 Peter Arnett, "Alert Marines Dowse at Khe Sanh," *The European Stars and Stripes*, March 5, 1968, 3; "477 Reds Die in Fighting All Along DMZ," *The European Stars and Stripes*, March 10, 1968, 1; Alex Lee, *Force Recon Command: 3d Force Recon Company in Vietnam, 1969–70* (New York: Ivy Books, 1995), 154–155.

5 Escalation

1 Operation Masher became Operation White Wing on February 4 when it grew from a single brigade action to a divisional operation employing two brigades and six battalions of infantry. R.W. Apple, Jr. "Division-Size Unit Widens GI Drive on Vietnam Coast," *New York Times*, February 5, 1966, 1; *Combat Operations After Action Report (RCS MACV J3/32)*, April 28, 1966, 15, Item Number 1710118001, Folder 18, Box 01, Operation Masher/Operation White Wing Collection, The Vietnam Archive, Texas Tech University. Online version on March 25, 2009, available through the online catalog at www.virtualarchive.vietnam.ttu.edu/virtualarchive/.

2 "VC Retreat as Marines Push Inland," *The Pacific Stars and Stripes*, February 6, 1966, 6; "US Explains New Tactic," *New York Times*, February 22, 1966, 2; "B52s, 1st Cav. Hit Viet Cong Stronghold," *The Pacific Stars and Stripes*, February 23, 1966, 24; "Making Contact," *Time*, February 25, 1966; *Combat Operations After Action Report (RCS MACV J3/32)*, 16–17, 22–23; US Army, *Employment of Riot Control Agents*, July 1966, 39–41; Neilands, "Vietnam: Progress of the Chemical War," 218; Hay, *Tactical and Materiel Innovations*, 37.

3 Charles Mohr, "Foxholes Prove the GI's Best Friend," *New York Times*, July 4, 1966, 2; Hay, *Tactical and Materiel Innovations*, 36.

4 Dispersers were essentially sprayer/duster systems used to discharge bulk quantities of powdered agent on a target. Only one of these sprayers could be carried by an individual soldier, the other two had to be mounted in a helicopter or the back of a truck.

5 Using both pods to drop all 336 grenades, a helicopter could generate a cloud that would saturate a square that was about 170 yards on a side. Under optimal conditions, the cloud would last for about ten minutes.

6 MACV, *Vietnam Lessons Learned Number 51*, 4; *Operation Crazy Horse: 16 May–5 June 1966*, Binh Dinh Province, Republic of Vietnam, September 10, 1966, 67, Item Number 1070802002, Folder 02, Box 08, Glenn Helm Collection, The Vietnam Archive, Texas Tech University. Online version on March 25, 2009, available through the online catalog at www.virtualarchive.vietnam.ttu.edu/virtualarchive/; United States Army Headquarters, *Flame, Riot Control Agents and Herbicide Operations, Field Manual 3–11* (Washington, DC: Government Printing Office, August 19, 1996), B.8; and Perry Brake, *My Experiences: The Vietnam War*. Online version on January 20, 2008 at www.perrybrake.com/Vietnam1.html.

7 US Army, *Employment of Riot Control Agents*, April 1969, chapter 2.

8 The commanding general of 1st Field Force Vietnam had already taken the initiative on May 7, 1966 and delegated this authority to all division and separate brigade commanders under his command. He reported this action did not have any major effect on the employment of riot-control agents in his operational area since any request to use them prior to this directive had routinely been granted. Headquarters, 1st Field Force Vietnam, *Operational Report for Quarterly Period Ending 31 July, 1966, RCS CSFOR-65*, August 25, 1966, 26.

9 Gary L. Telfer, Lane Rogers and V. Keith Fleming, Jr., *US Marines in Vietnam: Fighting the North Vietnamese, 1967* (Washington, DC: Government Printing Office, 1984), 111–118; Herbert L. Bergsma, *Chaplains with Marines in Vietnam, 1962–1971* (Washington, DC: Government Printing Office, 1985), 150–151.

10 US Army, *Employment of Riot Control Agents*, April 1969, 27, 39–41; United States Military Assistance Command, Vietnam, *Vietnam Lessons Learned Number 83: Guide for Helicopter Tactics and Techniques for Use with Reconnaissance Teams*, October 12, 1970, 12–13, 33; Headquarters, 11th Combat Aviation Group, *Operational Report – Lessons Learned (OR-LL) of the 11th Combat Aviation Group for the Period Ending 30 April, 1972, RCS CSFOR-65 (R2) (U)*, May 10, 1972, 5; Jack Shulimson, Leonard A. Blasiol, Charles R. Smith and David A. Dawson, *US Marines in Vietnam: The*

Defining Year, 1968 (Washington, DC: Government Printing Office, 1997), 483–485.

11 Although the war had officially ended twelve days earlier, the US military considers operations associated with the rescue of the Mayaguez and her crew as part of the Vietnam War.

12 Even though the ownership of the islands was disputed, also being claimed by Thailand and Vietnam, the Cambodians were using them as a basis to extend their territorial water limits. Such limits had been established in the seventeenth century to allow ships to travel the high seas without interference from every country with a coastline. However, it was not until 1982 that the United Nations standardized the limit at twelve miles.

13 In 1968, North Korea seized the electronic surveillance ship Pueblo and held the crew for almost a year. The eighty-two surviving crew members were tortured and forced to sign "confessions" that they had been spying for the CIA. After eleven months, they were freed, but only after the United States apologized to the North Koreans for "grave acts of espionage." The incident damaged the image of the US both at home and abroad.

14 "A Chronology of the Mayaguez Episode," *New York Times*, May 16, 1975, 14; Sydney H. Schanberg, "Mayaguez Captain Tells Story of Rescue," *New York Times*, May 18, 1975, 1; "Mayaguez Cargo is Inspected and Found Not to Be Weapons," *New York Times*, May 24, 1975, 2; "A Strong but Risky Show of Force," *Time*, May 26, 1975; "The Captain's Log: A Tale of Terror," *Time*, May 26, 1975; United States House Committee on International Relations, Subcommittee on International Security and Scientific Affairs, *War Powers: A Test of Compliance Relative to the Da Nang Sealift, the Evacuation of Phnom Penh, The Evacuation of Saigon, and the Mayaguez Incident*, 94th Congress, 1st Session, May 7 and June 4, 1975, 105–114; Thomas D. Des Brisay, "Fourteen Hours at Koh Tang," Monograph 5 in *USAF Southeast Asia Monograph Series Volume III*. Reprint (Washington, DC: Government Printing Office, 1985); "'Mayday' for the Mayaguez," in *The Marines in Vietnam, 1954–1973: An Anthology and Annotated Bibliography*, 2nd edn. (Washington, DC: Government Printing Office, 1985), 240–258; George R. Dunham and David A. Quinlan, "Recovery of the SS Mayaguez," in *U.S. Marines in Vietnam: The Bitter End, 1973–1975* (Washington, DC: Government Printing Office, 1990); American Merchant Marine at War, *Capture and Release of SS Mayaguez by Khmer Rouge Forces in May 1975*, June 5, 2000, www.usmm.org/mayaguez.html (February 5, 2008).

15 The fratricide rate from fragmentary weapons during the Vietnam War has been estimated at nearly 11 percent of total American casualties. Kenneth K. Steinweg, "Dealing Realistically With Fratricide," *Parameters* (spring 1995), 4–29.

16 "Nitze Supports Burning of Huts," *New York Times*, August 15, 1965, 3; Headquarters, United States Military Assistance Command, Vietnam, *Vietnam Lessons Learned Number 71: Countermeasures Against Standoff Attacks*, March 13, 1969, 1, 56–57; Headquarters, United States Military Assistance Command, Vietnam, *Vietnam Lessons Learned Number 77: Fire Support Coordination in the Republic of Vietnam*, May 20, 1970, C60; Hay, *Tactical and Materiel Innovations*, 31; US Army, *Flame, Riot Control Agents and Herbicide Operations*, 7.3, B3–B4.

17 Cecil, *Herbicidal Warfare*, 122, 148; Buckingham, *OPERATION RANCH HAND*, 162.

18 B.P. McNamara, E.J. Owens, J.T. Weimer, T.A. Ballard and F.J. Vocci, *Toxicology of Riot Control Chemicals – CS, CN, and DM, Edgewood Arsenal Technical Report 4309*. Medical Research Laboratory, Edgewood Arsenal, November 1969, 21; US Army, *Flame, Riot Control Agents and Herbicide Operations*, 6.6; Sidell *et al.*, eds., *Medical Aspects*, 310–311; "A Chronology of the Mayaguez Episode"; Schanberg, "Mayaguez Captain Tells Story of Rescue"; "Mayaguez Cargo is Inspected and Found Not to

Be Weapons"; "A Strong but Risky Show of Force"; "The Captain's Log: A Tale of Terror."

19 "Squad Loses to Bees," *The Pacific Stars and Stripes*, May 31, 1967, 27.

20 Unlike many weapons, the effectiveness of chemical agents is highly influenced by minor changes in the weather. Key factors are wind speed and atmospheric stability. Optimal conditions for an effective attack are wind speeds less than ten miles per hour with an inversion layer over the target area. As the wind speed increases or the atmosphere becomes less stable, the continuity of the cloud decreases. Other atmospheric factors, such as cloud cover, precipitation, temperature and humidity, can also affect the stability of the agent cloud and the persistence of the contamination produced after the cloud has passed. The least favorable conditions are heavy rains with lapse atmospheric conditions and wind speeds greater than twelve miles per hour. Even the time of day can play a critical role. In the afternoon, after the sun has warmed the soil, there can be significant convection currents causing the cloud to rapidly rise off the target. These vertical currents are typically not present at night, in the early morning hours or when the sky is overcast. US Army, *Flame, Riot Control Agents and Herbicide Operations*, 6.5.

21 Headquarters, United States Military Assistance Command, Vietnam, *Vietnam Lessons Learned Number 69: Analysis of Enemy Positions at Khe Sanh and Evaluation of the Effectiveness of Weapons Systems Against Enemy Fortifications*, September 10, 1968, 28–29.

6 Niches

1 Robert M. Smith, "US Command in Saigon Rejects Pentagon View That Use of Tear Gas Reduces Civilian Casualties," *New York Times*, September 29, 1969, 11.

2 Department of the Army, Army Concept Team in Vietnam, *Final Report of Miniature CS Disseminator and XM58 CS Pocket Grenade*, November 18, 1968, 7; Don Ericson and John L. Rotundo, *Charlie Rangers* (New York: Ivy Books, 1989), 37–38, 54, 77; Lee, *Force Recon Command*, 54, 57–58.

3 US Army, *Employment of Riot Control Agents*, April 1969, 27; MACV, *Vietnam Lessons Learned Number 83*, 12–13, 33.

4 Transcript of "Valley of Death," *Newsstand: CNN & Time*, June 7, 1998. Online version on June 8, 1998 at www.cnn.com/US/9806/07/valley.of.death/transcript. html; April Oliver and Peter Arnett, "Did The U.S. Drop Nerve Gas?," *Time*, June 15, 1998. Online version on June 8, 1998 at www.pathfinder.com/time/maga-zine/1998/dom/980615/world_did_the_us_drop.html; United States Department of the Air Force, *Air Force History Report on Operation Tailwind*, Air Force History Support Office, July 16, 1998; United States Department of Defense, *Review of Allegations Concerning "Operation Tailwind,"* July 21, 1998; "CNN Producer Says She's the Victim," *Yahoo!News*, February 14, 2000. Online version on February 16, 2000 at http://dailynews.yahoo.com/h/ao/20000214/cr/20000214031.html.

5 1st Field Force Vietnam, *Operational Report for Quarterly Period Ending 31 July, 1966*, 26–27; "The Quickening Pace," *Time*, June 24, 1966.

6 Headquarters 25th Infantry Division, *Operational Report for Quarterly Period Ending 31 July 1967 (RCS CSFOR-65) (BC)*, August 19, 1967, 31. Online version on January 8, 2008 at http://25thaviation.org/history/id768.htm; Headquarters 2nd Brigade, 25th Infantry Division., *Operational Report of the 25th Infantry Division for the Period Ending 30 April 1969, RCS CSFOR – 65 (R-1)*, May 1, 1969, 12. Online version on January 8, 2008 at http://25thaviation.org/history/id752.htm.

7 Gene Roberts, "'People Sniffer' Follows Scent of Enemy from Copter in Delta," *New York Times*, August 18, 1968, 3; Gene Roberts, "Search-and-Destroy Missions Gaining Flexibility," *New York Times*, September 10, 1968, 2; Headquarters 2nd Brigade, 25th Infantry Division, *Combat Operations After Action Report (RCS: MACJ3*

K-1), March 10, 1969. Online version on January 8, 2008 at http://25thaviation.
org/history/id769.htm; United States Army Headquarters, "Personnel Detection
Operations," in *Employment of Riot Control Agents*, April 1969; "Arsenal in Action,"
Time, November 18, 1966; Mangold and Penycate, *Tunnels of Cu Chi*, 201–202; F.
Clifton Berry, Jr., *Gadget Warfare* (Toronto: Bantam Books, 1988), 76–79; Julian J.
Ewell, and Ira A. Hunt, Jr., *Sharpening The Combat Edge: The Use of Analysis to Rein-
force Military Judgment* (Washington, DC: Government Printing Office, 1995), 109.

8 John W. Finney, "Pentagon Scored on Chemical War," *New York Times*, April 22,
1969, 2; "Ex-Aide Scores US on Tear Gas In War," *New York Times*, September 23,
1969, 32; Smith, "US Command in Saigon Rejects Pentagon View"; Robert M.
Smith, "Use of Gas in War Assailed in House," *New York Times*, November 19,
1969, 9; Week in Review, "Banning Tear Gas ...," *New York Times*, December 21,
1969, E14; "Pentagon Defends Use of Tear Gas," *New York Times*, March 23, 1971,
3; Raymond D. Gasti1, *Toward the Development of A More Acceptable Set of Limits For
Counter Insurgency*, Hudson Institute, Inc., Croton-on-Hudson, New York, August
8, 1967, 15–16; Monte L. Stuck, *Future US Use of Nonlethal Chemical Agents in
Warfare*, Air Warfare Office, Defense Research and Engineering Directorate, October
20, 1972, 4–5, E2.

9 A force multiplier is anything that amplifies one's own capabilities by diminishing the
effectiveness of the enemy. In this regard, tear gas is much more effective than smoke
for limiting the ability of soldiers to clearly see targets since it actually affects their
eyes. For this reason, it also prevents the efficient operation of equipment. Although
a gas mask will prevent exposure to the agent, it will also impair a soldier's efficiency
and still reduce the effectiveness of their operations. For inexperienced troops, a mask
can reduce their ability to communicate, their efficiency with a weapon and even
increase their sense of isolation. Since air must be forcefully drawn into the mask
through filters, there is increased effort to breathe. This can reduce their stamina and
inhibit effective counterattacks. So, either with or without a mask, the overall reduction in fighting capabilities typically ranges from 25 to 100 percent.

10 *Operation Crazy Horse*, 6, 38–40, 67.

11 MACV, *Vietnam Lessons Learned Number 51*, 4; ibid., 67; Headquarters, 173rd Airborne Brigade (Separate), *Combat Operations After Action Report for Operation Toledo*,
December 15, 1966, 11–12; Lieutenant Colonel Alvin R. Hylton, Division Chemical Officer, 1st Infantry Division, interviewed by Captain George E. Creighton,
17th Military History Detachment, transcript of a tape-recorded interview, March 3,
1967, Vietnam Interview Tape Collection Number 38, U.S. Army Center of Military History, Fort Lesley J. McNair; Headquarters, 101st Airborne Division Headquarters, *Combat Operations After Action Report, Operation Malheur (MACV/RCS/
J3/32)*, September 2, 1967, enclosure 5.

12 Headquarters, 1st Infantry Division, *Operational Report – Lessons Learned 1 May–31
July 1966*. August 15, 1966, 17, 32; Headquarters 2nd Brigade, *After Action Report
(RCS: MACJ3 K-1)*; Headquarters, 4th Infantry Division, *Operational Report – Lessons
Learned 4th Infantry Division, Period Ending 30 April 1970, RCS CSFOR-65 (R2) (U)*,
May 31, 1970, 24–25; Tolson, *Airmobility*, 141; Hay, *Tactical and Materiel Innovations*,
38; Rogers, *Cedar Falls-Junction City*, 72.

13 United States Army Headquarters, *Operational Reports – Lessons Learned*, United States
Army Combat Developments Command, July 24, 1969, 3–13; US Army, *Employment of Riot Control Agents*, April 1969, 37, 40.

14 B.O. White, Jr., *USAF Cargo Aircraft Dispenser For XM925 CS System*, November
1969; Headquarters, 101st Infantry Division, *Operational Report – Lessons Learned,
Headquarters 101st Airborne Division (Airmobile), Period Ending 31 July 1970, RCS
CSFOR-65 (R2) (U)*. April 15, 1970, 9; Ray L. Bowers, *Tactical Airlift* (Washington,
DC: Government Printing Office, 1983), 389.

15 Headquarters 2nd Battalion, 12th Infantry Division, *Combat After Action Report (MACV/RCS/J3/32)*. March 15, 1968, 13. Online version on January 8, 2008 at http://25thaviation.org/history/id764.htm.

16 MACV, *Vietnam Lessons Learned Number 56*, 5–9; US Army, *Employment of Riot Control Agents*, July 1966, 11–13; MACV, *Vietnam Lessons Learned Number 69*, passim.

17 MACV, *Vietnam Lessons Learned Number 56*, 10; Swearengen, *Tear Gas Munitions*, 523–525; Hay, *Tactical and Materiel Innovations*, 37; Headquarters, 1st Cavalry Division, *1st Cavalry Division – Vietnam* (Tokyo: DIA Nippon Printing Company, 1970; Reprint, Nashville: Turner Publishing Company, 1995, 194); Reece, *Analysis of Tunnel Warfare*, 33; Lindberg, "Use of Riot Control Agents," 53.

18 Hay, *Tactical and Materiel Innovations*, 38; US Army, *Flame, Riot Control Agents and Herbicide Operations*, 7.3–7.4.

19 "Old Fort Survives 5 Wars," *The Pacific Stars and Stripes*, May 15, 1967, 7.

20 Charles R. Smith, *US Marines in Vietnam: High Mobility and Stand-down, 1969* (Washington, DC: Government Printing Office, 1988), 139.

21 Joel M. Klein and James D. Wilcox, *Pelletized CS-2 for Terrain Denial: A Preliminary Feasibility Study, Edgewood Arsenal Special Publication 1200–5*, Edgewood Arsenal Chemical Laboratory, Edgewood Arsenal, Maryland, July 1972.

22 "GIs Seize Rice Cache," *The Pacific Stars and Stripes*, June 17, 1968, 7; "'Battle of Graveyards' Ends in Tons of Rice for Friendlies," *The Pacific Stars and Stripes*, July 5, 1968, 7; Rogers, *Cedar Falls-Junction City*, 57.

23 Depending on the model, the CH-47 could lift between five and ten tons, and had a flight time of between fifty-five minutes and 2.5 hours. The UH-1H could only lift a little over one ton and had a flight time of 2.3 hours. Headquarters, 101st Airborne Division (Air Assault), *The Air Assault Handbook*, 4th edn. (Washington, DC: Government Printing Office, 1986), 1.4, 1.9.

24 United States Military Assistance Command, Vietnam, *Counterinsurgency Lessons Learned Number 68: Viet Cong Base Camps and Supply Caches*, July 20, 1968, 18; "Cav. Ambushes Reds," *The Pacific Stars and Stripes*, November 6, 1965, 1; "Hitting the VC Where It Hurts – The Belly," *The Pacific Stars and Stripes*, December 14, 1965, 7; "GIs Grab Huge VC Rice Cache," *The Pacific Stars and Stripes*, October 31, 1966, 24; Jim Shaw, "Attleboro Battered Reds' Supply System," *The Pacific Stars and Stripes*, November 28, 1966, 6; "Biggest Rice Cache Found," *The Pacific Stars and Stripes*, January 5, 1968, 7; "Battle of Graveyards"; Rogers, *Cedar Falls-Junction City*, 34.

25 United States Army Headquarters, *Training: Operations – Lessons Learned, Army Pamphlet No. 350–15–1* (Washington, DC: Government Printing Office, October 1966), 13; "US Sprays Herbicide on South Vietnamese Rice Crop," *FAS Newsletter*, 19 (January 1966), 1; MACV, *Counterinsurgency Lessons Learned Number 68*, 20.

26 Headquarters 3rd Brigade Task Force, 25th Infantry Division, *Operational Report for Quarterly Period 31 July 1967 (RCS-CSFOR-65)*, August 10, 1967. Online version on January 8, 2008 at http://25thaviation.org/history/id769.htm; MACV, *Counterinsurgency Lessons Learned Number 68*, 17–18; Rogers, *Cedar Falls-Junction City*, 72; US Army, *Flame, Riot Control Agents and Herbicide Operations*, 6.3.

27 MACV, *Counterinsurgency Lessons Learned Number 68*, 18.

28 Ericson and Rotundo, *Charlie Rangers*, 226–230.

29 Lynn Newland, "Khe Sanh Pullout – A Lot Easier This Time," *The Pacific Stars and Stripes*, April 8, 1971, 6.

30 Richard A. Durkee, *CHECO Report: USAF Search and Rescue, July 1966–November 1967 – Continuing Report, 19 January 1968*, Item Number 0390216001, Folder 16, Box 02, Contemporary Historical Examination of Current Operations (CHECO) Reports of Southeast Asia (1961–1975), The Vietnam Archive, Texas Tech University,

19–20; Tilford, *Search and Rescue in Southeast Asia*, 95–96; US Air Force, *Air Force History Report on Operation Tailwind*.

31 United States Air Force, *Air Force History Report: Operation Tailwind*. July 16, 1998. Online version on January 22, 2008 at www.fas.org/man/dod-101/ops/docs/tailwnd.htm; US Air Force, *Air Force History Report on Operation Tailwind*.

32 LeRoy W. Lowe, *USAF Search and Rescue Operations in SEA, 1 January 1971–31 March 1972*, Directorate of Tactical Evaluation, Pacific Air Force Headquarters, October 17, 1972, 63–66, 75.

33 Tilford, *Search and Rescue in Southeast Asia*, 95; US Air Force, *Air Force History Report on Operation Tailwind*.

7 Urban combat

1 Moss, *Vietnam*, 272–273; Norman L. Cooling, "Hue City, 1968: Winning a Battle While Losing a War," *Marine Corps Gazette* (July 2001), 65; George W. Smith, *The Siege at Hue* (Boulder: Lynne Rienner Publisher, 1999), 24–25.

2 G.R. Christmas, "A Company Commander Reflects On Operation Hue City," in *The Marines in Vietnam, 1954–1973: An Anthology and Annotated Bibliography*, 2nd edn. (Washington, DC: Government Printing Office, 1985), 159; Keith William Nolan, *Battle for Hue: Tet 1968* (New York: Dell Publishing Company, Inc., 1985), 22, 23; D. Mclaurin, Paul A. Jureidini, David S. McDonald and Kurt J. Sellers, *Modern Experience in City Combat, Technical Memorandum 5–87*, United States Army Human Engineering Laboratory, Aberdeen Proving Ground, Maryland, March 1987, 67–68; Jack Shulimson, *Tet-1968* (Toronto: Bantam Books, 1988), 91–94; Moss, *Vietnam*, 279; Smith, *Siege at Hue*, 10–14, 26; Cooling, "Hue City," 64–65; William G. Robertson, ed., *Block by Block: The Challenges of Urban Operations* (Fort Leavenworth, Kansas: US Army Command and General Staff College Press, 2003), 124–126.

3 The Republic of Vietnam was divided into four corps tactical zones, each of which was a political as well as military jurisdiction. I Corps bordered the Demilitarized Zone and was made up of the five northernmost provinces of South Vietnam: Quang Tri, Thua Thien, Quang Nam, Quang Tin and Quang Ngai. It covered 10,000 square miles.

4 Autonomous cities were outside the jurisdiction of the tactical corps commanders and were under the control of mayors who reported directly to the government in Saigon. The autonomous cities were Hue, Da Nang, Saigon, Dalat, Vung Tauo and Can Ranh.

5 The initial North Vietnamese forces involved in the battle consisted of six infantry battalions, two sapper battalions and two mortar battalions. There were also six Viet Cong main force battalions. The Communists eventually brought in five more North Vietnamese battalions from the Khe Sanh battlefield, which brought their strength in and around Hue to two divisions.

6 Christmas, "A Company Commander Reflects," 159; Nolan, *Battle for Hue*, 156; Cooling, "Hue City," 66–67; Robertson, ed., *Block by Block*, 131–132, 444.

7 The M48 Patton was classified as a medium battle tank. It was about thirty feet long and twelve feet wide. The top of the turret was ten feet above the ground. It weighed nearly fifty tons and had a crew of four. Its armor was about 4.9 inches thick and it was armed with a 90-mm main gun, a 0.50-caliber machine gun and a 0.30-caliber machine gun. It had a top speed of just under thirty miles per hour and could travel almost 290 miles without refueling. Answers.com, *M48 Patton*. Online version on January 29, 2009 at www.answers.com/M48+tank?initiator=IE7:SearchBox.

8 The Ontos was a lightly armored tank destroyer armed with six 106-mm recoilless rifles and a 0.30-caliber machine gun. The recoilless rifles could be fired independently,

in sequence or all together. The guns had to be loaded manually from outside the vehicle, exposing the loader to hostile fire. Four of the recoilless rifles had 0.50-caliber "spotting" rifles that could be fired to insure that the main guns were lined up with an enemy target. It could only carry eighteen 106 mm rounds in the ammunition storage area, limiting the number of fire missions it could undertake without restocking. Answers.com, *M50 Ontos*. Online version on January 29, 2009 at www.answers.com/ Ontos.

9 Nolan, *Battle for Hue*, 33–55; Shulimson *et al.*, *The Defining Year*, 171–179; Cooling, "Hue City," 72.

10 It would have required about sixteen infantry battalions just to secure the perimeter of the city. This figure does not include the units necessary to enter Hue and defeat the entrenched forces within.

11 Nolan, *Battle for Hue*, 74–76; Cooling, "Hue City," 68; Robertson, ed., *Block by Block*, 136.

12 Robertson, ed., *Block by Block*, 1, 3, 9, 447; United States Army Headquarters, *Military Operations on Urbanized Terrain (MOUT)*, Field Manual No. *90–10* (Washington, DC: Government Printing Office, August 15, 1979), 1.7–1.8; United States Army Headquarters, *An Infantryman's Guide To Combat in Built-Up Areas*, Field Manual No. *90–10–1* (Washington, DC: Government Printing Office, May 12, 1993), 1.4–1.5.

13 Nolan, *Battle for Hue*, 69; Eric M. Hammel, *Fire in the Streets: The Battle for Hue, Tet 1968* (Chicago: Contemporary Books, 1991), 97; Cooling, "Hue City," 64, 73, 75; Robertson, ed., *Block by Block*, 128–129, 151–152.

14 Retired from the Marine Corps as a Lieutenant General in 1996.

15 Christmas, "A Company Commander Reflects," 160.

16 John M. Taylor, *Hue: A 1989 Analysis* (United States Marine Corps University Command and Staff College, 1989); Cooling, "Hue City," 69; Robertson, ed., *Block by Block*, 136.

17 Much like the Battle of the Bulge in World War II, weather was a big factor. It was unusually cold, about fifty degrees Fahrenheit with a constant misty drizzle that occasionally became a cold, drenching rain. Cloud cover and fog hampered all forms of aviation – jets, airplanes and even helicopters. The low overcast hovered over the city for much of the battle and the only days when the weather was clear enough to permit the use of jets for close air support were February 14–16. Nolan, *Battle for Hue*, 56–57; Hammel, *Fire in the Streets*, 59; Shulimson *et al.*, *The Defining Year*, 207.

18 Quoted in Smith, *Siege at Hue*, 103.

19 Hammel, *Fire in the Streets*, 88–89; Shulimson *et al.*, *The Defining Year*, 173–174; Smith, *Siege at Hue*, 141.

20 The 3.5-inch rockets were a World War II vintage weapon commonly called "bazookas." These weapons had been replaced by the Light Anti-Tank Weapon, or LAW. The LAW was a single-shot disposable weapon that fired a 66-mm high-explosive warhead with a shaped charge capable of penetrating one foot of steel armor or two feet of reinforced concrete. However, during the Battle of Hue, the marines resurrected the older weapons because they could blast through the thick building walls, whereas the LAWs did little damage.

21 The B40 fired a rocket-propelled grenade with a shaped charge capable of piercing thin armor plate. Although it was too small to penetrate the main armor of an M48 tank, it could still damage the tracks and disable it. The impact on the armor also created a horrendous din inside the tank, described as something similar to being inside a ringing bell. After several impacts in quick succession, a crew would become dazed and "punch drunk."

22 *Battle for Hue*, 83, 86–88; Shulimson, *Tet-1968*, 108–112; Hammel, *Fire in the Streets*, 141, 147, 148; and Shulimson *et al.*, *The Defining Year*, 180.

23 On the previous day, Captain Christmas had placed his M60 machine guns and

rocket launchers with the assaulting elements. This is an example of a tactic that worked well in the jungle but was a disadvantage in urban combat. As part of the assault, they could not provide effective supporting fire and were easily suppressed by the entrenched enemy. Hammel, *Fire in the Streets*, 154.

24 This was a superb display of gunnery. Because of the restrictions of the urban terrain, the mortars had to fire so that the round would come directly down on the enemy positions. To achieve this, the mortars were moved to within *minimal* firing distance. Using the least possible powder charge, the rounds were fired almost vertically, allowing the prevailing breeze off the Perfume River to carry them over and down onto the enemy positions. Ibid., 155–156.

25 Because of their weight, these weapons had to be mounted on small flatbed vehicles called mules so they could maneuver around the battlefield.

26 Various versions of the account credit a tank, a recoilless rifle gun crew or an individual firing 3.5-inch rockets with the destruction of the gate and the door.

27 Christmas, "A Company Commander Reflects," 161; Nolan, *Battle for Hue*, 82–83; Shulimson, *Tet-1968*, 108–112; Hammel, *Fire in the Streets*, 141, 154–175; Shulimson et al., *The Defining Year*, 180–185; Smith, *Siege at Hue*, 100–101, 146–147; Robertson, ed., *Block by Block*, 139–141.

28 Nolan, *Battle for Hue*, 105–106, 168; Smith, *Siege at Hue*, 143–144; Hammel, *Fire in the Streets*, 175; Shulimson et al., *The Defining Year*, 183; Cooling, "Hue City," 69, 74.

29 Hammel, *Fire in the Streets*, 183–186; Smith, *Siege at Hue*, 147; Nolan, *Battle for Hue*, 92; Christmas, "A Company Commander Reflects," 161.

30 Hammel, *Fire in the Streets*, 218–219, 224–225, 290.

31 Nolan, *Battle for Hue*, 56; Christmas, "A Company Commander Reflects," 162; Hammel, *Fire in the Streets*, 232; Shulimson et al., *The Defining Year*, 189.

32 Christmas, "A Company Commander Reflects," 162; Nolan, *Battle for Hue*, 117–120; Shulimson, *Tet-1968*, 120; Hammel, *Fire in the Streets*, 228–238; Shulimson et al., *The Defining Year*, 189–190; Robertson, ed., *Block by Block*, 143.

33 Hammel, *Fire in the Streets*, 251; Shulimson et al., *The Defining Year*, 211.

34 Commonly called the "four-deuce," the M30 was much larger (about 670 pounds with a 4.2-inch bore) and more powerful than the 81-mm mortars (about 120 pounds with a 3.2-inch bore) carried by an infantry battalion. The 4.2-inch high-explosive shells contain up to six-times more explosive than their 81mm counterparts. Unlike other mortars, the M30 had a rifled bore and used the spin imparted to the rounds to stabilize them in flight instead of fins, which made them very accurate. The maximum range of the tube depended on the type of round fired; high-explosive rounds had a range of about 4.2 miles, while CS rounds could only reach about 3.5 miles. The minimum range for all of the rounds, an important issue in the Battle of Hue, was just under one-half-mile. Leo P. Brophy, Wyndham D. Miles and Rexmond C. Cohrane, "Chemical Mortars and Shells," in *The Chemical Warfare Service: From Laboratory to Field* (Washington, DC: Government Printing Office, 1968); Brooks E. Kleber and Dale Birdsell, *The Chemical Warfare Service: Chemicals in Combat* (Washington, DC: Government Printing Office, 1990), 418; United States Army Headquarters, *Mortars, Field Manual 23–90* (Washington, DC: Government Printing Office, March 1, 2000).

35 Nolan, *Battle for Hue*, 136–138, 164–165; Shulimson et al., *The Defining Year*, 194.

36 The limited and predictable avenues of approach also made the tanks easy targets for the B40 gunners; by the end of the battle, every tank had been hit at least a dozen times. Nolan, *Battle for Hue*, 207.

37 Ibid., 204–205; Shulimson et al., *The Defining Year*, 168, 192, 197–198, 201; Cooling, "Hue City," 69–70; Robertson, ed., *Block by Block*, 146.

38 General LaHue told Major Thompson that he thought they would be finished and

out of Hue in just a few days. In fact, it would be almost two weeks of some of the bloodiest fighting of the Vietnam War until the Battle of Hue was over and the marines left the city to return to war in the jungle.

39 Nicholas Warr, *Phase Line Green: The Battle for Hue, 1968* (New York: Ivy Books, 1999), 102, 104.

40 Every marine in 1/5 had been issued a protective mask prior to being deployed to the Citadel. Unaware of the extensive use of CS during the battle, the line marines began spreading rumors that the masks were necessary because the North Vietnamese had chemical weapons. Ibid., 84.

41 The effectiveness of artillery in the urban environment was not everything that was anticipated. Naval guns had a relatively flat trajectory and either hit the outside of the Citadel wall or passed over the target. The marine howitzers, on the other hand, were accurate but were firing at extreme range from the south and into the face of the attacking marines. This meant that there was a high risk of friendly casualties due to normal variations in the trajectory of shells. Nolan, *Battle for Hue*, 206; Shulimson et al., *The Defining Year*, 200; Smith, *Siege at Hue*, 198.

42 "Allies Storm Hue Citadel," *The European Stars and Stripes*, February 16, 1968, 1; "Marine Jets Pound Citadel to Soften Up Red Defenders," *The Pacific Stars and Stripes*, February 16, 1968, 13; Nolan, *Battle for Hue*, 183–185, 194; Shulimson et al., *The Defining Year*, 199–200.

43 Company D was also operating at reduced strength. A platoon had been assigned to a security detail for trucks moving between Hue and Phu Bai. Nolan, *Battle for Hue*, 185.

44 Swift boats were small, shallow water vessels operated by the US Navy during the Vietnam War. They had aluminum hulls, were fifty feet long and thirteen feet wide with a shallow draft of about five feet. They were equipped with two 0.50-caliber machine guns and a normal crew complement of one officer and five crewmen.

45 Nolan, *Battle for Hue*, 185–192; Shulimson et al., *The Defining Year*, 200–201.

46 Nolan, *Battle for Hue*, 194; Shulimson et al., *The Defining Year*, 201–202; Smith, *Siege at Hue*, 196, 198; Warr, *Phase Line Green*, 110; Robertson, ed., *Block by Block*, 146.

47 Shulimson, *Tet-1968*, 142; Shulimson et al., *The Defining Year*, 202–203.

48 An unusual aspect of combat in the Citadel was that very little happened after dark. Whereas nightly patrols, ambushes and counter-ambushes were a routine occurrence in the jungle, in Hue US forces would fight until dark then fall back to defensive positions for the night. The North Vietnamese were also generally content to take the night off and wait for daylight. In some instances, realizing that the marines had broken off their attack, they would leave their daytime positions and move to a more comfortable area to spend the night. Then, like civilian industrial workers, they would return just before daybreak and set up for the next day's battle.

49 Nolan, *Battle for Hue*, 231; Hammel, *Fire in the Streets*, 336–337; Shulimson et al., *The Defining Year*, 206–208; Warr, *Phase Line Green*, 151.

50 US Army, *Flame, Riot Control Agents and Herbicide Operations*, 7.3; Warr, *Phase Line Green*, 222–229; Eberhart, "Tear Gas Quandary."

51 Shulimson et al., *The Defining Year*, 208–209, 211, 213.

52 Charles Mohr, "Foe Invades US Saigon Embassy," *New York Times*, January 31, 1968, 1; Peter Arnett, "US Diplomat, 56, Kills VC in Embassy Duel," *The European Stars and Stripes*, February 1, 1968, 3; Joseph L. Dees, "The Viet Cong Attack that Failed." *Department of State News Letter*, May 1968.

53 Hay, *Tactical and Materiel Innovations*, 38.

54 US Army, *Flame, Riot Control Agents and Herbicide Operations*, 7.3.

55 Fighting in Hue consumed an inordinate amount of all types of ammunition, almost ten-times the normal combat rate experienced during rural fighting. Nolan, *Battle for Hue*, 208; Shulimson, *Tet-1968*, 114; US Army, *Flame, Riot Control Agents and Herbicide Operations*, 7.3; Cooling, "Hue City," 75.

56 During 1968, as much CS was consumed in Vietnam as in all the previous years of the war put together. Between 1968 and the end of 1970, nearly three-times as much CS was purchased by the US Army for use in Vietnam as there was between 1963 and the end of 1967. Stockholm International Peace Research Institute, *Ecological Consequences of the Second Indochina War* (Stockholm: Almqvist & Wiksell, 1976), 54.

57 As quoted in Keith William Nolan, *House to House: Playing the Enemy's Game in Saigon, May 1968* (St. Paul: Zenith Press, 2006), 81.

58 Ibid., 312–314, 341–343.

59 "Reds Sink Navy Gunboat Off Viet," *The Pacific Stars and Stripes*, June 18, 1968, 24; "Last VC Holdouts Routed in Saigon," *The Pacific Stars and Stripes*, June 19, 1968, 1; Shulimson, *Tet-1968*, 142.

60 USAF 1967–1968, *Defense of Saigon* Part 2, no date, 69–70, Item Number 168300010908, Folder 01, Bud Harton Collection, The Vietnam Archive, Texas Tech University. Online version on August 19, 2009, available through the online catalog at www.virtualarchive.vietnam.ttu.edu/virtualarchive/.

61 Robinson, *CB Weapons*, 190; Hay, *Tactical and Materiel Innovations*, 38; Cooling, "Hue City," 64; and Robertson, ed., *Block by Block*, 149–150.

8 Communist chemical operations

1 Memorandum from the Joint Chiefs of Staff to Secretary of Defense McNamara, "Chemical Crop Destruction, South Vietnam," July 28, 1962, Document 251, Baehler *et al.*, eds., *Foreign Relations 1961–1963, Volume II*, 553–554.

2 Headquarters, United States Military Assistance Command, Vietnam, "NVA CBR Capability," dated August 25, 1966, in *Records of the Military Assistance Command Vietnam, Part 2. Classified Studies from the Combined Intelligence Center Vietnam, 1965–1973*, edited by Robert Lester (Central Michigan University Library, Frederick, Maryland: University Publications of America, 1988), microfilm, Reel 30, F40–F41, F52–F54; Headquarters, United States Military Assistance Command, Vietnam, "VC/NVA CBR (First Update)," dated February 16, 1969, in *Records of the Military Assistance Command Vietnam, Part 2. Classified Studies from the Combined Intelligence Center Vietnam, 1965–1973*, edited by Robert Lester (Central Michigan University Library, Frederick, Maryland: University Publications of America, 1988), microfilm, Reel 22, F834–F836; Headquarters, United States Military Assistance Command, Vietnam, "VC/NVA CBR Equipment Identification Guide," dated April 1, 1971, in *Records of the Military Assistance Command Vietnam, Part 2. Classified Studies from the Combined Intelligence Center Vietnam, 1965–1973*, edited by Robert Lester (Central Michigan University Library, Frederick, Maryland: University Publications of America, 1988), microfilm, Reel 30, F299–F301; *Captured Documents (CDEC): Anti-Chemical Medicines and Defoliation Powder*, January 7, 1967, Item Number F034600320422, Folder 0422, Box 0032, Vietnam Archive Collection, The Vietnam Archive, Texas Tech University. Online version on November 11, 2008, available through the online catalog at www.virtualarchive.vietnam.ttu.edu/virtualarchive/; *Captured Documents (CDEC): NVA Armored Regiment 202 Chemical Warfare Training in NVN*, January 10, 1967, Item Number F034600422443, Folder 2443, Box 0042, Vietnam Archive Collection, The Vietnam Archive, Texas Tech University. Online version on November 11, 2008, available through the online catalog at www.virtualarchive.vietnam.ttu.edu/virtualarchive/; *Captured Documents (CDEC): Detection of Chemical Warfare Agents in NVN*, January 10, 1967, Item Number F034600422439, Folder 2439, Box 0042, Vietnam Archive Collection, The Vietnam Archive, Texas Tech University. Online version on November 11, 2008, available through the online catalog at www.virtualarchive.vietnam.ttu.edu/starweb/virtual/vva/servlet.starweb?path=virtual/vva/virtual.web; *Captured Documents (CDEC): NVA Chemical,*

Biological and Mediological [sic] Information, April 19, 1967, 3, Item Number F034600900461, Folder 0461, Box 0090, Vietnam Archive Collection, The Vietnam Archive, Texas Tech University. Online version on November 12, 2008, available through the online catalog at www.virtualarchive.vietnam.ttu.edu/virtualarchive/; MACV, Vietnam Lessons Learned Number 69, 30.

3 US Army, Flame, Riot Control Agents and Herbicide Operations, 7.3.

4 "GIs Hit Caves, Nab N. Viets," The Pacific Stars and Stripes, August 26, 1967, 6.

5 Headquarters, United States Military Assistance Command, Vietnam, "The VC Capability for Chemical Operations in the RVN," dated May 13, 1966, in Records of the Military Assistance Command Vietnam, Part 2. Classified Studies from the Combined Intelligence Center Vietnam, 1965–1973, edited by Robert Lester (Central Michigan University Library, Frederick, Maryland: University Publications of America, 1988), microfilm, Reel 29, F511; Recently, the US Imperialists and their Henchmen Have Intensified their Destructive Activities in NVN, November 21, 1969, 46–47, Item Number 6340110008, Folder 10, Box 01, Admiral Elmo R. Zumwalt, Jr. Collection: Agent Orange Articles, The Vietnam Archive, Texas Tech University. Online version on May 14, 2008, available through the online catalog at www.virtualarchive.vietnam. ttu.edu/virtualarchive/; Captured Documents (CDEC): Training Lesson Plan on Chemical Effects and Precautions, November 26, 1966, Item Number F034600391834, Folder 1834, Box 0039, Vietnam Archive Collection, The Vietnam Archive, Texas Tech University. Online version on November 11, 2008, available through the online catalog at www.virtualarchive.vietnam.ttu.edu/virtualarchive/; Captured Documents (CDEC): Translation Report of Chemical Training, April 13, 1967, Item Number F034600852080, Folder 2080, Box 0085, Vietnam Archive Collection, The Vietnam Archive, Texas Tech University. Online version on November 12, 2008, available through the online catalog at www.virtualarchive.vietnam.ttu.edu/virtualarchive/; Captured Documents (CDEC): Instructions Pertaining to Chemical Prevention and Countermeasures, January 7, 1966, Item Number F034600160905, Folder 0905, Box 0016, Vietnam Archive Collection, The Vietnam Archive, Texas Tech University. Online version on November 12, 2008, available through the online catalog at www.virtualarchive.vietnam.ttu.edu/virtualarchive/; VC Defense Analyst, July 17, 1970, Item Number 2250212005, Folder 12, Box 02, Douglas Pike Collection: Unit 03 – Technology, The Vietnam Archive, Texas Tech University. Online version on May 14, 2008, available through the online catalog at www.virtualarchive.vietnam.ttu.edu/ virtualarchive/.

6 One reference warned against using dogs as test animals since they could apparently tolerate more of some toxins than humans. According to the document, several individuals had taken ill after consuming food that had been consumed with impunity by a village mutt. It suggested switching to other animals that were more sensitive to harmful chemicals, such as small fish. US Imperialists and their Henchmen, 31–33, 35.

7 Captured Documents (CDEC): Draft of Report on Toxic Chemicals, December 11, 1966, Item Number F034600872866, Folder 2866, Box 0087, Vietnam Archive Collection, The Vietnam Archive, Texas Tech University. Online version on November 11, 2008, available through the online catalog at www.virtualarchive.vietnam.ttu. edu/virtualarchive/; Captured Documents (CDEC): Information Pertaining to Chemicals and Preventive Measures, October 28, 1966, Item Number F034600161531, Folder 1531, Box 0016, Vietnam Archive Collection, The Vietnam Archive, Texas Tech University. Online version on May 14, 2008, available through the online catalog at www.virtualarchive.vietnam.ttu.edu/virtualarchive/; Detection of Chemical Warfare Agents in NVN; Captured Documents (CDEC): Circular Prepared by the Chemical Prevention Section of T2, January 27, 1967, Item Number F034600590321, Folder 0321, Box 0059, Vietnam Archive Collection, The Vietnam Archive, Texas Tech University. Online version on November 12, 2008, available through the online catalog at

www.virtualarchive.vietnam.ttu.edu/virtualarchive/; *Captured Documents (CDEC): Translation Report of Strength and Weapons of Cong Truong 9 Division*, April 2, 1967, 8, Item Number F034600970919, Folder 0919, Box 0097, Vietnam Archive Collection, The Vietnam Archive, Texas Tech University. Online version on November 12, 2008, available through the online catalog at www.virtualarchive.vietnam.ttu.edu/virtualarchive/; *Translation Report of Chemical Training*; *NVA Chemical, Biological and Mediological* [sic] *Information*, 3–4; *PLAF/PAVN Urban Military Tactics August 1969*, August 1969, 24–25, Item Number 2131007010, Folder 07, Box 10, Douglas Pike Collection: Unit 02 – Military Operations, The Vietnam Archive, Texas Tech University. Online version on November 12, 2008, available through the online catalog at www.virtualarchive.vietnam.ttu.edu/virtualarchive/; *VC Defense Analyst*; Mangold and Penycate, *Tunnels of Cu Chi*, 80–81.

8 *US Imperialists and their Henchmen*, 31–33, 35; *Captured Documents (CDEC): Report on the Captured Chemical Equipment*, no date, Item Number F034600570764, Folder 0764, Box 0057, Vietnam Archive Collection, The Vietnam Archive, Texas Tech University. Online version on November 12, 2008, available through the online catalog at www.virtualarchive.vietnam.ttu.edu/virtualarchive/; *Draft of Report on Toxic Chemicals*; R.W. Apple, Jr., "2,000 Men Bolster Viet Cong," *New York Times*, July 12, 1966, 2; Mangold and Penycate, *Tunnels of Cu Chi*, 81.

9 *Instructions Pertaining to Chemical Prevention and Countermeasures*; *Captured Documents (CDEC): Preventive Measures Against Poisonous Chemicals*, August 10, 1966, Item Number F034600071096, Folder 1096, Box 0007, Vietnam Archive Collection, The Vietnam Archive, Texas Tech University. Online version on November 11, 2008, available through the online catalog at www.virtualarchive.vietnam.ttu.edu/virtualarchive/; and *Draft of Report on Toxic Chemicals*.

10 Interview with Lieutenant Colonel Alvin R. Hylton; MACV, "The VC Capability for Chemical Operations in the RVN," dated May 13, 1966, F506, F517-F518.

11 *Preventive Measures Against Poisonous Chemicals*; *Instructions Pertaining to Chemical Prevention and Countermeasures*; *Draft of Report on Toxic Chemicals*; *PLAF/PAVN Urban Military Tactics,* 25; MACV, "The VC Capability for Chemical Operations in the RVN," dated May 13, 1966, F518–F521.

12 *US Imperialists and Their Henchmen*, 35–41.

13 Headquarters, United States Military Assistance Command, Vietnam, "Technical Intelligence Bulletin, First Edition," dated May 22, 1966, in *Records of the Military Assistance Command Vietnam, Part 2. Classified Studies from the Combined Intelligence Center Vietnam, 1965–1973*, edited by Robert Lester (Central Michigan University Library, Frederick, Maryland: University Publications of America, 1988), microfilm, Reel 29, F506; "Nonpoisonous Gas used by Viet Cong," *New York Times*, November 11, 1966, 1; "Gas Attack Confirmed," *New York Times*, November 12, 1966, 5; "VC Use Tear Gas 1st Time," *The Pacific Stars and Stripes*, November 12, 1966; "Viet Cong Deny Use of Tear Gas on GIs," *New York Times*, November 16, 1966, 2; "Arsenal in Action"; "The Giant Spoiler," *Time*, November 18, 1966; "Bar on Poison Gas Backed 101–0 in UN," *New York Times*, November 24, 1966, 12; interview with Lieutenant Colonel Alvin R. Hylton; Jozef Goldblat, *CB Disarmament Negotiations, 1920–1970* (Stockholm: Almqvist & Wiksell, 1971), 238–241.

14 "Gas Grenades Used By Vietnamese Foe," *New York Times*, January 18, 1967, 1; "Viet Cong Hurl Tear Gas, But Fail to Halt US Attack," *The Pacific Stars and Stripes*, January 19, 1967, 1; "86 Incidents Mar Tet Truce," *The Pacific Stars and Stripes*, February 11, 1967, 6.

15 "Reds Make Big Use of Tear Gas, Maul GIs," *Chicago Tribune*, March 1, 1967, 6; "GI's and Enemy in Sharp Fighting," *New York Times*, March 1, 1967, 2; "VC Use Tear Gas on US Troops," *The Pacific Stars and Stripes*, March 3, 1967, 6.

16 "Gas Grenades Used By Vietnamese Foe"; interview with Lieutenant Colonel Alvin

R. Hylton; Leon Cohan, Jr., "Vulnerable," *The Marine Corps Gazette* (April 1967), 33–35.

17 Headquarters, 4th Infantry Division, *Combat After Action Report – Operation Francis Marion*, November 25, 1967, Enclosure 6, "Chronological Summary of Significant Activities," 1; "Red Bridge Raid Rapped," *The European Stars and Stripes*, April 8, 1967, 2; "Reds' Pop-Bottle Gas Attack Stymied by Quick-Acting GIs," *The Pacific Stars and Stripes*, April 9, 1967, 6; "Use of Gas Spray by Foe Reported," *New York Times*, July 9, 1968, 5; "VC Use Gas on Viet Troops," *The Pacific Stars and Stripes*, July 14, 1968, 7.

18 *Draft of Report on Toxic Chemicals*; Headquarters, 1st Battalion (Mechanized), 5th Infantry, *Combat After-Action Report (RCS: MACV J3–32)*. September 14, 1966. Online version on October 10, 2008 at http://25thaviation.org/history/id747.htm; Headquarters 1st Brigade, 25th Infantry Division, *Combat Operations After Action Report*, September 29, 1966, 15, 18. Online version on October 10, 2008 at http://25thaviation.org/history/id743.htm; Mangold and Penycate, *Tunnels of Cu Chi*, 73.

19 Lindberg, "Use of Riot Control Agents," 54; Ericson and Rotundo, *Charlie Rangers*, 118.

20 US Army, *Employment of Riot Control Agents*, April 1969, 35.

21 "VC Routed by their Own Gas," *The Pacific Stars and Stripes*, January 25, 1968, 6; Headquarters 25th Infantry Division, *Combat Operations After Action Report* (Operation Yellowstone), March 21, 1968. Online version on October 10, 2008 at http://25thaviation.org/history/id763.htm.

22 "Marines Chase Reds After Con Thien Fight," *The European Stars and Stripes*, October 15, 1967, 1; Telfer *et al.*, *Fighting the North Vietnamese*, 135–136.

23 Also known as Puff the Magic Dragon. It carried three 7.62-mm mini-guns, each capable of firing up to 6,000 rounds per minute.

24 Shulimson *et al.*, *The Defining Year*, 377–380.

25 In addition to claymore mines interspersed throughout the barbed wire, camp defenses included two 4.2-inch mortars, seven 81-mm mortars, nineteen 60-mm mortars, two 106-mm recoilless rifles, four 57-mm recoilless rifles, 100 M72 LAW rockets, two 0.50-caliber machine guns and numerous smaller-caliber machine guns. The defenders had also coordinated defensive fires with marine artillery units at Khe Sanh.

26 The PT-76 was a light tank with a boat-like hull originally developed for reconnaissance. The crew consisted of a driver, a loader and the commander, who also operated the main gun. It was powered by a V-six diesel engine with a five-speed manual transmission and capable of a top speed of about twenty-seven miles per hour on land and six miles per hour in the water. It could travel up to 230 miles before needing to refuel. The upper armor consisted of 0.4 inches of rolled steel while the lower plate was 0.5 inches thick. The thickness of the armor on the turret ranged from 0.8 inches in the front to 0.4 inches elsewhere. It was armed with a 76.2-mm main gun capable of firing about seven rounds per minute and a 7.62-mm coaxial machine gun. Military Today, *PT-76 Amphibious Light Tank*. Online version on November 7, 2008 at www.military-today.com/tanks/pt76.htm; Enemy Forces, *Light Tank PT-76*. Online version on November 7, 2008 at www.enemyforces.net/tanks/pt76.htm.

27 "North Vietnamese Troops Control Supply Highway," *Great Bend Daily Tribune*, Great Bend, Kansas, February 8, 1968, 1; "Tanks Surprised Lang Vei Troops," *Tri-City Herald*, Pasco, Washington, February 8, 1968, 15; "Fall of Lang Vei," *Time*, 16, February 1968; Willard Pearson, *The War in the Northern Provinces, 1966–1968* (Washington, DC: Government Printing Office, 1975), 74–76; John A. Cash, "Battle of Lang Vei," in *Seven Firefights in Vietnam* (Washington, DC: Government Printing Office, 1985).

28 *PAVN and PLAF Weapons and Weapon Use*, November 1969, 7, Item Number 2250101012, Folder 01, Box 01, Douglas Pike Collection: Unit 03 – Technology, The Vietnam Archive, Texas Tech University. Online version on May 14, 2008, available through the online catalog at www.virtualarchive.vietnam.ttu.edu/virtualar-chive/; Headquarters 25th Infantry Division, *Combat Operations After Action Report* (Operation Yellowstone); Headquarters, 25th Infantry Division, *Combat Operation After Action Report* (Operation Quyet Thang), May 20, 1968. Online version on October 10, 2008 at http://25thaviation.org/history/id740.htm; "Allies Kill 282 Red Attackers," *The European Stars and Stripes*, September 28, 1968, 2; B. Drum-mond Ayres, Jr., "Enemy Offensive Still Seesawing," *New York Times*, April 2, 1969, 3; "Green Beret Camp Shelled," *The European Stars and Stripes*, June 24, 1969, 2; "70 Enemy Attacks in South Vietnam Reported by US," *New York Times*, February 2, 1970, 1; 101st Infantry Division, *Lessons Learned Period Ending 31 July 1970*, 20, 70, 81; "70 Reds Die in Outpost Attack," *The Pacific Stars and Stripes*, June 11, 1971, 6; Alan L. Gropman, "Airpower and the Airlift Evacuation of Kham Duc," monograph 7 in *USAF Southeast Asia Monograph Series Volume V. 1976*. Reprint (Washington, DC: Government Printing Office, 1985), 29; Lindberg, "Use of Riot Control Agents," 54.

29 *CDEC Document Training Principles*, January 16, 1970, Item Number 2310305014, Folder 05, Box 03, Douglas Pike Collection: Unit 05 – National Liberation Front, The Vietnam Archive, Texas Tech University. Online version on May 14, 2008, available through the online catalog at www.virtualarchive.vietnam.ttu.edu/virtualar-chive/; Bernard Weinraub, "Marines Repulse Bayonet Attack," *New York Times*, September 8, 1967, 9; "Marines Battle 4,000 Reds: Casualties Heavy," *The European Stars and Stripes*, September 8, 1967, 2; "Outnumbered Marines Kill 92 After Ambush," *The European Stars and Stripes*, September 9, 1967, 2.

30 "The Massacre at Fire Base Mary Ann.," *Time*, April 12, 1971; Al Hemmingway, *Sixty Minutes of Terror*, March 1996. Online version on October 23, 2008 at www.americal.org/sixtymin.shtml; Keith William Nolan, *Sappers in the Wire: The Life and Death of Firebase Mary Ann* (New York: Pocket Books, 1996), 143–181, 246–264; Kelly Bell, *Deadly Sapper Attack on Fire Support Base Mary Ann During the Vietnam War*, October 2006. Online version on October 23, 2008 at www.historynet.com/deadly-sapper-attack-on-fire-support-base-mary-ann-during-the-vietnam-war.htm.

31 Fox Butterfield, "Besieged Anloc is Said to Repel Another Assault," *New York Times*, April 21, 1972, 1; Malcolm W. Browne, "Highlands Bases Evacuated," *New York Times*, April 26, 1972, 17; "The Fierce War on the Ground," *Time*, May 1, 1972; David K. Shipler, "Vietnamese Sides Battle in Cambodia for 3rd Day," *New York Times*, May 3, 1974, 3; James H. Willbanks, *Thiet Giap! The Battle of An Loc, April 1972* (Washington, DC: Government Printing Office, 1993), 22, 39–40.

32 Shipler, "Vietnamese Sides Battle in Cambodia for 3rd Day."

9 Conclusion

1 John Duffett, ed., *Against the Crime of Silence: Proceedings of The International War Crimes Tribunal* (New York: Simon and Schuster, 1970), 341; Rose, *CBW*, 90–91.

2 Gerard Van der Leun, "Type VX," *Earth Magazine*, April 1972, 26–27.

3 Memorandum From William Trueheart, the Deputy Director for Coordination, Bureau of Intelligence and Research to Stanley Hughes, the Director of the Bureau of Intelligence and Research, "Developments in Operations Against Vietnam," October 9, 1967, Document 350, Kent Sieg, ed., *Foreign Relations of the United States, 1964–1968, Volume V: Vietnam, 1967* (Washington, DC: Government Printing Office, 2002), 873–875; Memorandum From General Earle Wheeler, Chairman of the Joint Chiefs of Staff, to President Lyndon Johnson CM-2944–68, "Khe Sanh,"

February 3, 1968, Document 51, Kent Sieg, ed., *Foreign Relations of the United States, 1964–1968, Volume VI: Vietnam, January–August 1968* (Washington, DC: Government Printing Office, 2002), 117–120.

4 Force Health Protection and Readiness Policy & Programs, *Chemical–Biological Warfare Exposures Site, Project 112/SHAD Fact Sheets*. Online factsheets on June 30, 2010 at http://fhpr.osd.mil/CBexposures/factSheets.jsp.

5 *US Imperialists and their Henchmen*, 16–17; Headquarters, 25th Infantry Division, *Operational Report for Quarterly Period Ending 31 January 1968 (RCS CSFOR-65) (BC)*, February 14, 1968. Online version on November 11, 2008 at http://25thaviation.org/history/id753.htm#quarterly_report_ending_31_jan_68.

6 F.J. Dyson, R. Gomer, S. Weinberg and S.C. Wright, *Tactical Nuclear Weapons in Southeast Asia, Study S-266* (Institute for Defense Analyses, Jason Division, March 1967), 7–8.

SELECTED BIBLIOGRAPHY

Internet resources

The History Place. The Vietnam War. www.historyplace.com/unitedstates/vietnam/index.html (November 16, 2007).

Infoplease. Vietnam. www.infoplease.com/ipa/A0108144.html (January 8, 2008).

Leonard, Ron. 25th Aviation Battalion, After Action Reports. http://25thaviation.org/history/home.htm (January 8, 2008).

Parsch, Andreas. Designations of U.S. Aeronautical and Support Equipment. June 23, 2006. www.designation-systems.net/usmilav/aerosupport.html#_ASETDS_Component_Listings_Alpha (January 22, 2008).

Public Broadcasting Service. Battlefield: Vietnam. www.pbs.org/battlefieldvietnam/history/index.html (January 8, 2008).

Smith, Ray. Ray's Map Room, Vietnam Areas of Operation, Topographic Digital Map Images. www.rjsmith.com/topo_map.html (January 8, 2008).

Vets with a Mission. www.vwam.com/index.html (November 16, 2007).

Journals, newspapers and magazines

Chicago Tribune, 1965–1969.

The European Stars and Stripes, 1967–1970.

FAS Newsletter 1964–1967.

Joiner, Charles A. "South Vietnam's Buddhist Crisis: Organization for Charity, Dissidence, and Unity." *Asian Survey* 4 (July 1964), 915–928.

Lindberg, Kip. "The Use of Riot Control Agents During the Vietnam War." *Army Chemical Review* (January–June 2007), 51–55.

Marine Corps Gazette, 1966–2001.

Neilands, J.B. "Vietnam: Progress of the Chemical War." *Asian Survey* 10, **3** (1970), 209–229.

The New Republic, 1965–1967.

New York Times, 1955–1975.
The Pacific Stars and Stripes, 1965–1971.
Time, 1965–1975.
Washington Post, 1965–1972.

Documents

Army Concept Team in Vietnam. "Letter Report of Evaluation – Large Capacity Tunnel Flushers." November 25, 1966.

Army Concept Team in Vietnam. "CS Munitions: Cartridge, 4.2 Inch: Tactical, CS, XM630." September 1, 1968.

Army Concept Team in Vietnam. "CS Munitions: Fuze and Burster Bomb: System SM920E2." October 1, 1968.

Army Concept Team in Vietnam. "Final Report of Miniature CS Disseminator and XM58 CS Pocket Grenade." November 18, 1968.

Army Concept Team in Vietnam. "CS Munitions: Cartridge 40mm: Tactical CS, XM651 and XM651E1." December 1, 1968.

Combat Operations After Action Report (RCS MACV J3/32). April 28, 1966, Item Number 1710118001, Folder 18, Box 01, Operation Masher/Operation White Wing Collection, The Vietnam Archive, Texas Tech University. Online version on March 25, 2009, available through the online catalog at www.virtualarchive.vietnam.ttu.edu/virtualarchive/.

Durkee, Richard A. *USAF Search and Rescue in Southeast Asia, July 1966–November 1967*. Directorate of Tactical Evaluation, Pacific Air Force Headquarters, undated (*ca.* 1968).

Headquarters, United States Army Infantry School, Fort Benning, Georgia. *Lessons Learned (Vietnam)*. Undated (*ca.* 1967).

Headquarters, United States Continental Army Command. *Education and Training: Operations – Lessons Learned, USCONARC Pamphlet No. 350–30–2*. Washington, DC: Government Printing Office, December 15, 1965.

Headquarters, United States Military Assistance Command, Vietnam. "NVA CBR Capability," dated August 25, 1966, in *Records of the Military Assistance Command Vietnam, Part 2. Classified Studies from the Combined Intelligence Center Vietnam, 1965–1973*. Edited by Robert Lester. Central Michigan University Library, Frederick, Maryland: University Publications of America, 1988. Microfilm.

Headquarters, United States Military Assistance Command, Vietnam. "Technical Intelligence Bulletin," dated May 22, 1966, in *Records of the Military Assistance Command Vietnam, Part 2. Classified Studies from the Combined Intelligence Center Vietnam, 1965–1973*. Edited by Robert Lester. Central Michigan University Library, Frederick, Maryland: University Publications of America, 1988. Microfilm.

Headquarters, United States Military Assistance Command, Vietnam. "The VC Capability for Chemical Operations in the RVN," dated May 13, 1966, in *Records of the Military Assistance Command Vietnam, Part 2. Classified Studies from the Combined Intelligence Center Vietnam, 1965–1973*. Edited by Robert Lester. Central Michigan University Library, Frederick, Maryland: University Publications of America, 1988. Microfilm.

Headquarters, United States Military Assistance Command, Vietnam. "VC/NVA CBR Equipment Identification Guide," dated January 22, 1969, in *Records of the Military Assistance Command Vietnam, Part 2. Classified Studies from the Combined Intelligence*

Center Vietnam, 1965–1973. Edited by Robert Lester. Central Michigan University Library, Frederick, Maryland: University Publications of America, 1988. Microfilm.

Headquarters, United States Military Assistance Command, Vietnam. "VC/NVA CBR Equipment Identification Guide," dated April 1, 1971, in *Records of the Military Assistance Command Vietnam, Part 2. Classified Studies from the Combined Intelligence Center Vietnam, 1965–1973.* Edited by Robert Lester. Central Michigan University Library, Frederick, Maryland: University Publications of America, 1988. Microfilm.

Headquarters, United States Military Assistance Command, Vietnam. "VC/NVA Munitions Production in the Republic of Vietnam," dated September 13, 1970, in *Records of the Military Assistance Command Vietnam, Part 2. Classified Studies from the Combined Intelligence Center Vietnam, 1965–1973.* Edited by Robert Lester. Central Michigan University Library, Frederick, Maryland: University Publications of America, 1988. Microfilm.

Headquarters, United States Military Assistance Command, Vietnam. "VC/NVA CBR Capability in the Republic of Vietnam (First Update)," dated February 16, 1969, in *Records of the Military Assistance Command Vietnam, Part 2. Classified Studies from the Combined Intelligence Center Vietnam, 1965–1973.* Edited by Robert Lester. Central Michigan University Library, Frederick, Maryland: University Publications of America, 1988. Microfilm.

Headquarters, United States Military Assistance Command, Vietnam. *Vietnam Lessons Learned Number 45: Viet Cong Tunnels.* February 12, 1965.

Headquarters, United States Military Assistance Command, Vietnam. *Vietnam Lessons Learned Number 51: Operational Employment of Riot Control Munitions.* April 24, 1965.

Headquarters, United States Military Assistance Command, Vietnam. *Vietnam Lessons Learned Number 52: Operational Employment of the Mity Mite Portable Blower.* November 22, 1965.

Headquarters, United States Military Assistance Command, Vietnam. *Vietnam Lessons Learned Number 56: Operations Against Tunnel Complexes.* April 18, 1966.

Headquarters, United States Military Assistance Command, Vietnam. *Counterinsurgency Lessons Learned Number 61: Salient Lessons Learned.* January 27, 1967.

Headquarters, United States Military Assistance Command, Vietnam. *Vietnam Lessons Learned Number 68: Viet Cong Base Camps and Supply Caches.* July 20, 1968.

Headquarters, United States Military Assistance Command, Vietnam. *Vietnam Lessons Learned Number 69: Analysis of Enemy Positions at Khe Sanh and Evaluation of the Effectiveness of Weapons Systems Against Enemy Fortifications.* September 10, 1968.

Headquarters, United States Military Assistance Command, Vietnam. *Vietnam Lessons Learned Number 71: Countermeasures Against Standoff Attacks.* March 13, 1969.

Headquarters, United States Military Assistance Command, Vietnam. *Vietnam Lessons Learned Number 77: Fire Support Coordination in the Republic of Vietnam.* May 20, 1970.

Headquarters, United States Military Assistance Command, Vietnam. *Vietnam Lessons Learned Number 83: Guide for Helicopter Tactics and Techniques for Use with Reconnaissance Teams.* October 12, 1970.

Hedden, E.M. and D.C. Hawkins. *CBU-30/A Incapacitating Munitions System, AFATL-TR-67–178.* Air Force Armament Laboratory, Eglin Air Force Base, Florida, October 1967.

Lowe, LeRoy W. *USAF Search and Rescue Operations in SEA, 1 January 1971–31 March 1972.* Directorate of Tactical Evaluation, Pacific Air Force Headquarters, October 17, 1972.

Mclaurin, R.D., Paul A. Jureidini, David S. McDonald and Kurt J. Sellers. *Modern*

Experience in City Combat, Technical Memorandum 5–87. United States Army Human Engineering Laboratory, Aberdeen Proving Ground, Maryland, March 1987.

McNamara, B.P., E.J. Owens, J.T. Weimer, T.A. Ballard and F.J. Vocci. *Toxicology of Riot Control Chemicals – CS, CN, and DM, Edgewood Arsenal Technical Report 4309.* Medical Research Laboratory, Edgewood Arsenal, November 1969.

Operation Crazy Horse: 16 May–5 June 1966, Binh Dinh Province, Republic of Vietnam. September 10, 1966, Item Number 1070802002, Folder 02, Box 08, Glenn Helm Collection, The Vietnam Archive, Texas Tech University. Online version on March 25, 2009, available through the online catalog at www.virtualarchive.vietnam.ttu. edu/virtualarchive/.

The RAND Corporation Memorandum RM-5271-PR – A Translation from the French: Lessons of the War in Indochina. Vol. 2, May 1967, Item Number 12050110001, Folder 10, Box 01, Vladimir Lehovich Collection, The Vietnam Archive, Texas Tech University. Online version on March 25, 2009, available through the online catalog at www.virtualarchive.vietnam.ttu.edu/virtualarchive/.

Recently, the US Imperialists and their Henchmen Have Intensified their Destructive Activities in NVN. November 21, 1969, Item Number: 6340110008, Folder 10, Box 01, Admiral Elmo R. Zumwalt, Jr. Collection: Agent Orange Articles, The Vietnam Archive, Texas Tech University. Online version on May 14, 2008, available through the online catalog at www.virtualarchive.vietnam.ttu.edu/virtualarchive/.

Reece, Allen D. *A Historical Analysis of Tunnel Warfare and the Contemporary Perspective.* United States Army Command and General Staff College, December 1997.

Riot Control Munitions. No date (*ca.* March 1965), Item Number 3670812011, Folder 12, Box 08, George J. Veith Collection, The Vietnam Archive, Texas Tech University. Online version on December 9, 2008, available through the online catalog at www. virtualarchive.vietnam.ttu.edu/virtualarchive/.

Schwendeman, James L. and Ival O. Salyer. "Composition and Method for Generating Stabilized Lacrimating Foam for Tunnel Denial." United States Patent 3814808, June 4, 1974.

United States Air Force. *Air Force History Report: Operation Tailwind.* July 16, 1998. Online version on January 17, 2000 at www.fas.org/man/dod-101/ops/docs/tailwind.htm.

United States Army Corps of Engineers. *Did You Know: How Army Engineers Cleared Viet Cong Tunnels?, Number 62.* US Army Corps of Engineers Office of History, undated.

United States Department of the Air Force. *Air Force History Report on Operation Tailwind.* Air Force History Support Office, July 16, 1998.

United States Department of Defense. *Review of Allegations Concerning "Operations Tailwind.* July 21, 1998. Online version on January 28, 2000 at www.fas.org/irp/news/1998/07/980721-tailwind.htm.

United States House Committee on International Relations, Subcommittee on International Security and Scientific Affairs. *War Powers: A Test of Compliance Relative to the Da Nang Sealift, the Evacuation of Phnom Penh, The Evacuation of Saigon, and the Mayaguez Incident.* 94th Congress, 1st Session, May 7 and June 4, 1975.

VC Defense Analyst. July 17, 1970, Item Number: 2250212005, Folder 12, Box 02, Douglas Pike Collection: Unit 03 – Technology, The Vietnam Archive, Texas Tech University. Online version on May 14, 2008, available through the online catalog at www.virtualarchive.vietnam.ttu.edu/virtualarchive.

Books

Baehler, David M. and Charles S. Sampson, eds. *Foreign Relations of the United States, 1961–1963, Volume II: Vietnam, 1962.* Washington, DC: Government Printing Office, 1990.

Bergsma, Herbert L. *Chaplains with Marines in Vietnam, 1962–1971.* Washington, DC: Government Printing Office, 1985.

Berry, F. Clifton, Jr. *Gadget Warfare.* Toronto: Bantam Books, 1988.

Bowers, Ray L. *Tactical Airlift.* Washington, DC: Government Printing Office, 1983.

Brophy, Leo P., Wyndham D. Miles and Rexmond C. Cohrane. *The Chemical Warfare Service: From Laboratory to Field.* Washington, DC: Government Printing Office, 1968.

Buckingham, William A., Jr. *OPERATION RANCH HAND: The Air Force and Herbicides in Southeast Asia 1961–1971.* Washington, DC: Government Printing Office, 1982.

Cash, John A., John Albright and Allan W. Sandstrum. *Seven Firefights in Vietnam.* Washington, DC: Government Printing Office, 1985.

Cecil, Paul Frederick. *Herbicidal Warfare: The RANCH HAND Project in Vietnam.* New York: Praeger, 1986.

Cosmas, Graham A. and Terrence R. Murray. *U.S. Marines in Vietnam: Vietnamization and Redeployment, 1970–1971.* Edited by William R. Melton and Jack Shulimson. Washington, DC: Government Printing Office, 1986.

Des Brisay, Thomas D. "Fourteen Hours at Koh Tang," Monograph 5 in *USAF Southeast Asia Monograph Series Volume III.* Reprint. Washington, DC: Government Printing Office, 1985.

Dunham, George R. and David A. Quinlan. *U.S. Marines in Vietnam: The Bitter End, 1973–1975.* Washington, DC: Government Printing Office, 1990.

Ellison, D. Hank. *Handbook of Chemical and Biological Warfare Agents,* 2nd Edition. Boca Raton: CRC Press, 2008.

Ericson, Don and John L. Rotundo. *Charlie Rangers.* New York: Ivy Books, 1989.

Ewell, Julian J. and Ira A. Hunt, Jr. *Sharpening the Combat Edge: The Use of Analysis to Reinforce Military Judgment.* Washington, DC: Government Printing Office, 1995.

Hammel, Eric M. *Fire in the Streets: The Battle for Hue, Tet 1968.* Chicago: Contemporary Books, 1991.

Hammond, William M. *Public Affairs: The Military and the Media, 1962–1968.* Washington, DC: Government Printing Office, 1988.

Hammond, William M. *Reporting Vietnam: Media and Military at War.* Lawrence: University of Kansas Press, 1998.

Hay, John H., Jr. *Tactical and Materiel Innovations.* Washington, DC: Government Printing Office, 1974.

Headquarters, United States Marine Corps. *The Marines in Vietnam, 1954–1973: An Anthology and Annotated Bibliography,* 2nd Edition. Washington, DC: Government Printing Office, 1985.

Huber, Thomas M. "Lethality in Motion: Tactics," in *Japan's Battle of Okinawa, April–June 1945.* Washington, DC: Government Printing Office, 1990.

Humphrey, David C., ed. *Foreign Relations of the United States, 1964–1968, Volume IV: Vietnam, 1966.* Washington, DC: Government Printing Office, 1998.

Humphrey, David C., Edward C. Keefer and Louis J. Smith, eds. *Foreign Relations of the United States, 1964–1968, Volume III: Vietnam, June–December 1965.* Washington, DC: Government Printing Office, 1996.

Humphrey, David C., Ronald D. Landa and Louis J. Smith, eds. *Foreign Relations of the United States, 1964–1968, Volume II: Vietnam, January–June 1965.* Washington, DC: Government Printing Office, 1996.

Keefer, Edward C., ed. *Foreign Relations of the United States, 1961–1963, Volume IV: Vietnam, August–December 1963.* Washington, DC: Government Printing Office, 1991.

Keefer, Edward C., ed. *Foreign Relations of the United States, 1964–1968, Volume XXVIII: Laos.* Washington, DC: Government Printing Office, 1998.

Keefer, Edward C. and Louis J. Smith, eds. *Foreign Relations of the United States, 1961–1963, Volume III: Vietnam, January–August 1963.* Washington, DC: Government Printing Office, 1991.

Keefer, Edward C. and Carolyn Yee, eds. *Foreign Relations of the United States, 1969–1976, Volume VI: Vietnam, January 1969–July 1970.* Washington, DC: Government Printing Office, 2006.

Landa, Ronald D. and Charles S. Sampson, eds. *Foreign Relations of the United States, 1961–1963, Volume I: Vietnam, 1961.* Washington, DC: Government Printing Office, 1988.

Lee, Alex. *Force Recon Command: 3d Force Recon Company in Vietnam, 1969–70.* New York: Ivy Books, 1995.

Lee, Alex. *Utter's Battalion: 2/7 Marines in Vietnam, 1965–66.* New York: Ballantine Publishing Group, 2000.

MacGarrigle, George L. *Combat Operations: Taking the Offensive, October 1966 to October 1967.* Washington, DC: Government Printing Office, 1998.

Mangold, Tom and John Penycate. *The Tunnels of Cu Chi.* New York: Berkley Books, 1986.

Mangold, Tom and John Penycate. *Tunnel Warfare.* Toronto: Bantam Books, 1987.

Moss, George Donelson. *Vietnam: An American Ordeal,* 3rd Edition. Upper Saddle River: Prentice Hall, 1998.

Nolan, Keith William. *Battle for Hue: Tet 1968.* New York: Dell Publishing Company, Inc., 1985.

Nolan, Keith William. *House to House: Playing the Enemy's Game in Saigon, May 1968.* St. Paul: Zenith Press, 2006.

Office of the Federal Register. "Executive Order 11850 – Renunciation of Certain Uses in War of Chemical Herbicides and Riot Control Agents," in *Codification of Presidential Proclamations and Executive Orders: April 13, 1945, through January 20, 1989.* Washington, DC: Government Printing Office, 1989.

Patterson, David S., ed. *Foreign Relations of the United States, 1964–1968, Volume X: National Security Policy.* Washington, DC: Government Printing Office, 2001.

Pearson, Willard. *The War in the Northern Provinces, 1966–1968.* Washington, DC: Government Printing Office, 1975.

Ploger, Robert R. *US Army Engineers 1965–1970.* Washington, DC: Government Printing Office, 2000.

Robertson, William G., ed. *Block by Block: The Challenges of Urban Operations.* Fort Leavenworth: US Army Command and General Staff College Press, 2003.

Robinson, Julian Perry. *The Rise of CB Weapons.* Stockholm: Almqvist & Wiksell, 1971.

Rogers, Bernard William. *Cedar Falls-Junction City: A Turning Point.* Washington, DC: Government Printing Office, 1974.

Shulimson, Jack. *Tet-1968.* Toronto: Bantam Books, 1988.

Shulimson, Jack and Charles M. Johnson. *U.S. Marines in Vietnam: The Landing and the Buildup 1965.* Washington, DC: Government Printing Office, 1978.

Shulimson, Jack, Leonard A. Blasiol, Charles R. Smith and David A. Dawson. *U.S. Marines in Vietnam: The Defining Year, 1968.* Washington, DC: Government Printing Office, 1997.

Sidell, Fredrick R., Ernest T. Takafuji and David R. Franz, eds. *Medical Aspects of Chemical and Biological Warfare.* Washington, DC: Office of the Surgeon General, Department of the Army, 1997.

Sieg, Kent, ed. *Foreign Relations of the United States, 1964–1968, Volume V: Vietnam, 1967.* Washington, DC: Government Printing Office, 2002.

Sieg, Kent, ed. *Foreign Relations of the United States, 1964–1968, Volume VI: Vietnam, January–August 1968.* Washington, DC: Government Printing Office, 2002.

Smith, Charles R. *US Marines in Vietnam: High Mobility and Stand-down, 1969.* Washington, DC: Government Printing Office, 1988.

Smith, George W. *The Siege at Hue.* Boulder: Lynne Rienner Publisher, 1999.

Smith, Louis J. and David H. Herschler, eds. *Foreign Relations of the United States, 1969–1976, Volume I: Foundations of Foreign Policy, 1969–1972.* Washington, DC: Government Printing Office, 2003.

Son, Pham Van and Le Van Duong, eds. *The Viet Cong Tet Offensive 1968.* Translated by the J5/JGS Translation Board. Republic of Vietnam: Printing and Publications Center, July 1, 1969.

Swearengen, Thomas F. *Tear Gas Munitions: An Analysis of Commercial Riot Gas Guns, Tear Gas Projectiles, Grenades, Small Arms Ammunition, and Related Tear Gas Devices.* Springfield: Charles C Thomas, Publisher, 1966.

Telfer, Gary L., Lane Rogers and V. Keith Fleming, Jr. *US Marines in Vietnam: Fighting the North Vietnamese, 1967.* Washington, DC: Government Printing Office, 1984.

Tilford, Earl H., Jr. *Search and Rescue in Southeast Asia, 1961–1975.* Washington, DC: Government Printing Office, 1980.

Tolson, John J. *Airmobility: 1961–1971.* Washington, DC: Government Printing Office, 1973.

United States Army Headquarters. *Employment of Riot Control Agents, Flame, Smoke, and Herbicides in Counterguerrilla Operations, Training Circular No. 3–16.* Washington, DC: Government Printing Office, July 1966.

United States Army Headquarters. *Employment of Riot Control Agents, Flame, Smoke, Antiplant Agents and Personnel Detectors in Counterguerrilla Operations, Training Circular No. 3–16.* Washington, DC: Government Printing Office, April 1969; reprint, Stockholm: Swedish Medical Aid Committee for Vietnam, 1970.

United States Army Headquarters. *Counterguerrilla Operations, Field Manual No. 90–8.* Washington, DC: Government Printing Office, August 29, 1986.

United States Army Headquarters. *40mm Grenade Launcher, M203, Field Manual No. 23–31.* Washington, DC: Government Printing Office, September 20, 1994.

United States Army Headquarters. *Flame, Riot Control Agents and Herbicide Operations, Field Manual No. 3–11.* Washington, DC: Government Printing Office, August 19, 1996.

United States Army Headquarters. *Grenades and Pyrotechnic Signals, Field Manual No. 23–30.* Washington, DC: Government Printing Office, September 1, 2000.

Van Staaveren, Jacob. *Interdiction in Southern Laos, 1960–1968: The United States Air Force in Southeast Asia.* Washington, DC: Government Printing Office, 1993.

INDEX